THE ROAD TO

GORDON HASKELL

the road to harry's bar

Forty Years on the Potholed Path to Stardom

MAINSTREAM
PUBLISHING
EDINBURGH AND LONDON

First published in Great Britain in 2006 by
MAINSTREAM PUBLISHING COMPANY
(EDINBURGH) LTD
7 Albany Street
Edinburgh EH1 3UG

ISBN 1 84018 987 8

A catalogue record for this book is available
from the British Library

Typeset in OptiCivet and Sabon

Printed in Great Britain by
William Clowes Ltd, Beccles, Suffolk

For my friend,
Martin Smith (1946–97)
He enjoyed life and pitied the tyrants that
seemed hell-bent on destroying it

Acknowledgements

My thanks to Neil Marr, David Nobbs, Mary Hionides, Bill Gerber, Susan George, Arif Mardin, Peter Knight, Bryn Haworth, Keith Guster, Tony and Judy Head, Cordelia Dade, Sally Smith, Robbie McIntosh and Hamish Stuart.

Contents

Foreword by David Nobbs

Gordon was a fan of the series of novels I wrote about Reggie Perrin. As we got to know one another, it gradually became clear to me that he identified with Reginald Iolanthe Perrin himself and that the stories I had created spoke to him and made him feel that there was a like spirit out there.

I soon began to feel that I, too, had found a kindred soul . . . in Gordon. I had something I had never expected or sought: I had a penfriend.

Gordon's letters began to give me a picture of his strange but never boring life. His image grew in my mind. I began to be able to see this humorous, romantic, over-sexed, itinerant, songwriting, guitar-playing insomniac as if he was one of my characters.

Insomniac? I don't know whether Gordon really is an insomniac, but his letters to me seemed to be mostly written in the middle of the night: 'It's 6.30 a.m. and I can't sleep.' One of them contained an entirely blank page except for the words, right in the middle of it, 'It's 5 a.m. Whoops!'

Itinerant? Almost every letter came from a different address. Once or twice, at times of comparative prosperity, Gordon wrote on paper embossed with company names such as *Ridiculous Music Limited* or *Wilderness Records*, but by the time the second letter arrived, the printed London address on the headed paper would be crossed out and something picturesque in Dorset substituted. Sloane Square and Biddulph Mansions in London alternated with the Kingfishers; Windwhistle Cottage; Friar Hayes Farm Cottage; and Pond Cottage, Dorset. I used to long for the next letter just to find out where he was living.

All the time, a picture was emerging of a wild man of music. He always seemed to have just broken up with some lovely woman – perhaps he didn't have time to write to me until they had broken up. He was always struggling against bad luck and a greedy, ruthless music business. He sent me a couple of his CDs and I liked them, but what did I know about music? If they'd been any good, they'd have been successful.

The communications seemed to tail off a bit at the end of the last millennium and the beginning of this one. Either he was doing much better and sleeping much better . . . or he had taken his identification with Reggie one stage too far and left his clothes on one of his beloved Dorset beaches.

And then, as I idly flicked through the pages of Ceefax one winter's day, I found him in the Christmas charts – No. 2, Gordon Haskell, 'How Wonderful You Are'. It truly was one of the most exciting moments in my life. I suddenly realised how fond I had become of this man I had never met.

And then I heard the record, and there it was, that familiar voice, and it was beautiful, and I knew that he had been good all the time; that he wasn't a deluded dreamer, he was a fine songwriter and singer, and had been all along. His success transformed how I saw him, retrospectively.

When we eventually met at my house, Gordon wasn't at all how I had imagined him. He was better-looking, larger, calmer and altogether more substantial. I knew immediately that I needn't have worried about meeting him.

I read Gordon's draft of this book with enormous interest. It filled in all the gaps in his intriguing life that I'd missed between his letters. It is a writer's book, created with a writer's eye and a writer's ear. It speaks to the reader directly and humorously. It's the story of a full life, a turbulent life, a life guided by passion and humility and warmth. It is laden with very funny observations of people. Gordon has an eye for the eccentric and clearly warmed to such people in his life. Another possible title, I think, would have been *Down and Out in the Music Business*.

This is a wonderful portrait of popular music from top to bottom.

We all know about the top end: our celebrity-obsessed media ensure that. And Gordon's life has fascinatingly brought him into contact with a few legends, including Cliff Richard, Jimi Hendrix, Paul McCartney and Brian Epstein. But this book also gives us an insight into the lousy pubs, ghastly clubs, strange lodgings, eccentric musicians, poverty, insecurity and stress that are just as typical of this vast industry.

Add a succession of extremely interesting women and you have an absolutely absorbing and illuminating read; a story of suffering, persistence and reward, steeped in the indestructibility of that greatest of all qualities . . . humour.

I thoroughly enjoyed this book. I hope you do too.

David Nobbs
Burton Leonard, Yorkshire

CHAPTER 1

I Have Winston Churchill to Thank for My Life

Churchill ordered Lord Dowding, head of the RAF's Bomber Command, to send 597 heavy bombers to Peenemunde in the Baltic on 17 August 1943 to destroy the V2 rocket sites and factory there. Dowding, who valued his crews greatly, argued that on a moonlit night, such as it was, the mission was plain suicide; the planes would be in full view of German artillery. Churchill was adamant, so the order was followed despite the wise advice of experts.

That summer evening Wing Commander Walter Ralph Haskell DFC kissed his beautiful young wife, Kathleen, and his two children, Heather and Digby, goodbye. He took off from an airfield in Lincolnshire, leading all the squadrons of Lancasters, and never came home. Just as Dowding had predicted, 40 bombers were shot down that night, with the loss of 270 crew. Ralph Haskell was one of the brave young men posted as missing.

Kathleen was 24 years old when she received notification at the garden gate. The messenger gave her an open railway ticket and her first cigarette. Any money due to her would be frozen for six months until they could be certain of her husband's death. They were sorry. It was nothing personal. At that moment, Heather was four and Digby, named after the airfield in Lincoln where they were stationed, was just over a year old.

The very same night, a German air raid reduced the family's rented ground-floor flat to rubble. They escaped unhurt. Lucky, I guess.

Homeless, widowed and clutching her two small children, a pushchair and a small suitcase, she left the debris of her life in Lincoln and took the train south.

Her mother and father lived in Verwood, a small village in Dorset where she had attended school and where she had been the childhood sweetheart of her beloved husband. She hoped she would find sanctuary there from the madness. The next two years of her life remain a family mystery. Digby was looked after by her sister, Pat. Kathleen, it is believed, returned to Lincoln with Heather.

In 1945, she joined Pat in West Moors, a village four miles from Verwood. Her sister had rented two rooms for herself and her two children along with Digby in a house belonging to a retired judge. By all accounts, 'Judge', as they called him, was a wonderful character and a kind soul.

It looked as if the war was ending. It was a time to be thankful. Kathleen was living on a war pension and they had survived. It was time for a night on the town. The place to go was the Norfolk Hotel in Bournemouth, where people could listen and dance to the resident jazz trio. It was there that Kathleen met a man who looked just like Clark Gable in the uniform of the American Air Force. He was suave, sophisticated, intelligent and incredibly good-looking, and his name was Harry.

What better way was there to celebrate after the complete hell of the previous five years than to make love with total abandon to a handsome man?

I was born on 27 April 1946 in a nursing home near Bournemouth. Nineteen days later, the nursing staff there delivered another baby boy called Robert Fripp. Our lives were to be linked from that day to this. The building burned down shortly after Robert was born, destroying all record of our existence.

By this stage, Harry was working as a war correspondent for the *New York Times*. He had returned to America to try for Yale but they'd rejected him, so, instead, he studied ancient history at Oxford and became an expert on Byzantine art. He rose to professor of history and started work on one of several new dictionaries he would eventually publish. He was penniless, which was nothing new for him.

Born in Canton, Ohio, of Greek immigrant parents, he was raised with his brother, George, and sister, Mary, in Paterson, New Jersey. It was his love of Greece and England that had prompted him to volunteer for the Greek Air Force as war broke out in Europe. Even though he was an American, he flew planes for the British, the Greeks and the Canadians before joining the US Air Force when his home country entered the conflict.

While he was at Oxford, he would hitch a lift to Verwood to see my mother and me. He wanted to take me to America and it so worried my mother that she made me a ward of court when I was four to prevent any such action. By that decision, made swiftly and instinctively in a moment of great tension, she probably saved my life. As an American citizen, I would have been drafted to Vietnam and may have died there.

I vividly remember a distinct atmosphere whenever we visited my grandmother. My mother's family made her feel as though she should be ashamed for bringing me into this world; instead, she adopted the haughty air of an ex-wing commander's widow, which is why people in the village thought her a snob, whilst they sniggered behind her back. I sensed a general atmosphere of hostility towards my mother, whether standing at a bus stop or going into the village store. Their attitude, I suppose, was born of small-mindedness.

So when Harry appeared out of the blue, it was a breath of fresh air to me, even though I had no idea at this stage that he was my father. I have a clear recollection of only one of those meetings, which took place at my grandmother's. Even at four years old, I had a nose for things and Harry left his mark on me. He brought a warm optimism into the hostile environment I could sense around me and, as he lifted me high above his head, his gentle touch and smiling, handsome face filled my heart with love for him. We are told that our early experiences affect our futures, and that rare moment with Harry has never left me. I've always sought out such people and looked to have fun ever since. He laughed a lot and loved a lot and the world seemed dull when he left, as if the sun had gone behind a dark cloud.

This stark contrast was all the more noticeable at our regular Sunday afternoon family get-togethers, where I'd see my four aunts and three uncles, my lovely old grandfather on two sticks and the grandmother who terrified me. Of all the people in that overcrowded room, I liked my grandfather best. He was quiet and thoughtful, and would occasionally come out with one slowly spoken solitary line of wisdom whereupon his wife would holler, 'Shut up, Jack!'

She yelled at Jack Pannell partly because he was deaf and partly because he got on her nerves. My grandfather was one of the few people in the village who had built his own house; however, as a stoker working on the steamships of the Royal Navy, he had been at sea most of his married life. And now that he was retired, he was always there, getting under her feet.

Grandmother put on a lavish tea every Sunday and ran the whole show. She loved her food. There was enough on the table to feed a small town. From where I was standing, all of three feet high, she looked enormous, like a huge turkey with a saggy neck, squawking out loud to her husband, her massive arms flapping like wings as she raced in and out from the kitchen terrifying everybody. Whenever she approached, I'd cling to my mother's legs or run and hide under the table.

The aunts and uncles I saw as black-and-white. Aunt Margaret was warm and kind and gentle, with beautiful eyes, and her husband, Uncle Geoff, was a desert rat who was impatient to take her home and make love to her. Aunt Mary had married Uncle Charles and was regretting it. Charles was an evil-looking swine and made cruel remarks to her all the time. Uncle John was very funny but bored out of his mind having to listen to his wife, Auntie Pat, being bossy to all her younger sisters. She never laughed at his jokes and he never took any notice of her bossiness. Aunt Bobbie's Australian husband had returned alone Down Under and she seemed happy to remain a single mother in England. They all talked at once and nobody listened to anyone. Nobody was interested in anybody else. Everyone stood around the table filling their plates. They'd eat their sandwiches and cakes, have some trifle and two cups of tea and the desert rat would always be the first to go, dragging his beautiful wife out against her will. Then they'd all talk behind his back.

'I wouldn't get in that bloody car with him for all the tea in China. He drives it like a bloody tank. He's mad,' said Bobbie, wishing someone would drag *her* away and make love to her in the desert.

'Still thinks he's in the Sahara. I don't know how she puts up with him,' said Mary, wishing Charles would get lost in the desert.

Uncle John would laugh his head off and get dirty looks from everybody. My mother rarely said anything within earshot of the children. Grown-ups had secrets. She'd smoke a cigarette.

Granddad would stand up on his sticks at some point and get a verbal thrashing for daring to go to the toilet with the family still there. He'd escape to the back garden to check his traps. I saw many a hung rat by the woodshed. Granny was too big to get caught in one of his traps. He was going to have to wring her neck one day.

I was acutely aware that I was, for some reason, set apart from my mother's family. Another uncle called David rarely appeared, as he was a high-ranking naval officer and away at sea so much. On his odd visits, he seemed to take pleasure in pointing at me and saying, 'He's not blood.' I didn't know what he meant but I felt bad.

I never saw anyone show any affection for anyone. It wasn't their style. It was considered the normal way for a close family to behave.

Harry would never have been invited to a Sunday do in case he got somebody else pregnant. He was different – and so was I. By this time, unbeknown to any of us, Harry had returned to New York and married there. It was 1950.

I spent the next ten years believing my father was Wing Commander Haskell and still wondering why I felt so alienated at those weekly family get-togethers.

When I was four, I went to my first school. It was run by two brilliant gentlewomen, a Miss Tippetts and a Miss Marriott, spinsters of their parish. Miss Tippetts was the loud one and Miss Marriott the quiet but more effective; I learned very early in my life that those who shout the loudest say the least.

I learned much more quickly with Miss Marriott and excelled in mathematics. They had twenty-four pupils and ran their school from a private house using two rooms with twelve children in each. It worked perfectly and would probably be against the law today. In Miss Marriott's classroom there were six Dachshunds in baskets placed either side of the fireplace.

Every so often, a strange, confused-looking woman would interrupt the class by sticking her head around the door and saying, 'Can I have some gas money, please?' She was odd but homely and I looked forward to her interruptions. The schoolhouse felt friendly and welcoming to me and a place to cherish learning. Like everything in this life, you can perform much more effectively when you relax. 'This is better than my grandmother's,' I thought. 'Her gas never runs out.'

The interruptions for gas coins established my taste for the bizarre and surreal, and I smiled about the strange woman from upstairs as I worked quietly and diligently, glancing occasionally at the contented dogs licking each other's balls by the coal fire.

I remember I refused to speak when Miss Tippetts called my name from the register. I had answered 'Present' on the first day and had remained silent ever since. Miss Tippetts reported this to my mother, and Uncle Geoff was brought in first to investigate. My logical explanation to my favourite uncle was that, having been seen to be present on my first day, anyone with any intelligence or memory for faces would realise that I was present on the days that followed. The outcome was a hasty diagnosis by experts in the field of child psychology: I was in need of special treatment. An ambulance picked me up every Friday to take me to a clinic where I spent the entire day making things out of building bricks with Al Stewart's mother, who was a nurse there. (Al himself would have a hit in the '70s with his song 'The Year of the Cat'.)

I was still a little kid – between five and eight years old – and I remember thinking how odd grown-ups were to believe I needed special treatment just because I wouldn't answer a silly question at school like, 'Are you here, Gordon?' It wasn't as though I was any less chatty than the rest of the kids in any other way. I didn't know how to explain the ambulance to my pals when I hadn't a clue myself.

I remember one day when Harry sent a huge parcel in the post to me. There were lots of lovely American stamps on the box with pictures of aeroplanes on them. My mother opened it up as I stood by and watched with mounting excitement. It was a pedal car. It wasn't just any old pedal car, though; this was an American military jeep with a big star on the bonnet, not that common on a Dorset council estate in 1953. I had no idea then, of course, that the gift was from my father. I thought Harry was just an exotic friend of the family from an exciting country far away. Mum said nothing to enlighten me and, like all kids, I wasn't about to look a gift horse in the mouth. My mother must have sighed with relief when the bolts holding the pedals worked loose. I'd had hours of fun in it and now, at last, she could hide it away in the shed out of sight of the gossiping, sniggering neighbours.

When my weekly trips in the ambulance ended I had to go to school again on Fridays. I was used to a four-day week. The horror of Fridays was having to sit and listen to a radio programme called *Travel Talks* from the BBC, then write an essay on what we'd heard. Unfortunately, this time I hadn't heard a thing; I'd daydreamed for the entire hour. The realisation then filled me with terror because writing about where I went in my daydreams wouldn't have been appreciated. I eventually developed a genuine excruciating stomach pain every Friday morning.

When the third of these sudden Friday attacks struck our GP was baffled and admitted me to Bournemouth Hospital. Of course, my regular Friday pain had gone by Saturday morning, just as mysteriously as it had arrived. But I didn't let on to the doctors and nurses and faked it.

After seven days and seven injections, and a week of horrible hospital food and well-meant but unwelcome visits from local football stars and clergymen, I'd had enough and staged a miraculous recovery. The imagined illness had been real enough to me – but only on Fridays. Doctors these days would have immediately diagnosed it as psychosomatic and simply brought on by fear; possibly the most potent disease of all.

I drew some comfort from church and there were definite pleasures experienced by attending. The first was music that I had never noticed before. I loved the melodies, I loved the words. The words suggested there was love in the world and that by giving out love we would be loved. Songs like 'All Things Bright and Beautiful' had a sound of beauty, love and truth to them; attitudes I adopted right there in the church as a five year old. If that's sentimentality, that's where I found it and hugged it and treasured it, because it certainly removed my fears. Love had been hailed as the answer to everything for nearly 2,000 years by a few Greek philosophers and a carpenter called Jesus. I suppose the less fortunate children growing up in 2005 are more likely to hear the words 'fuck off' before they hear that all you need is love.

The vicar would preach a sermon along those lines and have a glass or three of wine as the congregation took the Sacrament. He then began to flirt with the girls sitting in the front pew. By the end of the service, he could barely walk in a straight line, his eyes sparkling as he smiled warmly at everyone. He lived in the largest, most beautiful house in the village and owned a shotgun. He explained this by saying, 'The big birds are always frightening the smaller ones away from my bird table, so I shoot them.'

I liked his style.

After evensong, he could be found in the Monmouth Ash pub next door to Granny's. He claimed that by frequenting the pubs he could talk to the villagers who hadn't turned up for his church service. That way he made his presence felt to everybody. My taste for wine, women, song and justice was born of the Reverend John Lyons of Verwood Church. My love of music began right there, together with my love for the beautiful words I was hearing for the first time.

The other nice thing about Sundays was meeting those girls who came to church with their parents. I found them attractive and I managed to talk and smile quite openly with them. I copied the vicar. He seemed like a sensible man. It was all so lovely compared to what I would face at my grandmother's house later in the day.

I remember her saying to my mother sarcastically, 'Isn't Gordon like Ralph [her late husband]?' knowing fully how it would hurt her. After losing everything in the war, my mother had to put up with being bombed by her own mother. To this day, if I am a witness to man's inhumanity to man, I will air my views. They never could quite correct that part of me at the 'Friday clinic'.

By the age of 11, I had so enjoyed working out some of life's mysteries and thinking I could solve all the unkindness in the world, I decided to be a policeman. I was always caring of victims and longing to finger the bad guys. Policemen represented love back then. Some of them still do.

I would return home after church and pick out tunes on the old piano in the bungalow the council had given us. My mother had pestered them for four years and they had finally caved in. The bungalow was huge by today's standards, standing detached in a large garden with three bedrooms and a sitting room large enough to take a three-piece suite, a dining table and chairs, a side table for the wireless set, and the piano which my sister was learning to play. After church, the wireless would be turned on for *Family Favourites* and I began hearing all kinds of songs among the many hymns. The piano was ideally placed to play along to some of them. However, my first composition on the piano was achieved by placing both arms over every single note below middle C and playing them all at once. It made the same sound as a squadron of Lancaster bombers flying directly overhead. When my mother rushed in from the kitchen and slammed down the lid, I decided to go back to just using my fingers.

I made many friends back then. John next door was a railway buff and we'd spend a lot of time on the railway tracks helping the Southern Railway keep the trees and gorse bushes down on the embankments by setting fire to them.

The steam railways introduced me to the world of travel as I soon grasped how simple it was to go anywhere on any day without anyone noticing my absence. I saw the beauty of the English countryside from the windows of the train on my many secret railway journeys and couldn't wait for the weekends and school holidays to come, knowing I could escape so easily and enjoy my solitude. I was a great saver in those days and with 2s 6d a week (just 12½ pence in today's money) and the odd birthday bonus, I never craved expensive toys when half-fare train travel seemed such good value.

There was the occasional real drama in Verwood. Joe the baker was on his bread round and came across an angry husband trying to murder his wife with a towrope and went to her rescue. There was a fierce fight and Joe put the rope around the husband's neck and unintentionally killed him. I wanted to be as heroic as that and rescue someone because everyone loved Joe and he was found not guilty, so life went on as before. Joe delivered bread to my grandmother's. She'd holler, 'Have you got a large brown, Joe?' Then she'd look pleased when everyone within earshot smiled at her. It was years later before I understood why. A 'Joe' was the local euphemism for a penis.

I looked everywhere for another murder, but the best I came up with was the case of a flasher who had been bothering a girl on the common. I went up there to catch him and hid in a disused air-raid observation post. I heard footsteps and peeped over the shelter wall to see who it was, only to be faced with her angry and reputedly violent father, who assumed I must have been the culprit. I still think it was amazing he took so long to accept my innocence, since I was only eleven. This confirmed my worst suspicions that many adults were mentally retarded.

If I felt any frustration, it was because I longed to be old enough to explore the world that I was finding so exciting whenever I slipped the tight leash I was kept on by my frightened mother. The fears she had developed from her war experiences were subtly passed to her children year by year but my old soul was kicking life into me and I longed for my school years to end.

I passed my 11-plus examination with ease, courtesy of Marriott and Tippetts, and started at Wimborne Grammar School. This was to be my first experience of male teachers, some of whom seemed terrifying at first. As it turned out, the most intimidating staff member was female. I'd also never participated in games or physical education and I was extremely nervous in the beginning. But I surprised even myself by adapting quickly and was soon in the school rugby and football teams, and doing well in them. I loved athletics and represented the school at discus, once coming third in the county; a natural, considering Harry's Greek extraction. Although the sports master was a bit of a bully I will always be grateful to him for making a sportsman out of me. The hell he put me through in that first year was an early lesson in endurance, courage, discipline and single-mindedness that would serve me well in the future.

It was on the discus field that I met Robert Fripp, the baby born just after me in the maternity ward. We became firm friends and saw each other out of school. We began playing 'fives' (like squash without rackets) at school and both became masters at the game. In the school championship, it was inevitable that we would be seeded through to fight it out for the cup. The winner would be the best out of three.

I won, but in my joy and love of the game, I said to Robert, 'Let it be the best out of five.'

He took the next two games. And he took the cup. That moment was a hint of the fundamental difference in our natures which, had I taken more notice, could have spared me years of grief in later life. I loved the game so much that winning had not been uppermost in my mind. And, incidentally, it still isn't. Little did I know then that coming second to Robert Fripp of King Crimson would become a lifelong habit.

After the first year at grammar school, we were graded into A, B and C streams. As fate would have it, Robert Fripp and I landed in the same class and he sat at the desk directly in front of me. We already knew each other, so it was natural that our friendship would develop and we started to hang around together all the time. It was at this stage that I discovered who my real father was.

I was 13 and during one geography period we inadvertently touched on human biology. The teacher, who suffered from a lisp, had become exasperated with his struggle to pronounce the phrase 'the Bosphorus Isthmus that leads up to Istanbul' and was determined to avenge himself on all those cruel boys who were smirking. He went on the attack.

'I'm going to go round the class today and ask each of you what your fathers do for a living.'

Robert, preceding me, answered accurately, 'An auctioneer, sir.'

I followed him, announcing proudly that mine was a wing commander and he'd been killed in 1943.

There was the sound of muffled giggles. The geography teacher looked relieved that we were no longer laughing at him and said, 'Then you are obviously too old for my class.'

He then rapidly moved on to the next boy. Nothing more was said but it had registered on my radar. As soon as I got off the school bus, I raced home knowing my mother was out at work as an auxiliary nurse. I had previously seen where she kept her private papers and I searched through her mail.

There I found letters in airmail envelopes with American stamps like those I remembered had been on the box of my pedal car, but to my disappointment no letters from the man I thought and hoped might really be my father.

He was a lovely friend of my mother's who visited us all every Sunday after we returned from Granny's. His name was Ken Harris and he was – and remains – the kindest, sweetest soul I've ever known. I had never noticed anything remotely like affection from my mother towards Ken but I was no expert on that subject, and as Granny's had been seen as the norm it wasn't something I expected. A peck on the cheek as he said goodbye was also the limit of Ken's expectations.

He'd arrive laden with vegetables and strawberries he'd grown in his garden, an OXO tin full of chocolate bars for our school lunches and sometimes he brought a lemon meringue pie he'd made. His efforts were rewarded with a direct order from my mother, disguised as a question, for him to mow both lawns, which were huge, and dig the back garden; oh, and to start a bonfire, as she didn't want piles of cuttings making the place look untidy.

He would do anything for anybody, free of any kind of reward. He played cricket, football, badminton and sociable bar games like dominoes, shove-halfpenny, darts and snooker, and everyone outside of the family loved and respected him. My mother snapped at him continually. She seemed mad at him all the time, as if every pitfall and catastrophe in her life was his fault. And still he would come back for more and never once answered her back.

He was an electrician on a humble salary and would listen as my mother told him how such-and-such had his own electrical business and three vans and a luxury house in Verwood. Ken would carry on reading the sports section and say nothing. I was devastated when he fell from a ladder and died at 55. The whole neighbourhood turned out for his funeral. My mother said he was a fool and always took unnecessary risks for his employers. Such-and-such would never be that stupid. She had nothing to say when such-and-such died ten years later and only six people turned up at the church. Famous people receive medals. Ken, I am in no doubt, was better than any of them. So I was hoping he was my father.

Then I found what I'd been looking for.

'That fateful night . . .' ran the letter written from a college within Oxford University and stating that Harry had completed his first dictionary and Collins had paid him £1,500 for it. He was enclosing something for her and his dearest Gordon. A stunning photograph, inscribed on the back 'To Kay and Gordon', was among the letters. He looked like a movie star. For all I knew, he was a movie star.

The first person I told was my girlfriend – yes, I had begun to have girlfriends – and it seems ridiculous, looking back, that I gingerly said, 'You might not want to go out with me any more . . .'

Instead of confronting my mother and risking a half-truth from her, I became a sleuth. My childhood ambition to become a Scotland Yard detective got out of hand. I bought an old trench coat from a second-hand shop in Ringwood and a magnifying glass, and started taking fingerprints around the house using my mother's talcum powder. If Harry had visited when I was at school, there would be an odd set of prints in the bungalow that I couldn't match. But Harry must have been too smart to leave prints.

With my fascination for railways and all things steam, I had bought a railway timetable. It wasn't unusual for me to disappear for the whole day and jump on and off trains. By the age of 14, I knew my way around the whole of the south of England, including London. For £3 10s, I could buy a ticket that lasted a week and enabled me to travel anywhere on the Southern Region. One Saturday I dressed in my trench coat and boarded a train bound for London.

On arriving at Waterloo Station I walked, as I imagined all great detectives walked, with authority and a degree of stealth, to the taxi ranks. As the cab approached, I grabbed the door handle before it had even stopped and, raising my voice above the din of the traffic, I said, 'Scotland Yard.' I remembered to glance behind me in case I was being followed. We arrived at the Yard and I paid the cabbie, then looked up at the famous façade. I looked around to see if anyone was watching and got on a bus and went back to Waterloo, caught the train home, took a few engine numbers to satisfy my mother that I'd only been trainspotting and felt, all in all, that I'd had a successful day. I'd been working undercover and nobody knew. I was obviously good at this.

My next move was to go to the local library and find Harry's dictionary. There were now several from which to choose. He had been busy during the last 14 years. The most successful and therefore the easiest to find was the Collins English–Greek standard edition. Looking in the preface, I jotted down the New York address of the publishers. Later that day, I wrote my first 'Dear Harry' letter and posted it care of Collins.

My school work was beginning to go downhill. I had been in the top three for three years and now I was slipping towards the bottom. I had lost interest and felt as long as I could get into the police force I didn't really care about passing eight or nine O-level examinations.

All I needed for the Met was English and mathematics, both of which I could have passed at 11 years old.

My mother put it down to my distractions with girlfriends and my new interest in music. I felt it was the time to ask about Harry. She handled it well and told me I was a 'love-child'. I longed to ask, 'So, Heather and Digby are what?'

By now, I had begun dating my first serious girlfriend and my attention was primarily on her, as she was extremely experienced for 14. Belinda had already made a name for herself with one of my classmates for doing things I barely knew about or understood. She lived in a caravan with her mother and father, and had given me the eye in the playground at school and invited me to her home. I had been flattered. I was attracted to her, so had gone to see her.

We sat in the caravan alone and she began twiddling her thumbs and hinting for me to get started. She had chosen ten records that she stacked on the automatic changer of her little record player. Peggy Lee would sing 'You give me fever' and Belinda would look at me adoringly. After kissing and panting she took my hand and walked me out of the caravan to the woods nearby. She simply threw us both down onto a bed of autumn leaves and undid my trousers.

We loved each other and stayed together for 18 glorious months of regular love-making in those woods. It would never ever be that simple or innocent again. It was untainted by the world at large. It was a secret love all of our own and in some ways it has never been bettered. We parted when I became involved in music and groups. 'Belinda will never play second fiddle to a guitar,' her mother told me.

Robert Fripp had spoken about his desire to form a band and asked if I'd learn to play the bass so that we could get started. I began seeing live bands with him and was gaining interest, particularly in those playing rhythm and blues, and jazzy versions of 'September In The Rain'. The local big-name bands were Zoot Money and Dave Anthony, and they were terrific. They had a full line-up of musicians just as Fats Domino or Ray Charles or any great American band of the time tended to have, with a rhythm section, electric guitar, saxophones and a trumpet. They commanded the stage like veteran professionals but could only have been 19 year olds. In a less enlightened age, when the perceived roles of men and women were clearly defined, these acts impressed me greatly, not only musically but for the way women were drooling over them. They whetted my appetite and, though I thought

I'd never be able to afford the instrument, I sheepishly went along with Robert to Don Strike's guitar shop in Bournemouth to pick out a bass. I chose the cheapest available and agreed to a private hire-purchase deal sustainable from odd-jobbing.

Robert began teaching me some basics. As well as the limited knowledge I had gained from playing the piano, I'd played around with my sister's boyfriend's acoustic guitar at home, so it wasn't long before I began to feel and understand the instrument, and Robert and I practised together at his home. That's when the girl in the woods gave up on me.

Over the next two years, Robert and I played together in The Ravens and The League of Gentlemen. We played youth clubs, village-hall dances and nightclubs in the larger towns nearby. I was preoccupied with pretending to be Jet Harris, The Shadows' moody rebellious bass player with whom I identified. Although I did a fairly good impression of Jet, it had little to do with music and a lot to do with puberty. It was essentially white boys' music. I didn't start defining and developing a style of my own until I joined Les Fleur de Lys in 1965 when, incidentally, I met Jet Harris. He'd had a few too many and fallen off the stage into the orchestra pit during the famous Shadows' Walk . . . and therefore, likewise, fell from grace.

The Ravens' drummer Graham Wale acted as bandleader and secured our first date playing on Bournemouth beach. We plugged in the amps in the public convenience block. During his drum solo, his drum-kit sunk into the wet sand and turned over.

Tino Licinio was the singer and was popular with the girls for his sharp Italian looks and fine singing. I remember him mainly for the odd way he set his watch. He claimed by putting it three hours ahead and reading it as two hours behind, it gave him more time to get ready for a gig. He was an hour late for everything.

When we formed The League of Gentlemen we brought in Stan Levy on drums and Reg Matthews as lead singer. Stan was Scottish and nobody understood a word he said, and Reg was at one time a winner of Mr Universe. Reg wore a bright-red suit, sounded identical to Roy Orbison and lifted all the gear into the clubs on his own. Using a yoke, he could balance a speaker on each shoulder while carrying a sack on his back and an amplifier in each hand. We all had a fine time but it hadn't yet occurred to me to consider being a professional musician. Robert and I were preparing to take our GCE school exams.

* * *

Discovering my father's details had only one visible effect on my life. I used his surname in the local paper when The League of Gentlemen was getting some press. All a bit stupid really, as nobody could pronounce Hionides. Even I had to hazard a guess. I don't remember the time as one of deep psychological stress. I was excited by the fact I had a very glamorous and intelligent father who wrote dictionaries, but I could have shown more discretion and I regret embarrassing my mother further. My several efforts to make contact with him through Collins, his publishers, were rewarded when I received my first postcard from him. It had been posted in Venezuela and dated 30 October 1963.

> Dear Gordon,
> It was really a pleasant surprise getting your news. I hope and wish you every success in the music world. I am going for a few months to Argentina and Brazil and will drop you a line from there. I don't know whether I'll get the chance to return via London, but if I do I'll make a point of seeing you.
> Sincerely,
> Harry

I showed the card to my mother and I realised my ignorance when it dawned on me that I had not considered her feelings. Instead of being sensitive to her pain, I had revelled in the experience of being different, a delusion that I was somehow being singled out for something heroic. I hadn't thought for a minute what it must have been like for her. I began to warm towards her and ask her about the war years. As a detective, I brought her in for questioning.

The more I listened to her story, the more I understood her. Her days of dining at the Ritz on the arm of an RAF wing commander were gone; when the Lancaster bomber he was flying was obliterated from the skies, her status went with it. They had been sweethearts since the age of 13; as soon as he'd won his RAF wings they would go to a private airfield near Verwood and take joy rides in the most basic of single-engine aircraft. It had all been so thrilling. They were so full of life. Now she was faced with widowhood and raising three children in a council-estate bungalow, plus small-minded village whisperers and their gloating, and her mother's shame. All that was on offer was my handsome but penniless father. How could she justify marrying him? She would lose her RAF pension. How could Harry support her and three children? Why shouldn't she hate her life and chain-smoke and put on a la-di-da voice occasionally? A weaker woman would have hanged herself.

I'd often look at that postcard and wonder why there was no address. Where did Harry live and what was he doing in South America? Did he expect a reply via his publishers? Was it possible with his war background and Oxford University and the *New York Times* connection that he could be a spy? In a letter that was to follow, he mentioned he'd met the renowned spy Donald Maclean. The last thing he needed was a lost son turning up and blowing his cover. I decided to be patient and leave it alone for a while.

Robert and I parted company in 1962 when we both left school and the first incarnation of The League of Gentlemen was disbanded. I had passed my entrance examination for the Metropolitan Police College at Hendon and Robert was going into his father's estate-agency and auctioneer business.

Working with Robert had been fun and, though the band struggled sometimes with his inability or unwillingness to play like the other guitarists of the day, there were never any arguments nor was there ever any unpleasantness.

CHAPTER 2

🍥 🍥 🍥

That'll be a Shilling, Sir

My career in the Metropolitan Police lasted three days and I didn't even get a pension.

There wasn't a trench coat or magnifying glass to be seen anywhere. I was an idiot for thinking I could ever have joined up. I returned home with my tail between my legs and received a dressing down from my mother, who dragged me screaming to the Labour Exchange when I said I wanted to be a musician. She collected leaflets about the civil service, which I petulantly tore up in front of her. Eventually, I copied Robert and took a job in an estate agent's office in Bournemouth.

My experiences in the working world to date comprised a paper round and a Saturday milk round I'd had while still at school. I had suggested meekly to my mother that if I did the milk round, I could fit it in with my musical plans for the time being, but she said she hadn't worked all hours to pay for my education so that I could become a milkman or a musician. The wages at the estate agency were very low so I did continue helping out on the milk round at weekends because not only did it pay well but it was a light relief from the pomposity I was experiencing elsewhere.

The dairy belonged to Reg Shearing, who employed one other man, a Mr Hubert 'Uby' Sims. Reg's routine started late for a milkman, at 7.30 a.m., and he always seemed to be in a hurry to get home. Uby used a motorbike with a wooden sidecar made to measure for milk crates and was always laughing about somebody – very often it was about Reg and his flusters.

For the first hour we would all be together in the Morris 1000 van. I would be squeezed into the back on top of a milk crate. Reg coughed up phlegm for the whole of the first hour, occasionally spitting the larger offerings out of the window. Sometimes this anti-smoking advertisement would refuse to fly and get stuck to his fingers. Reg's fingers had been damaged in a fire as a child and he had difficulty removing the sticky mess. He always did his very best to hide such catastrophes. Uby would turn around to look at me and say 'Oarr' in his Dorset accent, nodding his head up and down, which used to make me have to stifle my laughter. That 'Oarr' taught me that comedy doesn't need a lot of dialogue.

Reg would be similarly embarrassed by his farts, which were silent and terrible, and which he would always blame on the drains. Uby would nod to Reg in agreement and turn around to give me a nod and a wink.

When it rained, Reg wore an immense amount of clothing. He had a vest, a shirt and tie, a short-sleeved pullover, a tweed jacket and grey trousers, on top of which hung the largest, longest raincoat I'd ever seen in my life. He wore the topcoat open with his moneybag hung in the gap. On his feet he always wore what he called his 'top boots', which were wellingtons with the tops folded down halfway. They were so old the tread on the soles had been worn flat by the high mileage he'd walked over the years. From the rear, as he raced up people's paths with his overcoat flapping open and his splayed flat-footed gait, Reg looked as though he was on waterskis.

One day after being soaked to the skin during the round, instead of getting out of his wet clothes at the end, he sat by the living-room fire for an hour. I walked in to collect my wages and he was almost hidden in clouds of steam and cigarette smoke. He always kept a Woodbine in his mouth. He'd mastered the technique of blowing the ash off as he spoke to customers. It would generally land on the pages as he was writing in his round book, at which point he'd brush it off with his damaged hand, still holding the pencil, while his other held the book firm.

In one of many memorable comedy moments, I remember Reg searching through over 50 empty Woodbine packets, all crammed together on the van dashboard, looking for a full pack he'd lost amidst them. Reg was always in a hurry, so he searched every one of those packets by throwing them this way and that, getting madder and madder as he became more desperate to find the full one. He left all the empty packets there; he would never make it easy for himself. And I'm glad, because it was a lovable quality. He was never boring.

I think the days I spent with Reg and Uby were the happiest, warmest and most entertaining of my whole life. It was like working with Max Wall and Tommy Cooper every day. Reg and Uby's sense of comedy shaped my own and would be used as a great comfort to me in the future. In the years to come, whenever I would rant and rave, I never saw it as anger and couldn't understand why everybody around me would get so upset. Couldn't they see how funny it all was?

My most vivid memory from working in the estate agent's office was seeing a woman go by every day taking her dogs for a walk. I counted 33 dogs, all on separate leads of varying lengths. She caused absolute chaos in the busy Bournemouth suburban streets when she crossed the road, which she delighted in doing every 100 yards as she spotted a shop that suddenly took her fancy on the other side. She called out the names of the dogs in a commanding, shrill, upper-class voice that rose above the din of the traffic. That, added to the sound of 33 barking mutts, ensured that you could hear her coming a mile away. It broke up the day. I looked forward to it. She'll never know how much pleasure she gave me by being ever so slightly do-lally-tap.

I missed being in a group so I reformed The League of Gentlemen. Robert was giving his career as an estate agent 100 per cent and attending business college in all his spare time, so I recruited my local hero Dave Anthony (who would eventually be the last singer of Les Fleur de Lys). We picked up gigs in the area easily enough but we were eager to move to London. For two nights one holiday, the singer Dave Anthony (his real name was Tony Head) and I slept on Zoot Money's floor in west Kensington – Zoot Money had already made a name for himself as one of the leading musicians of the London club scene. How were we to know that instead of a simple geographic shift of a few miles, it was a journey over light years to a new culture and lifestyle?

The music we were making now was more to my liking and we had more authority with Tony fronting the band. He was a wonderful singer and I felt proud to be backing him. The music was gutsy rhythm and blues and his knowledge of the genre educated me. We became good friends and socialised together. He was three years my elder and was a master at chatting up the girls in the ballrooms we regularly visited. As his sidekick, I learned a lot from him musically and socially, although neither of us had any idea what we were doing careerwise, so I returned to Bournemouth, leaving Tony to form Dave Anthony's Moods, which soon became a popular eight-piece London band.

A year had passed with the estate agency when I took a gig with another local act, The Dowlands. The band had a small hit with a cover of the Beatles song 'All My Loving', produced by the lunatic and legendary Joe Meek, and they were fun to be with.

Joe had been enormously successful as the first truly independent record producer in Britain. 'Telstar' by the instrumental group the Tornadoes had made No. 1 all around the world, including America. John Leyton had reached No. 1 with 'Johnny Remember Me' and Meek was making a fortune. He lived with his mother in an upstairs flat in Highbury and recorded the artists in the bathroom. He was outrageously gay for those days and highly innovative, reversing tapes and experimenting long before The Beatles arrived. He'd recorded The Dowlands but they sounded too much like The Everly Brothers for him, so he speeded up the tape. He got them a hit.

A troubled soul, Joe shot himself in 1967.

The Dowlands was a highly professional band that toured around the country and my day job was getting in the way. If I was ever going to take the bold step of living the life of a truly professional musician, I was going to have to quit. On the day they offered me the bass gig, I was ready to jump. I just didn't go back to the office after lunch. I received a stern letter in estate agent-speak saying this act had 'besmirched' my former character. My mother was not amused and insisted I maintain some kind of 9-to-5 existence. I said I wanted to be a professional musician but agreed to do any old job to satisfy her until I was 18.

She didn't hold me to that and the first of many silly jobs I did while playing for The Dowlands was as an ice-cream retail officer on Bournemouth beach. It was a cloudy day and there wasn't a soul to be seen. I must have walked a mile gazing out to sea thinking, 'What the hell am I doing? All that education, all that early outstanding promise at the Misses Tippetts and Marriots . . .' My mind wasn't on the job. In the world of ice cream, I was a disappointment. When I finally found a customer, I opened up the box and pulled out a briquette as requested. It promptly went splat in the man's hand and dripped down his wrist as he attempted to put it to his mouth. Every one of the ice creams had melted. I'll never forget his bewildered look as I told him, without a hint of humour, 'That'll be a shilling, sir. Oarr.' It didn't work quite as well as Uby's 'Oarr' but it was a good try. And he paid and walked away.

'I'll go labouring,' I thought. 'It's good money, I hear.'

A friend who drove the band around said he knew a bricklayer who needed a labourer, so I got the job. I felt exhilarated to think I had already made such distinctive connections within the music business. No one else shared my enthusiasm, least of all dear Mum. The money I earned would buy me a Fender bass guitar, which in those days was like owning a Porsche – well, to us musicians anyway. My cheap, nasty bass was now an embarrassment.

A JCB digger picked me up at my gate and we travelled six miles to the building site. I felt like Eisenhower sitting up on the bright-yellow mudguard of that mighty machine. The deal was simple enough: fill a wheelbarrow with breezeblocks, wheel it over the rutted ground and hand them to the bricklayer as he built a high wall. It was hard work with little rest because the boss worked quickly. By five o'clock, I could barely walk, let alone lift a loaded wheelbarrow and push it over the ruts.

'One more and we're done,' said the man with the trowel and the mortgage.

I reached the wall for the last time; by now it was over six feet high and I had to stretch myself to pass each block to the bricklayer. As I lifted the very last one and tried to pass it up to him, the combination of its sheer weight at the end of that long, hard day and a rogue rut beneath my feet made me trip and lose my balance. To stop myself from falling, I put my hand out onto the newly built wall. Wet mortar and cement is known for its hostility to musicians and ex-policemen, and the combined weight of the block and me was too much for that marvellously built, straight-and-true solid breezeblock masterpiece. I saw myself gently easing the entire structure over as it yielded to gravity. It fell into a hundred pieces with me on top. How I longed to be playing 'Roll Over Beethoven' and doing the duck walk like Chuck Berry.

'Are you hurt?' asked the brickie.

'Yes, my arms are bleeding.'

'Good. You're sacked.' Then he screamed at me with the direst threat I had yet been given in my life. 'You'll never lay bricks in Bournemouth again.'

Struggling for a UK record for the most jobs in a week, I found a promising position as a laundryman in Bournemouth. I'd be out and about on my own and I reckoned it would be similar to delivering milk. 'Once you have memorised the route, you should be able to do it blindfolded,' I told myself. (The advertisement in the newspaper had promised unique opportunities.)

Initially, I was sent out with the experienced roundsman I would be replacing. He seemed friendly enough and we were getting along fine. He would stop outside someone's house and ask me to wait in the van while he collected the baskets, leaving an empty one for the customer to fill for the following week.

The next day I arrived at the laundry only to be shown into the manager's office. There I was introduced to Sergeant Baker from Bournemouth CID. I briefly imagined myself in the role and thought how much prouder my mother would have been had I become a policeman. Apparently, I was a suspect in an investigation into several burglaries in the neighbourhood. They had all occurred the day before and they all just happened to be on my round. The driver was given two years in prison for housebreaking. I was as innocent as a lamb.

I hung on to the job and was getting on quite well when an unexpected gig was booked and, to make it to the venue, I needed to leave work at midday. The boss refused to give me the afternoon off, as it was their busiest day; Hurn Airport was a huge contract they couldn't afford to lose and it was vital I collect the laundry. I delivered the clean package to the airport and picked up the dirty one, but dumped the van there and went to the gig. I thought I could pick it up in the morning and no one would be the wiser, but the van was spotted parked at the airport and I was sacked. Big Brother was just starting out then. Watching laundry vans was the thin end of the wedge.

I was finding and losing jobs so fast I managed to get through twenty-one in three months, which may have deserved an entry in *The Guinness Book of Records*. But I kept my last job the longest and it was back with dear old Reg the milkman, who took me on full-time. It worked perfectly with the bands, as the round was always finished by 2 p.m. and that left me time for a sleep before a gig. But even that came to a sticky end when I was offered two weeks away for good money in a rocking ballroom in Weymouth. Reg was very upset; he thought music was a precarious way to make a living and didn't want to lose me. It was nice to be wanted for a change.

He was right, of course, and, ironically, had I continued as a milkman and bought a field in that village, I would have become a very rich man with the minimum of effort, as Verwood became a developer's dream. Unigate came in and offered Reg a sizeable sum for the dairy. He and Uby retired. Fields that cost them next to nothing to buy years before were changing hands for a quarter of a million. Sometimes the gold mine is right under your nose.

But music was my destiny and I had little say in the matter.

The Weymouth summer season with The Dowlands was fabulous fun; it was a novel experience to be earning my living solely from music. We could be on the beach all day and fit in a two-hour rehearsal before each show. I was getting better at playing the bass now that I was with different musicians. As a professional, more was expected of me and I became interested in musical theory. As soon as I'd learned to play chords on an acoustic guitar, I began to write songs. I started reading *Melody Maker* and noticed that there were lots of jobs ideally suited to me in the adverts on the back pages. Manfred Mann was there openly looking for a bass player. Jack Bruce, who rose to prominence with Cream, got the job. I was beginning to realise that if I wanted a really top job, I would have to move up to London. For now, though, I was quite happy.

Brothers Peter and Michael Giles were respectively the original bass player and drummer of The Dowlands. They had left to form Giles, Giles and Fripp, not a firm of estate agents but the embryo of the hugely successful cult band, King Crimson. Peter Giles had also left behind his band suit and The Dowlands wanted me to wear it. He was much taller than me, so they got an excellent seamstress in Southampton they knew to make the necessary alterations. We picked it up on the way to the gig in Camberley and I put it on with confidence. The trousers were skintight; visualise Max Wall and you'll be close. Thinking the jacket would hide some of the damage, I hurriedly put it on. We were due onstage in ten minutes. The 'excellent seamstress' had taken a pair of garden shears to it and simply cut the jacket in half in a straight line across from the centre button. We just laughed for the whole gig. As no doubt the audience did too. Why me?

The music around us pre-Beatles had been the very same music that had inspired the band itself. There was a healthy mixture of jazz standards, skiffle, early rock 'n' roll, black rhythm and blues, white vocal groups and romantic balladeers. Hence we got 'Please, Please Me', ''Til There Was You', 'Roll Over Beethoven', 'Long Tall Sally' and 'Yesterday'. If you loved a record you heard on the radio, you went and found it waiting for you in the record shop. Records sold because they were great songs. They all provided the backdrop to dancing and making love, and the lyrics were there to help you through the obstacle course of dating.

After being a 13-year-old fan of Cliff Richard and The Shadows, regular visitors to Bournemouth, I became even more excited as I discovered the roots of it all and saw all the kings of rock 'n' roll, like Jerry Lee Lewis, Little Richard and Chuck Berry (all on the same bill and not a political thought between them). Elvis Presley, Fats Domino and jazz artists like Peggy Lee and Nat King Cole led to my eventual all-time favourite, Ray Charles. I felt all his pain as my own. When The Beatles mixed all these ingredients together, the whole scene exploded and we were reaping the benefit of the new interest in groups. I'd heard virtually every kind of song anyone could ever write by the time I was 18 and held a healthy, broadminded view of how brilliant they all were in their variety. As Humphrey Lyttleton, one of the fathers of British jazz music, said so succinctly at the time, 'There is only good and bad music.' There was so much good music all around, past and present, and everybody's aim seemed to be to reach for the same high standards that had been set for us all over the past 30 years.

It was 1964 and I was approaching my 18th birthday. Soon I would be allowed to leave home. Mum had given up trying to talk any sense into me about security, like getting a proper sensible job in the civil service.

My brother, Digby, joined HM Customs and Excise, and enjoyed going on ships and searching them and drinking with the captains, or being in airports at the gates of Great Britain. When they brought in VAT a few years later, he had little choice but to be transferred as a VAT officer – still a safe, sensible career, but very different to the romance of ships and aeroplanes that had attracted him as a young man.

My sister, Heather, seven years older than me, who had looked after me so many times while Mum was at work, found a pleasant enough job at the Ministry of Pensions. But she was transferred to the Child Support Agency and was terribly stressed at seeing families torn apart. Grown men were reduced to living in bedsits, some even committing suicide in their despair.

Mum gave her husband to His Majesty's Government and spent a lifetime with a broken heart; my sister and brother gave themselves to the civil service and were pushed from pillar to post; yet it was still me that my mother thought to be in danger of wasting my life. Mum's disappointment was obvious when I quit the police force after only three days. That, combined with my guilt for adding more pain to her already traumatic life, was one of many reasons I never gave up. And it was all the more significant when she became part of the story of 'How Wonderful You Are' so many years later.

I met many musicians on the road with The Dowlands, particularly in roadhouses, motorway cafés and popular granny-style bed-and-breakfasts. One was called Martin Smith, or 'Cuddles', as he was nicknamed by the fans in Bournemouth, and he and I were immediately connected by our sense of humour and mutual respect. He was in a band called The Meddy Evils. Virtually everyone I met was working non-stop and he was no exception. It was the gold rush, but nobody was focused on cash; we were overwhelmed with happiness to be part of a thriving community where there were no jealousies, rival factions or *egos* (the word hadn't entered the musician's vocabulary at that time). When I first met Martin, we had a typical conversation about the great records we were listening to and what a great gig such-and-such had done: 'Did you get to meet Andrea yet at Margate?' 'What about the caretaker at Dunstable?' and so on. It was that kind of mutual, harmless good-natured gossip that was becoming the common experience for us all. Bands stood around in car parks talking for hours. As groups arrived for fry-ups in the greasy-spoon cafés, we watched and laughed as each compared the vans that were already parked there, scrawled with messages of love from adoring girls. That year we must have seen every top-20 act pull into the Blue Boar motorway café. Martin would sometimes point to a band arriving and say they hadn't actually played anywhere, that they weren't even a band, they were just pretending to feel part of the family. After rubbing shoulders with a few stars they'd go back home to the estate around the corner. Van sales were booming.

We were both working for the same well-known Southampton music agency, Avenue Artists, and there were lots of stories about the antics of the owner, Len Canham, who was the first of many homosexuals I came across working in the music business. Back then, homosexuality still carried a stigma and was largely kept secret. But at a time when the whole music scene was in a state of revolutionary change, and everyone involved had a political and social agenda, homosexuals felt more inclined to come out of the closet. In this more liberal atmosphere, they were accepted by those of us who saw truth as a mission and freedom as a right.

Len added colour and amusement to the excitement of the time. Martin was one of his favourites – he just wished Len wouldn't keep calling him Cuddles.

Inevitably, with all the dozens of opportunities for musicians in the area, Martin told me of a gig going with another Southampton band called Les Fleur de Lys. They were being managed, were with Avenue Artists and had already released 'Moondreams', a Buddy Holly track. They had signed a deal with the very trendy Immediate Records in London, which was gaining popularity with musicians and the music-buying public because it was breaking new ground: the company would take a chance on a new artist or a new style. We felt they were on our side against the more staid recording establishment. Added to that, Fleur had lots of work.

I auditioned and got the gig, which meant leaving home, although I was only travelling 30 miles away to a village near Southampton. It was late 1965 when I left Verwood and The Dowlands, and my friends and family, and began the long journey into the unknown. I was very excited.

My mother, however, was clearly devastated by my determination to risk becoming a derelict, begging in the mean streets of the New Forest. I would end up as a hobo, living in the hedges of Dorset, bringing embarrassment on her friends at work, stealing chickens to eat. I'd get involved with dreadful girls from whom I'd catch the most dreadful, incurable diseases and die of syphilis, bringing even more shame on the family than she had. I was going to be captured by ruthless homosexual gangs roaming the south coast and sold into the slave trade in the Middle East. She would never be able to pay the ransom money. I would bring it all on myself. Her parting words were, 'Don't ever come back if you fail.' I remember them stinging a wee bit.

But it was exciting; the real '60s were about to happen. In nine months' time, I'd be living with Jimi Hendrix and having the time of my life.

Les Fleur de Lys was a four-piece group formed by Frank Smith a year before I joined. Danny, the bass player I was replacing, was tall, dark and handsome and a big hit with the girls; he was a hard act to follow, especially since I felt I was short, awkward and ugly. It did make me focus on the music more, as I tried to compensate for my shortcomings.

Frank said I could stay at his home in Southampton with his mother, father and pet monkey. There was never any mention of rent and his parents welcomed me as warmly into their comfortable home as they did Frank's monkey. We both roamed freely in our strange new environment. The monkey lived on nuts and I lived on beans. We both suffered from wind. They forgave the monkey.

Frank's father was a successful builder and supplied the band with a new, gleaming white Commer Dormobile. His mother was the sexiest woman I'd ever seen and I was stupid enough to flirt with her at every opportunity. She made living away from home for the first time much easier. Unfortunately, *The Graduate* hadn't yet made it out of the Hollywood studios, so I didn't dare believe my juvenile fantasies could come true, although it was nice being under the same roof, knowing I might bump into her in her bathrobe one night. Of course, I only ever bumped into the monkey. They gave their son Frank anything he asked for. He wanted to be the leader of a band, so they helped him to achieve that. He was the singer and guitarist, full of confidence and personality, and popular with the girls. He was fearless. Some called it arrogance. All I knew then was that he was much better equipped for life than I was. I walked in his shadow and cleaned the van willingly, falling comfortably back into being dominated.

Frank talked me into buying a Rickenbacker bass, which was very expensive – I could have done without the burden of hire purchase – and he fussed with my hair. He was image-conscious and I was letting the side down. This was all new to me and I found it uncomfortable and unnatural; it was destabilising my already fragile confidence and self-esteem. I would never look like a Mod, no matter what you did to my hair. Just to make matters worse, Frank chose a hideous green check jacket for me, which made me feel like Coco the Clown. Maybe he was secretly ensuring that no girl would ever take her eyes off him. It worked. For him, that is.

I had entered the modern world of popular music having only recently discovered the old one. I stubbornly tried to cling to the imagery of the early rock 'n' rollers. They were kings to me. I had seen them work; I had bought their records. The Beatles had come along and now groups were changing yet again. What made it worse was Frank was right and I was wrong. The new look meant that record companies could sell the same genre of music to teenage girls just by having a new, young artist perform it. The kids wouldn't have bought Elvis because their mums liked him, and that meant he belonged to another, older generation. But they would accept similar music by someone brand new on the scene. The clever artist packaging and promotion that was becoming such a major part of the industry meant record companies could sell black music to white kids.

This was my first lesson in marketing to adolescents and a hint of the politics working in the boardrooms of big business. If I hadn't been so naive, I would have enjoyed the band more because we were extremely popular everywhere we played, particularly with teenage girls. We gigged a lot all over the country in fabulous venues, usually with a famous band headlining. The ballrooms and clubs were smart and there was a comfortable atmosphere. The general feeling among the performers, dancers and audiences was that there was fair play for all: money for value and value for money. Nobody felt cheated or badly used.

Compared to Dorset, Southampton was a city buzzing with the latest trends. There were so many bands working and, with London only an hour away, I felt I'd made an entry into the professional music business. I must have been stupid not to want to change with the fashion. We all got paid and we all got laid . . . except me. That made me even less confident and even shyer.

We were then offered a month's work in Germany. As The Beatles had cut their teeth there, every band thought it was a good career move. The Germans had never had it so good and exploited the situation. We arrived in Dortmund at a grubby little club and were shown to an equally grubby old farmhouse miles out of the city, where we were to stay for four weeks. I was reluctant to try out the different foods on offer and lived entirely on sausages. By the end of the four weeks, my mouth was full of ulcers, my tongue had swollen so much it was blocking my windpipe and I had difficulty breathing. But I forgot all about it when I walked into a club and saw and heard a giant talent. His name was Phil Sawyer. He played a beat-up old Fender Esquire with all the flair of Eric Clapton (who was barely known at the time). Phil sang like a black soul singer. I didn't realise at the time he was already pretty well known and greatly admired on the music scene, and he went on to great things. He looked as wild as Jimi Hendrix would in months to come. The girls swooned.

He and I hit it off. Keith Guster, the drummer of Les Fleur de Lys, was keen to ask him to join us when he was back in England. He was leaving his current band, so came and stayed at the farmhouse with us. He seemed keen to get back home and willingly joined the band. Our organist Alex was the victim and left. Actually, 'victim' is too strong a word; he hadn't enjoyed the experience in Germany and was on the verge of pulling out anyway, so nobody's feelings were badly hurt.

Germany had indeed served its purpose. We now had a much more dynamic band with Frank and Phil the standard two guitars, me on bass and Keith on drums. The band was then asked to record a Who song, as they'd run into legal problems over who had rights to their work. While two competing record labels squabbled over the issues, The Who gave us the song to save it going to waste.

We went to IBC studios to make the record – my first visit to a top recording studio and it couldn't have been better. Frank and Phil had written a song for the B-side similar to 'Shotgun', a Junior Walker tune we'd seen Phil doing in Germany. Junior was huge at the time. He was knocking us all out with some of the first real funky music. The engineer on the session was Glyn Johns – not well known at the time but he later became the engineer/producer of choice of the Rolling Stones and The Eagles. Frank stayed as lead singer and played rhythm guitar but Phil took over the lead guitar and played a blinding intro and solo. Glyn Johns was bowled over along with the rest of us and a week later it was being reviewed and in the shops. My first record had taken only three hours to record and a week to release. It was called 'Circles'. It remains a classic version of the song and is valued at £200 by collectors these days. I played bass and sang back-up. 'How Wonderful You Are' was recorded 35 years later using exactly the same principles as we used that day when I was a novice.

Shortly afterwards, the band split into two camps. Keith and I left Frank in Southampton and went to London to be with Phil. Frank was now in Phil's shadow and the band was moving away from his fashionable ways towards the black-influenced music Keith and I preferred. I could easily accept being dominated by a giant talent such as Phil Sawyer; in fact, I relished it and worshipped him. I was proud to share the same stage as him. We took Les Fleur de Lys's name from Frank and reformed with Phil's mate Chris Andrews. It wasn't as though the name belonged to Frank, and, besides, he was moving into a career as a builder (in which he became very successful). Frank would never have moved to London anyway. He was happy to stay behind because, at home, his parents were giving him everything he wanted. The band didn't mean as much to him as it did to the rest of us. I've met him since and he did what he wanted to do, as we all did. We were just children playing at it in Southampton. It was too cosy to be taken that seriously.

For the first two weeks in London, Keith and I had a lousy time holed up in a crummy little place in Tooting that we grabbed in our eagerness to show Phil and Chris that we were serious. They each lived with their parents nearby. Being more laddish than us sweet boys from the country, they quickly turned our grotty flat into their private bordello, running back home after each party and leaving us to clean up the mess. We didn't mind too much. It was the start of our lives in a big city and we were eager to adapt. We found a good agent in Soho to take over the bookings from the Southampton agent and we all went out on the road. We were now viewed as a top London band simply because we had a serious London agent and he was able to sell us easily for good wages.

We met Pete Sears, a pianist and bassist, who started jamming with us. He was living in a broom cupboard in Notting Hill Gate. It was just big enough to take a single mattress and he shared it with his girlfriend, Lucy. The landlord charged them £2 10s 6d a week. He wore a candy-stripe suit and carried all he owned in a leather briefcase. Pete took Keith and me to see his parents in Beckenham and they kindly put us up for a couple of weeks so that we were spared any more of the Tooting experience. He was a kind soul and an excellent all-round musician. He attempted to play with us for six months, but his electric piano never worked. He tried desperately to get it working, fiddling with it all the time and spending each gig with a soldering iron in his hand. One music critic in Leicester actually wrote, 'Pete Sears used the strobe cunningly, enhancing the overall sound of the ground-breaking Les Fleur de Lys to good effect.' In six months, Pete never managed to get one single note out of it but we kept him on because he was such a laugh and thoroughly reliable in other areas, such as arranging the music and trying to mend the van.

One night, he positively beamed as he said he'd got the piano working. He was so excited; he wanted to make up for all the nights he hadn't made an impression. He brought his hands down really hard on the keyboard for the first song in his grim determination to be dynamic. The legs gave way under the pressure and one of them rolled off the stage. It kept going all the way to the back of the dancehall to the entrance, whereupon someone stepped on it and roller skated into a bouncer who promptly threw him out. The legless piano smashed to pieces on the stage – the only thing that survived was Pete's soldering.

Chris never took anything seriously. He had come from playing the Artful Dodger in a production of *Oliver!* and he continually ribbed everyone. Whilst travelling in the back of the van, he would wait until Pete was asleep and set light to the string he used for laces in his shoes. When we stopped at the motorway café, Pete would wake up and step out of the van and wonder why his shoes were falling off his feet. Pete was very upset when we were forced to sack him because of the failing economics of the band, as we all were; it was sad to see him go. A week later, he flew to San Francisco, where he promptly auditioned for the legendary Jefferson Airplane and landed the job of bass player and pianist. He became a millionaire with them. We've all stayed in touch and still laugh about those days before everybody got so terribly serious. And there still wasn't a hint of drink or drugs anywhere except among the jazz musicians playing the cellars of Soho, whom we admired but for whom we felt sorry: the world was rejecting their immense talents as it turned all its attention to rock groups.

We continued as a four-piece and a regular gig was Margate's Dreamland Ballroom. We loved the caretaker. We were a big draw at the venue but he always liked to tell us who had been there before us. His peculiar habit was leaving the 's' off a band's name where it should have been and adding one where there wasn't. He would proudly say, 'We've had them all here, you know; the Manfred Manns, Brian Pooles and the Tremolo, The Hollie, Gerrys and the Pacemaker and the Animal.'

Nothing was happening with 'Circles', but it had attracted the attention of talented people within the industry. Kenny Barker, a song-plugger, and Nicholas Wright, a well-known 'pop' photographer, approached us and became our managers. They had plenty of contacts, and in particular knew a guy called Frank Fenter, who needed a back-up band for his protégé and wife, Sharon Tandy.

Before we knew what was happening, we were at the Finsbury Park Empire (later known as the Rainbow) for one night. We opened up the show along with Sharon for Sonny and Cher, who were No. 1 with 'I Got You Babe'. It all went well and Frank wanted to take the band with him to his new job at Atlantic Records, based in the Polydor building at Stratford Place. We grabbed the chance.

Frank seemed to know everybody of any importance. He put us into the Playboy Club in Park Lane, playing from 9 p.m. until 3 a.m., one half-hour on, one half-hour off. I had to sleep in the van in Hyde Park between three o'clock and eight in the morning for the first week, as we thought it would be stolen or towed away without someone on guard duty.

All sorts of glamorous people, including James Mason, visited the club and we all loved it. It was well run and nobody got shot, as far as I know, but it closed down shortly afterwards amidst rumours of Mob involvement and Met corruption.

We continually floated in and out of the West End, blind to all the criminal activity around us. We'd play The Cromwellian, a famous club on the Cromwell Road, and hear about protection rackets but not realise the notorious Kray Twins (even the most innocent country bumpkin had heard of them – they were always in the newspapers) were making a collection that very night, ostensibly for selling the club the furniture we saw neatly stacked in the corner. Our innocence brought us nothing but joy, even though the London gang bosses and their henchmen were right under our noses wherever we played.

Not every job was as glamorous but when we played for a cinema ad for Tuff Boots we met some interesting people. Guitar legend Jeff Beck arrived on the film set with his girlfriend, who was an actress. He gave us all a ride in his Stingray and told us how Phil Sawyer was rated around town. He said there were three guitarists in London: Eric Clapton, Jeff Beck and Phil. Keith and I felt privileged to be in such company.

Keith had always been the mainstay in Les Fleur de Lys, always solid as a rock, both in his drumming ability and in his quiet resolve. He was there from the very beginning when Frank Smith first formed the group to the day it finally folded. He was continually asked to join other, more successful groups but he always stayed. He never complained about anything. He nicknamed me 'Rupert the Bear', as I was always getting grumpy, but he always managed to cheer me up.

Our manager Nicky had recently been photographing the Animals and had become friends with them. They asked him to look after their flat at 27 Cranley Gardens in South Kensington, close to The Cromwellian, so he offered it to Keith and me while they were away in the USA. It was a beautiful place with three big bedrooms in a great location. The day we moved in we had one box of Smarties and one apple between us. We'd play venues like The Cromwellian or Blaises in Queensgate, then nip round to see Sharon Tandy for soup in Penywern Road in Earls Court, all within a mile of each other.

Frank Fenter, meanwhile, asked us in to record a song or two for

Polydor. Phil and Chris wrote a track called 'Mud In Your Eye' and we did 'I've Been Trying', a Curtis Mayfield song, on the B-side.

Back at Cranley Gardens, a fuzzy-haired black guy had taken one of the rooms. He introduced himself as Jimi Hendrix.

CHAPTER 3

◉ ◉ ◉

A Glimpse of Heaven

Chas Chandler, the bass player with the Animals, was managing
Jimi, and had given him a key to the flat. Chas was in America
doing another tour, so Jimi was literally on his own in a strange city
and could use some company. He needed to know where the guitar
shops were, as he only had an acoustic with him and he was going
to need an electric. We did our duty for mankind and dragged him
round Charing Cross Road. He never put out the garbage. I had to
tell him off about that. Well, you would, wouldn't you? He kept
himself to himself most of the time, drawing, or painting on the
floor of his room. He'd occasionally rattle off a tune on his acoustic
guitar just to make us feel good. He was left-handed and his talent
struck us as being up there with the likes of Phil Sawyer, who was
still amazing us all. Jimi was invited to play lead on a Curtis
Mayfield track we were recording called 'Amen' with producer
Hilton Valentine. Other tracks we did with him were 'Ring of Fire'
and 'You've Got To Earn It'. The session took place at Kingsway
Studios with Pete Sears on his faulty electric piano (before he left
for San Francisco), Keith on drums, me on a cheap Burns bass (my
Rickenbacker had gone missing) and Phil on vocals. Nobody knows
where the tapes went and half the band doesn't remember being
there. There was something strange about the coffee. I had an
acetate of the recordings but left it in Mum's council house in my
damp back bedroom cupboard. It went all mouldy, so I threw it

away about ten years later. It's buried in the landfill site on the B3082 near Ringwood, if anyone is interested.

I nearly did one gig with Fleur at a showbiz restaurant, where we were due to start at 9 p.m. after another band. The owner came over as the first group was getting its stuff off the stage, and said, 'You should be playing.'

I was cocky and said, 'Well, we're not, are we?'

'Get out of my restaurant!' he bristled and screamed back.

We shrugged our shoulders and took our kit back to the van, which was parked up the alley in St Anne's Court.

'I'm going back for the money,' I said in my best naive Jimmy Cagney heroic style. As I walked in, the owner came racing over, so I asked him for the money. 'Union rules,' I explained.

'Get out!' he shouted, drawing the attention of his ten-foot-tall bouncer.

The owner pushed me towards the door, so I pushed him back and the bouncer started to move . . . fast. I was out of there. I ran for the van shouting, 'Give me the keys! The keys!' but the guys in the van couldn't find them. They shook their heads . . . and Gorillaman was upon us. He started rocking the van and would have tipped it over, so I jumped out the other side and ran back up the alley. The owner was waiting. He stopped me long enough for Gorillaman to catch up. One blow from those massive fists of his sent me into a daze and I vaguely remember the second one landing as I was sinking to the ground. I caught the sound of the bottle being smashed and knew what was coming – the end of my face as I had known it.

But my guardian angel stepped in. I heard two burly policemen blow their whistles and I was saved. They took me to the station, where I was told that Gorillaman had claimed I'd hit him first. I was warned to stay out of the area, as they'd also been involved in a stabbing the week before – someone else who'd mysteriously hit them first.

I like to think that what happened to them the following week had something to do with either Frank or my guardian angel, but it's fanciful of me. Somebody got the better of both of those bastards and stuffed their heads into a huge saucepan of boiling fat. The restaurant closed shortly afterwards. I survived with a very swollen face for a few weeks but I took the advice of the police and never went near the place again. And we never did get the money.

Another night out with Les Fleur de Lys was ending at 2 a.m. in Portobello in London when we came across a wonderful café that was still open. Inside, it looked like the set from *Sgt Peppers*. There was a harmonium along one wall and I sat down to play it. It was the most wonderful sound and so 'Beatlish'. There, sipping a drink, was a guy with a Hendrix hairdo who asked us if we were a band. We told him who we were and he said he'd seen us play at The Marquee and that he liked our support group, Pink Floyd.

The Marquee was a prestigious club situated in Wardour Street, in Soho. Any band that secured a residency there was considered to be on its way to the top. We continually received offers from record companies but chose to stay with Frank at Atlantic Records. It was the 'coolest' record label in the world.

The freak in the café then said he and his friends were starting a new record label called Apple. At this point, Chris Andrews started nudging me and trying to make me laugh. He was always mimicking the kind of pseudo would-be managers who said, 'You're going to be big,' and this guy fitted the bill. We kept talking to him and he said, 'Maybe you need convincing.' He stood up and said, 'Follow me.'

We all piled into a long, black limousine with darkened windows, which pulled up outside a large white building, and we followed him down into the basement. Inside was a rehearsal room and in the corner was a set of drums. The name on the bass drum was The Beatles. It was all so far-fetched. We were still sniggering at his Mr Big act and silly hair. We walked around in disbelief and eventually said, 'Thanks a lot,' taking his telephone number and leaving.

His last words were, 'We are looking for a band, if you change your mind.'

Chris gave the number to a mate of his. His friend had a group and they became Grapefruit, the first signing The Beatles made to their new label, Apple. The guy with the silly hair was John Lennon's right-hand man, Terry Doran; we just didn't believe him. Smart, eh? Gifted, that's what we were. We had that special instinct that attracted failure.

Phil, like a lot of greats, was a confused boy and upset a lot of people in his early days. It had been a mystery where my Rickenbacker bass went because one minute it was in the van when Phil went up to the West End, and the next it had gone. It was stolen by persons unknown. Now, I certainly don't believe Phil stole it, but at 22 one leaps to conclusions, inevitably bad ones, and I suspected him. Thankfully, I didn't openly accuse him and kept my suspicions to myself.

It wasn't long before we lost Phil; he was too good to be struggling with us. He landed the gig with the Spencer Davis Group when Stevie Winwood left to form Traffic. Phil had a hit with the song 'Timeseller', but soon left the group when he met a lady who whisked him away from the record business. Suddenly, Phil was married and everything changed for him. He went to study symphonic music and has excelled musically, writing ballets and recording classical music for films and television.

Phil and I had shared the driving of our Ford Thames Dormobile, which Keith's father had bought on condition we kept up the payments and looked after it. None of us knew anything about vehicles, so we lived with the constant whining from the back axle. Everyone had joked that at least it was drowning out my own whining. One day, while driving through Salisbury, the entire drive shaft dropped off onto the A30, leaving the entire stream of traffic behind us hooting and hollering as they tried to avoid the huge piece of junk. After a pitstop for repairs, we became aware that we'd neglected such things as changing the oil and checking the radiator – normal servicing. The crunch came a few weeks later when the battery fell through the floor. The overflowing acid had begun to eat the surrounding metal. We had no choice but to sell it as scrap for £50; it was a year old. The dealer stopped the cheque, as we still owed £300 to the hire-purchase company.

With the demise of the van and without a guitarist, we could no longer tour, but good things started to happen in quick succession. Our first stroke of luck was when we met Bryn Haworth walking along Wardour Street with his guitar, looking lost, malnourished and as gentle as a lamb. He was unknown and on his uppers, but turned out to be quite brilliant. We stumbled across each other at just the right time – for him and us.

We loved him instantly. He came from the farmlands of Lancashire and had a sensitive nature similar to my own. I had found a soulmate. He eventually became Britain's top slide guitarist, featuring on records by Joan Armatrading and Gerry Rafferty, among others, and recorded several solo albums. He's still one of my closest friends.

We went to The Ship, the pub frequented by all the Marquee acts, bought him a beer and talked for hours. He came back with us and we played in the flat, then we told Frank we'd found Phil's replacement. We were on cloud nine. We now had three compatible musicians all locked into the same musical groove, the feel of the music coming from the southern states of America. All the acts on

51

Atlantic had it but it was rare to hear it coming from a British band. The timing couldn't have been better. Frank wanted to build a reputation with Les Fleur de Lys in exactly the same way Atlantic Records had built Booker T and the MGs in the USA.

Bryn, Keith and I now had the perfect band to back up any artists that came through the studios at Polydor. Frank put us on a wage of £15 a week each and we went to work every day.

Keith and I moved out of the Animals' flat, said goodbye to Jimi Hendrix and took a bed-sittingroom in Bayswater. It cost £7 10s a week. We could walk down Bayswater Road to Stratford Place in 20 minutes and live like kings on the rest of the money. We were chauffeured around all the favourite nightclubs of that time. There was the Speakeasy, the Bag O'Nails, The Scotch of St James and the Revolution, and we'd arrive in a black limousine that was all part of the Atlantic Records service to its personnel. Frank had us playing regularly at the Speakeasy, which was where we met Jimi again. He sat in and played Bryn's Fender Strat upside down. He was phenomenal. The Beatles, the Stones and Eric Clapton were in the audience. Eric was also one of Bryn's fans at the time.

We were on top of the world, hanging out with the crème de la crème of the industry and witnessing the birth of some of the world's finest artists. It was sheer bliss to see Hendrix's first gig, Clapton at his finest with Cream and the mighty Otis Redding. Frank was responsible for bringing so many acts from Memphis and New York and we were getting the education of a lifetime in the space of a few months. We were made to feel the equals of these giants in the making. But we were still virgins.

I never quite got over it. When I hear people use the expression 'cool' today, I think of those days in the Speakeasy and shake my head, remembering what cool really meant once. There was no arrogance. There were hugely talented artists all delivering what would become massive hits that would stand the test of time. They may have gone to Carnaby Street or Chelsea for their clothes but it was an afterthought. Fashion was very much the tail of the dog. The music was what people were buying and the spirit of goodwill was overwhelming. The word bullshit was never heard because there was none.

Isaac Hayes and David Porter, one of the most successful songwriting partnerships in the '60s, would rehearse songs with us to demo something they were working on for Otis or Sam and Dave. Once, we played all night with Isaac Hayes and he invited us all along to Paris with him the following day. What a privilege. I learned my craft from them. I learned the connection music has with our spirituality from those people and I would never forget it or trade it for the nonsense that was to follow. Right there and then, I learned all I needed to know to make *Harry's Bar*. I just didn't realise I'd have to fight so hard and for so long to make my point.

It's a minor miracle when the public gets a chance to buy what they really want and feel. Back there at Stratford Place, Johnnie Walker could walk in, go straight to Frank's office and pick up the latest Otis Redding, or the latest Aretha Franklin, or dozens of hidden gems for his radio shows. Then he could nip next door to Roland Rennie's office for the Polydor roster of Jimi Hendrix, Cream, The Who, BeeGees and oddballs like William E. performing 'Lazy Life' (written by G. Haskell). Next to Rennie was Clive Selwood's office representing the Elektra label with The Doors. How could a scene like that confuse any disc jockey? Try getting it wrong. You couldn't.

Bill Kimber, whom Frank had known as a star in South Africa, was to sing under the fictitious name William E. Bill came into the studio with his own song, 'Sunny Days', which was good, but he needed a B-side, so I played him and Frank 'Lazy Life', which I'd just finished. It was my first serious attempt at songwriting. It got their immediate approval and Les Fleur de Lys recorded it straight away with Bryn playing my acoustic. It recorded easily just as it was: guitar, bass and drums, with no need for overdubs. It was a perfect little record. The reaction was so strong when it was released in 1967 that it became the A-side. Johnnie Walker made it his record of the week on Radio Caroline and Polydor received thousands of orders for it.

Then fate played its hand. The factory went on strike and failed to meet an order for 10,000 records, which would have put it in the chart. I didn't even blink at the time. I wasn't bothered; I was just so happy to be around the enormous talent in the building. I didn't really think 'Lazy Life' was a hit. As it turned out to be No. 1 in both South Africa and Australia, I guess I was wrong. It would have been big in Britain.

Chris Andrews, who had found himself a producer and wanted to record a song written by Rod Lynton for EMI, approached Les Fleur de Lys. Chris wanted us to supply the backing, to which we agreed, but when they asked that the band's name appear on the single, we declined. He had been left in limbo when we had stopped touring – we didn't have a job for him, as we were continuing as session musicians – and, by using us, it was a way he could still have his old band around him. We hated the song but went along with it, and recorded one Bryn and I had written called 'Hold On' for the B-side. It was still only the second song I'd written and, so far, both had been recorded satisfactorily. Both tracks were recorded under the name Rupert's People, which Chris had created.

Bryn, Keith and I decided in our wisdom to keep the name Les Fleur de Lys for our Atlantic recordings. We still worshipped the label's stable of artists and had turned our backs on offers from the mighty EMI, who could boast The Beatles.

'Reflections of Charles Brown' was released on EMI with 'Hold On' on the B-side, and, of course, the damn thing went all over the radio. It entered one chart at 50, spread across the European charts and they were begging us to promote it, but we declined and it went away. The reviews were awful, accusing us of copying Procol Harum. We didn't get any prizes for our integrity in backing away from it either. The royalties for 'Hold On' were carved up so many ways neither Bryn nor I made anything out of it.

Many bands at the time were actually made up of experienced session men. A record company would pull together four or five musicians and have them recording all day long. Young boys would jump in at a low wage just to be part of a famous band. Promoting a record involves working all day for peanuts. Young boys would do that; hardened session men wouldn't.

We were happy working sessions for Frank Fenter and he had us involved in all kinds of projects all the time. He was charging Polydor the full-session rate, paying us a £15 retainer and pocketing the difference. One Christmas, we went up to the office to collect our money and Polydor had signed cheques to each of us for £375. We only found out about it because Frank was in the south of France on holiday. Looking back, I'm not surprised I got so mad with him. Frank laughed it off as all being par for the course. He was no worse than any of his breed back then. Musicians were innocents, grateful for the chances, dazzled by the glamour, careless of the money side . . . sitting ducks for any hard-nosed businessman with an eye for the main chance. Mind you, we did have a weekly buzz factor worth at least £375, plus music lessons from our heroes of the time.

Frank brought in a well-known producer and artist to work with us, whose name was Donnie Elbert, known at the time for his hit 'A Little Piece of Leather'. Donnie was the first man I ever saw make an acoustic guitar sound like a whole band. In years to come, when I started doing solo gigs, he would be my role model. He taught us a lot about studio work and we cut dozens of tracks with him either for his records or our own. One track of his was shipped over to the States for the legendary producer/arranger Arif Mardin to add a string arrangement. We were extremely proud to be associated with it. The single was called 'In Between the Heartaches', but it never surfaced. In five years' time, I would be working with Arif myself.

At this time, we also did a lot of work with Sharon Tandy. She came into the studio and we re-cut 'Hold On' with her. It caused a few ripples, as it still does in the rave clubs of Ibiza. By now, she and Bryn were living together and dabbling with drugs. Frank, who was still technically married to her, was with someone else, so everyone was happy. I behaved like Sharon's little errand boy. She let me stay in the spare room at her flat quite a lot and I liked her, but there had never been any attraction. I was detached from any form of relationship, not because I wasn't interested, but because I simply never seemed to get the opportunity. I was perfectly content to be immersed in music and enjoy everyone's company. I had my eyes on a woman called Janet in Frank's office, but she seemed so superior and aloof, and I was still so boyish compared to the men she was dating. Despite the fact that I had made love non-stop to Belinda for 18 months back when I was 14, I really didn't have a clue how to chat up girls and most of the girls I was meeting probably thought I was a virgin. I was what they called 'too nice' (I'm happy to report they don't say it any more).

Next, Frank decided it might be creative to put us in the studio with the New York band Vanilla Fudge and see what we came up with as a seven-piece. The Fudge were the loudest, heaviest band we'd ever seen. They were phenomenal at the Finsbury Park Empire and scored a big hit with their fantastic record 'You Keep Me Hangin' On'. We blew solidly all night and everything was recorded. I'd never played so hard and wild in all my time, nor have I since.

We recorded so much at Stratford Place and we never gave it a second thought; there must have been stacks of unused recordings in the vaults of that building, filed under 'non-commercial'. We had been immersed in a way of life that had nothing to do with money for us. Somebody was paying for it and for a reason, but the business side of things didn't interest us. We were cocooned in a blissful state of total contentment.

I never once had any problems getting on with people at Stratford Place. Maybe everybody was just so good at their jobs – like the dedicated Janet and Judy, who were not only the MDs' PAs, but also ran the fan clubs for the whole Atlantic scene. We would be recording across the corridor and, when we took a break, would go and see Jan (unavailable), Judy (unassailable) and gorgeous little Pat (unbelievable), and they'd all still be there at ten in the evening, dedicated to the music they were promoting. I began to fancy every girl that ever visited the office, but they all seemed involved with more glamorous men.

I took advantage of Atlantic's free booze cupboard and all the records you wanted. Keith Guster still has every single ever released from that office. Then, when we wrapped up, we'd all shoot off down to the Speakeasy in a limousine. Somebody great was always on the line-up. We never came across any poor acts anywhere we went. Everybody talked to each other affectionately and loved the music; sheer joy abounded from every corner. People who didn't 'get' any of it stayed away in their sad closets plotting the future. Margaret Thatcher would have been one of those alienated souls lost at sea, harbouring grudges and plotting how she would change it all one day.

The Beatles' 1967 album *Sgt Peppers* marks the pinnacle of the whole scene – from then on, it would all be downhill until music reached rock bottom with punk in 1977. The choice you had in the clothes shops was fantastic. The choice in music – brilliant music – was vast and still there were no categories, just the greatest ideas leaping out at you wherever you looked, wherever you went. The customised Minis, the Kings Road boutiques, the E-type Jaguars, the World Cup; everything revolved around London because London ruled the world. 'Buy British' ran the slogan, and we did.

The Beatles reached into places like the Soviet Union simply by their positive messages, and eventually wrote 'Back in the USSR' for them. It was irritating governments and interfering with the war games they so loved to play.

Years later, during a visit from my Uncle David, a Royal Naval Commander, he positively fumed at me, saying, 'We were ready for you lot. We had meetings at the Admiralty and discussed how we intended to put a stop to all your nonsense.'

I tended to believe his ranting. 'Why are you so sure that you're representing the good guys?' I replied, with as much contempt as I could muster.

London in 1967 through to 1968 felt like the happiest and most optimistic place in the world. Brian Epstein had taken possession of the Savile Theatre and when we played there, he came into our dressing-room to meet us and thank us. We thought, 'If Brian Epstein can have fantastic manners and talk to us small fry whilst managing The Beatles, why can't everybody?' All the greats we met during that time, and I include the businessmen, had a degree of good manners and class. These were the examples I remembered as time passed. This was the standard that was set for me. As the years went by, I saw the good manners of those days gradually disappear, along with the special relationships I'd had with the music business that made being a part of it so enjoyable for me. This was a moment when man could have seized the opportunity to enlighten the world. Millions of people were uniting in spirit, ruffling the feathers of world politicians and manipulators. Creativity was winning and it was making money; the old profitable wars and the negative, destructive thoughts and actions of the Establishment were on the rails.

Today's critics talk of naivety when discussing the '60s. Yes, we were naive . . . for not realising just how powerful we were and how powerful our enemies were. Divide and rule is how politicians sustain their world. I saw how they systematically dismantled the '60s ideal, trashing all the positive elements and focusing on the negative, ridiculing the notion that all you need is love. We stood by and allowed them to divide us with propaganda that created the vicious society we now live in.

The distraction of our never-ending social life in Les Fleur de Lys had a down side. Frank had given us all a free ticket to the greatest two years in popular music Britain had ever known . . . and paid us a retainer for the privilege. When we weren't recording for Polydor, Atlantic or outside companies, we were out on the town. It gradually dawned on Frank that I was neglecting my writing and, although he tried to encourage me, I was still mad at him for cheating us out of the money. I have always tended to react to dishonesty by going on strike, which never has any effect on the perpetrators, as the only person I ever hurt is myself; they just carry on with someone else. I had the ideal scene for songwriting and I blew it. I was still only 22 but should have seized the opportunity and got stuck in. I had started to sing more on some of the records we were making and none of it was costing me a penny. The studio was free, the musicians were free and I had a retainer. I was privileged and didn't realise it. I was too busy admiring everyone else instead of thinking that I might have had talent as well. And I had an unhealthy attitude towards money – it wasn't that important, was it? I was creating the blueprint for a lifetime of poverty when I had the foundations of a gold mine right under my nose. I was paving the way for money men.

Frank blamed it on the good life we were living and pulled in other writers.

I was becoming fascinated by musicians who quit or were fired from the top bands, believing they clearly weren't interested in the money, that they were the real rebels as opposed to the many who were merely acting for the sake of the cameras. It was a childish and destructive attitude to cling to and it took me years to see how stupid I was.

One of the great rebel stories around at that time was the case of John Gustafson, the bass player of The Big Three. Tall, dark and handsome, with outstanding ability as a singer and bassist, he was offered a huge solo deal by EMI and tipped as a major star of the future. On the way to Manchester Square to sign his deal, he had to pass the Marble Arch Cinema and there was a great movie showing, so he went to that instead.

Public rebels that came later, like the Sex Pistols, didn't fool anyone who had been around in the mid-'50s. James Dean, Marlon Brando, Elvis Presley, Jerry Lee Lewis and Little Richard – they were really wild and didn't need a PR firm to 'create' an image. I grew up before PR firms really got to grips with the rock 'n' roll industry. It was so new; it was more natural, 'organic' in today's language. Plenty of acts today have to hire PR to get heard or noticed and, as soon as they do, their 'act' is just that, an act. It's phoney. For me, the music business doesn't entertain real rebellion, so the whole premise of the cutting edge is contrived. It's generally the clue to warn you not to buy into it, because the Sex Pistols and their ilk can't usually write a good song; in my experience they can't even play a bad one well and can rarely hold a tune.

Donnie Elbert was a rebel in the camp in many ways. He'd read a lot on music-business law and kept a particular book on the subject in his room at Stratford Place. I'd go in there often and just talk about a lot of things. We were almost kin, certainly soulmates. He'd laugh a lot about how he'd always put in 'that back-door clause' that would allow him to escape being sued by a record company. While he was recording and being paid by Polydor, he was also recording elsewhere. These records would eventually enter the top 10 on EMI, on Avco, and . . . er . . . London Records. Donnie reached No. 8, No. 11 and No. 27 in the bestsellers with three different records and nobody could sue him. Frank wasn't happy about that. It was fine for

Frank to be smart with Polydor's money or Atlantic's, but not all right for a dumb artist to start playing that game. The business is so fond of telling everybody about how artists' egos are enormous, but in all my 40 years in the business I have never come across an ego larger than that of a record-company executive. They are like governments; they have to be in control. Donnie had to leave the country, and pretty fast. But he collected his royalties and it was said that he was escorted onto a plane at Heathrow with a gun held to his head and a warning that if he ever came back he would be killed. I missed him.

Otis had perished in an air crash along with his band and the last record we made with Donnie was a tribute album with him doing all the singing. The overall vibe, you could say, was turning sour. Conspiracy theories were rife. Mafia stories circulated. Frank conning us every week began to make me paranoid.

I had finally succumbed to smoking dope regularly with Bryn and it didn't suit me. I was already nuts. I was a screwed-up kid and dabbling with any drug would only exacerbate my condition – which it did with increasing regularity. I've known plenty of folks it doesn't affect badly and can only assume their brains are different to mine.

I'd been offered £45 a week for playing bass for The Flowerpotmen, a chart group which was enjoying its success with the hit 'Let's Go To San Francisco'. That, and my paranoid ravings, drove me to leave the best scene I could ever have hoped for, the best band I'd ever play with and some of the best friends I would ever make. A mistake. Or was it? When one looks at one's whole life and recalls such scenarios, the rational might call it foolishness, ignorance or even madness; the businessman might look at it simply and, without emotion, comment that I left because it was three times the money Frank was paying. For me, I ask myself, 'Did I lose my friends?' The answer is, 'No, I didn't.' I have remained close to all the good guys of that glorious time at Stratford Place. Donnie's dead now, and so is Frank. In a sense, a part of me died too. It was definitely the end of something for everyone involved.

Frank went to America and formed the Capricorn record label with Phil Walden. He had great success with the Allman Brothers Band and was involved with Jimmy Carter on the presidential campaign. Before leaving England, he sold all our songs to three different publishers, grabbing an advance from each. That alone took years to sort out. He was a player in a tough business and we were boys; it was like lambs to the slaughter. But, all in all, he gave us an education. He gave us the best time of our lives in the best years the London music scene has ever known. We bathed in his glory of bringing Stax label artists to the UK's attention. He gave me DJ Johnnie Walker, who would remember me, and that whole fantastic scene. When I had learned what I needed to learn in my life and I was ready, I would create a song and Johnnie would play it. That journey was to take another 33 years.

It was 1968. Keith and I were sharing the bedsit in Bayswater with our Baby Belling cooker. The two girls upstairs, who were Liverpudlians, kept flirting with us on the stairs. Whenever we came in from the studio, the one chasing me would say, 'Here comes creeping Jesus,' and I'd smile at her. The girl chasing Keith would offer us both beans on toast upstairs in their flat and sometimes we'd take them up on the offer because we were genuinely hungry and tired. Keith then wanted to be alone with his girl, so I would considerately return to my room alone and think how lovely Belinda had been all those years ago when I had made love for the first time. Why couldn't I find somebody like her?

There would come a knock on the door and I knew it was madam upstairs, who'd explain she couldn't play gooseberry with the other two. I would make an excuse and she'd get shirty and say I was stuck up. She was forever knocking on my door . . . and one day I let her in.

She got what she wanted. Then she decided she was in love and wanted to marry me. It was a thousand miles away from my idea of love, but it was typical of the times and as a bewildered idiot I handled the situation badly. I had no experience. Of course, she got pregnant.

Both Phil and Chris had had the experience of getting girls pregnant and life had carried on as normal for them. None of it felt real to me and I certainly didn't think of myself as a rogue or even a lovable Alfie type. I thought things would sort themselves out on their own. Could I marry someone I didn't love or even like? What did she expect? She wanted something she couldn't get and it was our destiny to have a beautiful daughter. I only remember sleeping with her once but I'm not surprised I don't remember anything pleasant. There was nothing to remember. It had never been a close relationship and marriage could never have worked. I don't regret my part in it, for my daughter is a jewel, but I regret not ever becoming friends with her mother. We could have got over the stupid part. And it was outstandingly stupid.

I wouldn't see my daughter for 32 years. It was meant to be. Her mother and I were ignorant and young and carefree, but we weren't criminals and it certainly doesn't justify a life sentence of bad feeling.

In the following months, Tony Head joined Les Fleur de Lys as the lead singer. We had spent time together in our Bournemouth days and I was glad to see him again. I wished I'd stayed with them all, but now I was with The Flowerpotmen. Les Fleur de Lys went on to back Aretha Franklin and supported The Beach Boys and did *Top of the Pops* with the Potter Dee song 'Two Can Make it Together'. It sold enough copies for it to have reached the No. 1 spot in today's market. Bryn was never happy after I left, so he followed Pete Sears to the USA, where he formed Wolfgang with Richie Hayward, who was soon to be known with Little Feat. Pete was getting hits with Jefferson Airplane. The band fell apart.

My days with Les Fleur de Lys remain the most perfect I have ever spent in the music business. It was a complete family affair, with Frank as the godfather and all of us doing what we did best. I loved the whole industry then. The success of the '60s was down to people who knew how to do their jobs well, artists and businessmen alike, pulling together as a team, neither interfering with the other. That's why the songs have stood the test of time and subsidised the incompetence of the generations that followed.

To deride that time and use the quote 'If you remember it, you weren't really there' is to miss the underlying point that it was extremely profitable as well. And continues to be. Not everybody was wrecked. As history has shown, the doers got on with the job.

Frank was on his path to American politics; Bryn and Frank's secretary, Janet, were embarking on more spiritual journeys, one towards Christianity, the other into Buddhism; while Keith looked towards a happy marriage, and Tony and Judy began 36 years of wedded bliss. People passing through on their chosen paths, yet linked spiritually from some distant past; a staging post for old souls meeting up before launching into the rest of their lives. It was a glimpse of heaven.

CHAPTER 4

🍥 🍥 🍥

In the Court of King Crimson

Little did I know as I joined The Flowerpotmen that they would be the catalyst to meeting the woman who was to become my wife. Mark Goddard, the band's road manager, had been a friend of Les Fleur de Lys through the days of Chris Andrews and Phil Sawyer, and he was now living in Bayswater with Keith and me. Mark had tipped me off that the Flowerpotmen's backing band was quitting to launch themselves as Deep Purple. Robert's Giles, Giles and Fripp, who'd just arrived in London, had auditioned for the gig, but a band led by drummer Carlo Little, who was highly regarded by the rock 'n' roll aristocracy, was chosen instead. Carlos was known for his work with Cyril Davies and the RnB All Stars featuring Alexis Korner, and Screaming Lord Sutch and The Savages. The Stones were Cyril Davies's support band at The Marquee. Because they were short of a drummer, Carlo helped them out by sitting in for them. They offered him the full-time job but he turned them down. In his defence, though, he doesn't need one: when they offered him the job, they weren't nearly as good as the big boys Carlo was playing with. The Stones, of course, eventually signed Charlie Watts.

As soon as I started rehearsals, I knew I'd entered the world of hardened professionals. And after the closeted spiritual life of Stratford Place, I found playing hard to enjoy in the same way. It was just a job to everyone and they performed in the knowledge that next month there'd be another job with a different name but essentially the same attitude and demands. It was about grown-up men earning their living, being highly competent. The intimacy I had enjoyed so much with Les Fleur de Lys had gone; socially, it felt more like workmates than soulmates.

Carlo was a tough guy on the outside, but we became closer and, in other circumstances, I could have formed an impressive heavy three-piece with him, like Cream. I soon got to like him and respected his undoubted authority. Our lives would be linked forever from the time of our first week together working in the Northeast, where he met his future wife, Iris, and I met Sally.

The job was doubling two swish clubs in the north of England, La Dolce Vita in Newcastle and the Stockton Fiesta, forty miles away in Stockton-on-Tees, for seven nights. That's fourteen shows each lasting forty-five minutes. There was just enough time to do the drive between towns and set up. Unfortunately, the Ford Transit couldn't cope and broke down in between and we were very late for one of the shows. At the end of the gig, we had to leave the van in Newcastle and go home on the night train to London.

Sally travelled back down south with us. She said she'd been appearing at a nightclub in Newcastle and I took her to be a cabaret singer, a style I had never enjoyed because it always seemed too showy to me to mean much emotionally. We slept most of the way and when we arrived at Kings Cross, she wanted to stay with me in London. I didn't argue, but I wondered why she stuck to me so quickly. We hadn't even kissed each other. She spoke with so much confidence and authority in a self-assertive, grand manner that I was bowled over; I was putty in her hands. 'Why me?' I thought again and went along with anything she suggested. I was a simple country boy at heart, way out of my depth. I had been viewed as a problematic child and a vulnerable, naive young man. I'd been nowhere special yet, so I was tremendously flattered to be treated as 'somebody' by Sally and her sophisticated friends. She had played Broadway, the London Palladium, had appeared on television. She was a star and I was dazzled. She reeled me in like a skilled angler. My personality was switched on from the moment I met her and my shyness evaporated.

By coincidence, Sally called me 'Bear' and I was reminded of Keith's nickname for me: Rupert – moody, cuddly, likes a bit of honey and extremely grumpy when poked with a stick.

Sally was more like a finishing school for me than a romance. She took little boy blue and made a man of him. Unfortunately, she loved little boy blue a little too much to allow him to become a man, but

I'm very grateful to her nonetheless. 'He's a child,' I could imagine all of her sophisticated friends saying.

Keith's face was a picture when we arrived back from Newcastle and walked into the bedsit. He was getting up as we arrived just after seven o'clock and Sally stood there in a mink coat. Neither of us had ever seen such a thing before. She was vivacious, shapely and a little under five feet tall, loud and shrieking with laughter. I was my quiet, timid self. I held out my arms to Keith in mock bewilderment and more than a little pride, like a kid who'd just caught a very big fish.

At that moment, I thought I must have made the right moves by leaving Les Fleur de Lys, because one week later I was being invited to 'the cottage in the country', which, at that time, only rock stars could afford. She owned a car even though she couldn't drive, so I was getting transport as well. It was this or stick around the flat and marry a pregnant girl I didn't like. I don't think I was equipped to handle either and, on reflection, I chose what I thought would be the easier option. At that age, I hadn't realised I could say 'no' to both offers.

'I don't know what's going on. I'll call you,' was how I left it with Keith.

Sally and I caught the train to Bookham in Surrey. Little boys are so impressionable. How I love being over 50.

The cottage turned out to be rented at £7 a week, the car was a Renault 1300 and she had two dogs and an overdraft. It didn't matter. I thought she was wonderful and everything I wasn't. Her initial spark may have blinded me, but on her own turf, out of the limelight, she was a good, kind, thoughtful, strong yet fragile person. She fascinated me. I had never met anyone like her before. She shone and the world smiled wherever she went. She was Judy Garland. You couldn't get a word in and life was a non-stop cabaret, even in the local butcher's shop. But at home alone it was like bathing in the warmest of waters. I was mystified and mesmerised by her double identity, yet she would always deny its existence when I brought up the subject.

Sally ran a fairly strict routine at the cottage. On waking, I would have to fetch a cup of tea for her in bed. Then she would cook a full English breakfast. She was a first-rate cook. It was always my job to wash up. This was followed by walking the dogs across the farmland surrounding the cottage. Her routine never varied and I never questioned it. The result was that my day could never start until after 2 p.m., but I quite liked it nevertheless. It was a different life from what I had known. She put me through an Open University degree course in lovemaking and after a year I passed my Ph.D. with honours.

One day as I was buying an amplifier in Hammersmith she went to the pet shop next door and bought another dog. I hadn't loved dogs up to that point but Flop became one of the greatest pleasures of my life and would bring me immense happiness for nine years.

I was still feeling the loss of Les Fleur de Lys but Sally loved 'the Pottymen', as she'd renamed them, and encouraged me to stay with them. The four frontmen were Tony Burrows, Robin Shaw, Neil Landen and Pete Nelson. When Pete left, they offered me the job as frontman, as I was always making them laugh. It was turning into a cabaret act and they thought I could bring some lunacy into it.

I was very close to agreeing when Robert Fripp popped up in my life again and took me to an audition for another chart group, Cupid's Inspiration. Their song 'Yesterday Has Gone' was a No. 4 hit in 1968 and they sounded great. I landed the bass gig but they didn't take Robert. He asked too many financial questions. He would've been able to outsmart them when he was 11 years old.

The first tour was a big deal, with Scott Walker topping the bill. He was the biggest thing on the scene at the time – a superstar with a string of smash hits. Three chart groups appeared in the first half of the show. There were four gigs a week for about three weeks or so. The management paid £1,000 a night for each band . . . but all we musicians saw, after creative accountancy had taken its customary toll, was thirty quid a week each. The accountant had done his job for the manager and the tour expenses had soaked up any profits. 'One day it'll all be different,' I thought. As the record business has shown me over 40 years, it won't. Fiddling the books seems to be human nature.

I did another nine weeks thinking it would sort itself out but it got worse. When the clapped-out old Transit spluttered to a halt at the end of the entire twelve-week tour, it was over. I looked around for someone to blame and remembered that it was Robert Fripp who had been instrumental in bringing such a shambolic outfit to my attention. It was entirely my own choice but I was only 23 and still playing the blame game as a child might.

Sally was appearing in a play at the Yvonne Arnaud Theatre in Guildford and to tide myself over I got a job in a fruit-and-vegetable shop in Bookham, as I wanted to show Sally I wasn't workshy. It was right on my doorstep. I rose early and drove into Covent Garden at

5 a.m. to fetch the produce in the firm's van. Although it felt odd not to be working in music, I knew it was only a temporary rest. I didn't go on the dole because I preferred not to get involved with the government. It was interesting to see a different culture at work at that time of the morning and everyone seemed cheerful in a world of his or her own. I'd go back to the shop and help out serving until 1 p.m., then go home and write music for the rest of the day.

My one memorable high point during this diversion was when a frail-looking lady in her 70s came in to buy vegetables. She was known by the other staff and they greeted her with their usual 'How are you?'

'I was burgled last night,' she said. 'They've taken all my silver.'

The manager of the shop quickly responded with, 'My dear, come and sit down. You must feel so shocked.'

'No, no, not at all,' said the lady. 'If I'd known they were there, I would have got up and made them a cup of tea. It is their job after all.'

I left the world of dirty vegetables soon afterwards when The Flowerpotmen offered me more work as their bass player. Their replacement singer had been Rick Woolf, an incredibly talented artist/writer from South Africa. Like most other musicians at the time, he had side projects running as well as his main gig – some guys played in three or four bands simultaneously – and we formed a recording band together. Our wages continued to come from The Flowerpotmen but our creativity was being channelled into something completely 'different and credible', the euphemism the industry uses when you're willing to starve for your art. Roger Cook, who sang with the big top-10 funky band Blue Mink, produced it at Air London Studios and it was a stunning album that was way too far out for the business. Still, it was credible. Rick was a Buddhist. He played a harmonium and had a voice full of spirituality, packed with a soulful punch that still knocks me for six every time I hear it. It remains one of my favourite albums, although it was never released or even given a title.

I was beginning to see the business for what it was. Now that 1969 was upon us, things were changing. The Beatles had started fighting, Epstein was dead, new people had entered the game and the light was fading fast. Rick Woolf could have brought some radiance back into the world but it wasn't to be. Pink Floyd filled the gap. Much as I like them, their message was negative; Rick's was positive and optimistic and a natural successor to The Beatles' mystical excursions.

Tony Burrows was doing so many vocal sessions he was on *Top of the Pops* in four different bands on the same night and they were all high in the top 10, including the No. 1, 'Love Grows' by Edison Lighthouse. He was so bored with being on the road and could earn a great living in London doing sessions while still being able to see his family, so The Flowerpotmen was broken up. Tony had the talent to be anything he wanted but the business pigeon-holed him into 'pop' when all he was doing was feeding his family. The critics expect us all to die for our art to give them something more interesting to write about. They can take the corporate wages and obey their editors but we're not allowed to. We have to become junkies and alcoholics to prove our sincerity. It's all bullshit from beginning to end. Tony has passed through life like a warm breeze, smiling to himself as he watched much lesser talents being lauded by fools, and, from 1969, the fool count was rising rapidly. I love Tony's character and he loves his cricket. We're still good friends. Some things are built to last. Rick went home to South Africa.

It's natural to assume The Flowerpotmen were just banal pop performers; the truth is that they were never given a chance to be who they really were as individual talents and they put their families first.

During my 12 weeks with Cupid's Inspiration, I worked on their album and contributed a song. Their producer listened to ten or more I'd written and thought I should do a solo album. I could hardly believe it and rushed home to tell Sally, who adored everything I was writing. To be fair on myself, some of the lyrics were very beautiful in their innocence but, at the time, I badly wanted to write something with more grit. I had little experience of real life and I wasn't impressing myself enough to get really excited.

I signed, or, to be absolutely accurate, the producer signed to CBS Records (he who signs gets the cheque). Two top arrangers were hired to work with me and the whole project was scored out before we entered the studio. That was often the method used to save costs, so an album could be recorded in a week. Yet again, I was flattered but, though I liked some orchestrated records, like those of Burt Bacharach, I hadn't reached the same class yet. Had I been confident, self-assured and assertive like my friend Robert, it might have been more successful. I had a knack for melody and lyrics, but continually spoiled the effect by allowing clumsy musicians to trample all over the bare bones. As it was, the album *Sail In My Boat* made record of the week on BBC Radio 1 and Wanda Arletti, a South African girl singer, did a cover of 'Zanzibar' which reached the No. 1 spot over there.

I was surprised and ridiculously slow at taking advantage of my success. I did nothing and I didn't even tell anyone about it. Sally and I had found happiness and I was daydreaming my time away in the beauty of the Surrey countryside. I wasn't focused enough on music. I headed for the comfort zone whenever I could, writing songs as if I hadn't a care in the world. It was pure but irrelevant compared to the massive talent of writers like Dylan and Paul Simon. But then, just as I was having a taste of happiness, Robert Fripp called to ask me to join his band King Crimson.

I had been to see King Crimson in 1969 at The Marquee. They were being hailed as the best band in the world and they'd only done a few gigs. They were startling. I felt I was in the presence of Satan. I stayed until the end and gave my compliments to the band, and went home hardly believing that this was the baby with whom I had shared a maternity ward and chummed with at school.

Why didn't I buy into it? Jealousy? No, I had never felt I was in competition with Robert Fripp – not even when we were kids playing fives – so there was no question of being envious of his huge success. I just didn't buy into the harshly negative Crimson message. I felt down when I was with them. All the music I'd heard throughout my life had lifted my spirits and spoken to me of love, unity and optimism. The Beatles had left us believing 'All You Need Is Love'. So the arrival of King Crimson's music, screaming destruction and hatred for the world and full of dread for the future was perfectly timed. It was the antithesis of the optimistic '60s revolution and its sheer power was enough to flatten anyone opposing those ideals. The band was the musical equivalent of those delightful people who orchestrate the world of politics, business and war.

King Crimson scared me. They depressed me. They epitomised the right wing. My soul was sure I had been in the presence of a real evil and I couldn't wait to get out of The Marquee. In the band's biography, the drummer, Michael Giles, speaks of a dark force present in the band and the discomfort they all felt, which was so intense no one but Robert wanted to carry on. The band was a huge international success, but disintegrated after a year, leaving Robert and his writing partner, Pete Sinfield, to pick up the pieces, using hired hands to continue their commitment to the record company.

During the making of the second album, I had done one vocal overdub for Robert, namely 'Cadence and Cascade'. He hadn't reformed the band but was considering his options. He was under enormous pressure. I received his call and he asked me to join as a full member, as bassist and lead singer. I was happy to hear from him. He'd sent a postcard from the USA when King Crimson was at the height of its success and we'd had so many close encounters I was able to talk to him as an old friend.

'That's fantastic, Bob, but you know it's not me. I like funky bass gigs and black influences, how could it possibly work?' was my immediate response.

He replied in his normal earnest manner, 'I want you in the band because your time is good, you never speed up when you're playing and I believe some of what you know can be useful.'

He had only known the little boy in me and I don't doubt he felt comfortable with that. Some little boys will follow orders and some little boys like to give them. We were both still schoolboys at 24.

Robert called to ask me again and I caved in against my will, my soul and my judgement, and in that single moment I put myself on a journey to hell. It would take me 27 years to honestly say to myself, 'I am over it.' And it was only my love of Robert that enabled me to do it at all. My period with the band has been accurately described in the excellent book *In the Court of King Crimson* written by Sid Smith. Going back into the fine detail will be very destructive but I do so with apologies to Robert because we're changed men.

I was paid £30 per week on the verbal understanding that I was to have a fifth share of the royalties. The plan was to rehearse the new material for the next album. We assembled in a basement in Fulham, where we would stay for three months until we were up to the job. Robert loved to say that King Crimson was a way of life and that there was nothing else around at the time comparable to the material being produced by the band.

Robert approached music using mathematical equations. We would spend the entire rehearsal counting as we played. Time signatures would change during a piece and, for example, run 4/4 for four bars, 5/4 for eight bars, 7/8 for eight bars and 4/4 for four bars. I can only describe it as bullshit because it was contrived; there was no involvement of the soul and it seemed deceitful. The adage 'blind them with science' sprang to mind.

The music was simple enough to understand mathematically but it remained firmly uninspired. It didn't *feel*. We had to think like mechanics. I was not privy to what the final piece of music would be, unlike a musician reading a score or the composer who had written it. Therefore the song remained meaningless to me. There were promises of thousands of pounds . . . but it's the same if you choose to be in pornography. It's never enough to change your gut feeling that you disapprove; it won't ever make you happy and you'll have to live with a negative force. You'll go through with the sadism and masochism of it all, sell a lot of copies and the art-school brigade will rave about it, put it on the front page and try hard to explain it all to lesser mortals. Welcome to the '70s, the age of bullshit. Glam rock was your other choice.

It was the direct opposite of everything I had learned at Stratford Place. Hate and coldness were created just as easily as the love and warmth I had experienced from the black musicians who always elevated me to a higher consciousness. Listen to Marvin Gaye's 'What's Going On?' and feel the difference. Robert and his followers were convinced they'd created something superior. They hadn't. Robert felt brutal, and so he expressed the feelings he harboured inside. Hate has impact. It's brash. It's loud. It wasn't making love; it was masturbation. The business was ready for something different, so we all had to suffer the satanic nonsense that was creeping up from the sewer.

Hate replaced love as a trend. That's all there was to it. And it was dressed up as intellectual. The lack of any ability to write a decent melody was disguised by pretensions and delusions of grandeur. Robert could impress a lot of people by playing faster than anyone in the country. With his mathematical mind, he was a genius at creating a scary noise on the guitar – akin to the sound and effect of a nuclear blast. You may think that's complimentary but I hadn't planned on a visit to Hiroshima. Everything I have learned in my life, before and after the King Crimson experience, confirms my belief that it was a well-considered, coldly commercial enterprise to showcase a musician's technical skill. The sum total of all the various parts was enough to create a sound that was unique yet destructive. That intellectuals insist this is superior to those composers who write memorable, meaningful music is the bane of my life. If it is so mundane to be Burt Bacharach, why can't the mundane do it?

There is nothing worse than knowing you've been duped and not being able to own up to it. I grew up with Robert. I know him. He was always frustrated by his shortcomings. He learned to compose by substituting a natural feel for music with mathematics, formulas and technical effects. It produced a unique sound, but no real musician would have called it music. I admire him immensely for making a huge success of his life. But at the time, I wasn't going to take my direction from him and I didn't care how famous he was. Once when I argued with him, he snapped at me, 'How many hits have you had?'

I could have said, 'Three, actually.' But I didn't. He wanted hits like the rest of us.

I couldn't bear what I felt to be his bullying attitude towards the drummer. Being intimidated by Robert was the King Crimson norm. I didn't need to associate with that for a little bit of fame. I would like to go back in time to that rehearsal room and confront him the way he deserved for behaving that way to a fellow human being. It was almost akin to torture. But we were boys.

We took our King Crimson Airfix kit into the recording studio and spent one whole day trying to get a drum sound. I suggested after 12 hours of banging drums and moving microphones that they could get the original drum sound they were seeking by using my dick. Nobody dared laugh. It was pathetic that no humour was allowed. It was as if I'd farted in front of the vicar in church.

When we finally got started, I was recorded with just the drums. It was the most boring recording experience I'd ever had and I felt it couldn't possibly work. It was heartless. I had to do the singing as well and not one of the songs meant a damn thing to me. They were all in the wrong key for my voice and at the end of one song I just started laughing. Robert and Pete thought it sounded freaky, so they kept it on the record. As a worshipper of truth, I can only say that I wasn't making some deeply poetic statement for the esteemed critics to recognise as 'art'. I was laughing because it was so appallingly bad in every single way. It was . . . well . . . laughable.

When *Lizard* was released, the headline ran, 'If Wagner were alive, he'd be playing with King Crimson.' Fans wrote and said it was their favourite King Crimson record. It sold thousands all over the world, making my name and forever linking me to a style of music I still believe is seriously flawed. I began a prison sentence from that day, chained to a wall where I would be fed on bread and water and tortured daily until my redemption. Had I been as tough as I am now, I could have spared myself a lifetime of pain and broken relationships. But it was the life I had chosen and it would become one of the parts of the whole driving force that would see me clamber out of my pit of despair to freedom in 30 years' time.

CHAPTER 5

You'll be Bigger than Neil Young

The King Crimson split occurred as we began rehearsing for our first concert tour of America. I refused to sing in the written key and wanted it transposed.

'I'll put your voice through the special-effects machine. No one will know,' Robert had said.

'That's the point. I'll know. And I'm not going onstage and conning people,' I replied.

'So, you want to leave then?' Robert applied his ice-cold stare.

'Yes, please.'

I never once appeared with them in public, I'm glad to say.

Two weeks later, the management, EG Records, together with three members of the band, took a vote on whether or not to pay me my royalties. It went 3–2 against. The score was the same as the championship fives game I had played with Robert at school. And he took the cup again.

There was Robert and there was Bob. I didn't like the new Robert and the whole sorry tale merely confirmed that my instincts can be trusted. I never should have joined.

Did I regret leaving? No. For a long time I regretted joining, but time has made me look at the whole picture and it did have a huge impact on my life. King Crimson was like a tower block. It made a fortune for the architect but it was hell for those who had to live in it.

In the spirit of the '60s, quitting on the grounds of your integrity was noticeably admired – Clapton left The Yardbirds to play the blues with John Mayall – but that attitude was now being trashed. I could no longer expect anything to be as I had known it at Stratford Place. Robert had dismissed everything I had learned from the Otis Redding crowd. Guitarists like those bluesmen were no longer relevant. For nine months, I had taken instruction from a critically acclaimed guitarist who, by his own admission, was tone deaf and didn't possess one ounce of rhythm. And his way was winning. It was all business, perfectly in tune with Robert's commercial-school background and training as a hard-sell estate agent. It was Robert's time, not mine.

In our individual ways, we were both reaching for the light. It was to occupy an enormous amount of my time, for my fascination is with the human mind and I have learned from experience how music can cure each and every one of us. I have healed others and I have healed myself simply by doing my job. It should never have been a competition between us. Just as the championship fives tournament at school had been so immensely enjoyable to me that I wasn't interested in the outcome, our lives continued based on old attitudes. I was never competing; I was in music for the sheer love of the game. But Robert wasn't playing; he was in it for the points he could score . . . for the winning.

Musically, Robert and I were diametrically opposed, which was entirely due to our backgrounds and the demands of our individual souls. Neither of us was to have it easy, no matter how it appeared to the outside world. He had to struggle with a different set of demons and has often said how he'd never had the time to waste thinking about me and bore me no ill will. I used to believe he'd say something like that to intentionally hurt and ridicule me, but he was merely stating facts. Thirty years on, I believe him. He was totally focused on the job he had to do and that's the only way one can pull it off.

We have both been difficult in completely different ways, two ends of a spectrum, yet I am convinced now that there is this need in both of us for love and an understanding of the world and all it contains, and that that was what drew us together as children. I believe I still love Robert for that reason and, just as I never gave up on music when all the odds were against me, I will never give up on Robert. When I hated him – and I did for far too long – I was really hating myself. I wish him well and congratulate him for an outstanding life and his contribution to the history of rock music. He's a one-off.

* * *

I felt relieved to be away from King Crimson and I was determined to carve out a life all of my own. I had to be more organised, so I started a routine of writing songs and thinking out my next moves. I was influenced by American music and kept wondering whether, had I been born an American as my father Harry had been, I would feel more at home. The English music scene had become the opposite of what I liked.

I met the record producer John Miller through fellow bass player John Wetton, who was doing sessions for him. I'd have been 25 at the time and John was also in the band Family, who had made the phenomenal album *Bandstand*. I now had a lot of new songs, dealing with my concerns for the survival of the planet, created from a strange blend of my love of American songwriting and the weird new English styles, and we felt we could make an album together. Out of the blue, he called to say he'd fixed an audition for me with Ahmet Ertegun, who was staying at the Dorchester Hotel in Park Lane.

Ahmet Ertegun, president of Atlantic Records, was moving with the times. He had signed King Crimson and Emerson, Lake and Palmer in the States even though he'd always been associated with music he loved, having found Ray Charles and Aretha Franklin. The new people who'd replaced Frank in London were corporate types. I found them cold and unemotional. The age of mergers was upon us. I left John in the foyer while I went up to Ahmet's suite. There I met the man all musicians regard as the greatest of all record-company men. I played six songs on my acoustic guitar.

'That's outta sight,' he said. 'I wanna produce you. We'll do it at Muscle Shoals, Alabama [where he'd done Aretha Franklin]. You'll be bigger than Neil Young. How much do you want?'

I said that I was £3,000 in debt because King Crimson hadn't paid me my royalties.

'I'll give you $10,000 and I'll get you your royalties,' he promised me. It felt like I'd won the pools.

I went back down to tell John the news. He was so pleased for me, he allowed me to take the offer, doing himself out of the producer's job. At that time of great confusion, I was able to follow my instinct to sign to Atlantic Records again and be back with the label I had enjoyed so much in the past. I was ecstatic and extremely proud to be signed by the most respected man in the record industry. Ahmet's endorsement of my work gave me the confidence I had been lacking. You couldn't get higher respect than his.

I took the good news back to Sally, paid off our debts and waited.

If only I'd known this was the beginning of a new world order and Ahmet was entering the corporate hemisphere. He called to say he couldn't produce me as he was in the middle of heavy negotiations with the Kinney Corporation, who were big in car parks, but I could choose any producer I liked. I still felt up about it all because when I asked for Arif Mardin, I got him without question. He was my favourite producer, arranger and engineer, so now nothing should go wrong.

Things were looking good again, with Sally back in the West End in what became my favourite musical, *Company*, written by that genius Stephen Sondheim. She was magnificent in it and the songwriting was out of this world. I drove her up to the theatre each night and saw the show over and over again.

Meanwhile, I sat around and waited and waited for Atlantic Records to tell me when we were recording. When the call finally came, they only gave me a week's notice to put a band together. The caller explained Arif Mardin was only in London for a fortnight and that the studio had been booked. The only option was to wait a further three months. I thought it was a strange way to arrange things but I managed to quickly pull together some good musicians and have a couple of days' rehearsal, then started getting nervous at the speed things were expected to happen. I went into Island Studios and met the brilliant Arif Mardin. I needn't have worried. He was a fabulous man, full of charm, suave and relaxed. He was a genius as an engineer and producer, as well as being one of the finest musical arrangers in the world. He made me feel he was proud to be working with me. I couldn't help thinking how Robert Fripp might have benefited from witnessing the humility of a real genius.

Ahmet Ertegun had supposedly booked Eric Clapton for the sessions to help sell the record but he didn't show up (this was at the height of Clapton's heroin addiction). The sessions were fairly good and there were some magic moments but it could and should have been a lot better. When the work was done, and just before Arif went back to the US, Atlantic threw a big party for me at The Dorchester to celebrate and I invited all my friends from Les Fleur de Lys. Arif scored some subtle strings as only he can and did some additional back-up vocals in New York with The Rascals, originally The Young Rascals, who'd had a huge hit on both sides of the Atlantic with 'Groovin''.

In the London office of Atlantic Records, Rob Dickins was taken on as a postal clerk. He would eventually rise to become the chairman of Warner Brothers. Johnnie Walker was still a frequent visitor and was roped in to take the photographs for the artwork. The album was to be called *It Is And It Isn't* and the front cover was supposed to depict the paradoxical nature of life. Instead, I had the most ridiculous sleeve I've ever seen, showcasing Spike Milligan's adopted tree in Kensington Gardens with gnomes sitting on its branches. You'd have to have been on acid to find the connection.

The mixes arrived from New York and they seemed tame compared to the impressions we'd all had during recording. Added to that scenario, the release was delayed for six months because of a corporate reshuffle when Atlantic in London was bought by the Kinney Corporation and was no longer independent. Atlantic proposed releasing 25 albums with the slogan 'The New Age of Atlantic'. Disc jockey Kid Jensen voted me 'brightest hope', an annual award sponsored by the press and judged by industry personalities, and the album went to No. 8 in the Radio Luxembourg top 20.

John Sherry of the Sherry Copeland agency became my agent. He had been a drummer in Bournemouth and was now one of the biggest agents in London. He put me on at the Rainbow (formerly the Finsbury Park Empire), where I appeared with the hugely popular progressive-rock bands Wishbone Ash and Mountain, who were stunning fans with excellent guitar work. Then there was a long and typically hectic tour with the innovative Stackridge and Audience.

The gig at the Rainbow was fantastic for me, as it had been on the first occasion when Les Fleur de Lys had appeared there. As I was fairly bonkers at the time (this was after spending ten months with Crimson), I went onto the huge stage with a lawnmower and an old bicycle, and left them on one side without ever referring to them. I have always been drawn to surrealism and anything of a bizarre, absurd nature. I sat down and played an acoustic guitar for thirty minutes in front of three Marshall amplifier stacks. The stage set was like a surreal painting. And the crowd cried out for more. In his review, John Peel wrote, 'I arrived just as Gordon Haskell was finishing.' I wanted him to say, 'He made a nice job of the grass.'

My first royalty statement showed the party Atlantic had thrown for me at The Dorchester had cost me £700. They hadn't mentioned they would bill me.

I didn't like the new age of Atlantic and wrote to Ahmet asking to be dropped, to which he agreed, after a few more months of waiting. I was free to be the captain of my ship again, albeit mightily disillusioned after such a promising break. The rough seas of the past two years had calmed, but calm seas don't necessarily make good sailors.

I also met Billy Fury back then. He was massive, a hero to everyone, musicians and fans alike. A real talent and as sexy as a young Elvis. Early in their career, The Beatles auditioned as his backing group, but although Billy loved them (well, Ringo was an old school chum), his manager turned them down. The Beatles and most others of the day were great admirers. It was a tragedy when Billy died in 1983, aged 43. But for years *Top of the Pops* carried on using in their opening credits that unforgettable silhouette of Billy perched on a stool with his jacket slung casually over his shoulder.

Billy came to the cottage at Bookham as he had been singing my near UK hit 'Lazy Life' in his act and thought I was the right man to produce him. I wish I'd had the confidence to oblige, but I felt completely out of my depth with post-Fripp mind-poisoning, so I backed away, which I regret. It was a sad day when he died. He was a really gentle soul and such a charismatic artist. I'd seen him countless times as a teenager: moody and magnificent, and one of the few really sexy all-male British rock singers.

I had auditioned for Marty Wilde when I was with The Dowlands (and accidentally smashed an expensive lamp as I was leaving his house) and here I was screwing up again with another big name. King Crimson had left me in a state of utter confusion and neurosis, not knowing where I wanted to go musically. I was trying to hang on to my R'n'B roots, wishing I was in the Average White Band but feeling I was no longer up to the job.

Just to worry me further, I had bought my first house on the strength of the Atlantic deal. Sally and I moved to Bramley, near Godalming, in 1972, yet I was to all intents and purposes unemployed; I was out of my contract with Atlantic and had a mortgage I'd no idea how to pay.

Sally always worked at Christmas. This year, she went away to play the lead in *Alice in Wonderland* at Stratford-upon-Avon and didn't come home. She and her lover had decided to have an adventure of their own. How apt, I thought.

I heard of a six-nights-a-week bass gig in a hotel in Euston paying £90 weekly and, after having earned only £30 with Crimson, jumped at it. The bandleader, Nico Findeisen, was a salesman first and a drummer second. On the very first night I heard his conversation with the restaurant manager and it was an education. He pulled himself up to his maximum height, put on a terribly important face and slammed his little briefcase onto one of the tables. He demanded to see the manager at once.

'Ve are renowned to be zee best trio in Europe. I haff reviews from our last sell-out European and Middle Eastern tours.' He had lived in England for 20 years but his German accent remained. 'Vould you please ensure ve haff a bottle of vine served vith our dinner in zee break? Red, I think, vould be nice. Do you haff German vine?'

The manager nodded graciously and was visibly shaken. Nico shook his hand hard, smiled and said, 'Thank you, sir, that's vunderful. You're a gentleman.' Then he bowed in respect.

Most hotel gigs like those in Park Lane insisted musicians use the rear entrance and forbade them from eating in the restaurant, in case they contaminated the clientele – 'You'll find a plate of sandwiches in the kitchen' was the normal greeting. Nico was ridiculous, but he wasn't going to stand for the disrespectful British.

None of us had played together before and the head waiter had swallowed the whole story. All I got from the keyboard player on that first gig as I prepared to play was the count in: '1, 2, 3 . . .' and we were off. We busked through an assortment of Jobim bossa novas and on through a selection of pop songs using the wrong words and chords and the wrong feel from the drums. I started laughing. A customer sent a note up to the stand that read, 'Are you joking, or can you really play?'

But, sure enough, in the break, our table was all perfectly laid out. The manager came over and Nico calmly said with utter confidence, 'Vat did I tell you? Aren't ve zee best?' The manager positively grovelled, pouring our wine for us and smiling ingratiatingly.

It continued like that for the six months I was there. We never rehearsed and it was fairly chaotic at times. Nico was the perfect German gentleman, living proof that confidence fools a lot of people, puts food on the table and, in my case, pays the mortgage.

Two major things happened during my six-month post-Crimson convalescence. My old friend John Wetton came to see me at the restaurant and was appalled that I could be playing such a place with such a trio after a world-class act like King Crimson. He'd just taken over my bass gig with the band and said Fripp was changing his attitude. I really couldn't have cared less. I didn't see Robert and Nico as that different, except the latter's manners were better. They were both selling something they believed in. One was not better than the other.

John had just joined King Crimson and was excited about it. Boz Burrell, my replacement, had had enough of Robert and gone on to the more successful rock outfit Bad Company. I could see from the constant line-up changes immediately after my departure that I wasn't the only one having problems with Robert Fripp. Something inside me was relieved I was in an average trio in central London. The pianist of that *average* trio, Winston Sela, went on to write 'Too Much Too Little Too Late', a worldwide smash hit for Johnny Mathis and Deniece Williams, which reached No. 1 in the US and No. 3 in the UK. Then, of course, the bass player wrote 'How Wonderful You Are'. Nico was not only a good salesman, he could spot talent. Perhaps we were worth the money and VIP treatment, after all. John and I didn't speak again for 25 years.

Sally and her Stratford lover split up and she was back two weeks later. But, by this time, I had decided to sell up the house we'd lived in together and buy my dream cottage in Dorset. I wasn't going to ask her permission about anything any more. I was looking forward to a fresh start. The tears had stopped falling and I began to relish the move. I hadn't met any great women in London and the idea of returning to Dorset filled me with hope and excitement.

The value of the house in Surrey had gone up by £7,000 in the six months we'd had it and places in Dorset were a lot cheaper, so I could afford to move, put down a deposit and reduce my mortgage. It was what I'd always wanted: a thatched cottage in the county I loved. I found the ideal one down a quiet leafy lane leading to open country in a hamlet called Stour Provost. It was the perfect size for me, but much too small for Sally to like. She hated every moment there and I started to feel I was punishing her too much.

Bryn Haworth, our old guitarist with Les Fleur de Lys, came to visit at this time. Sally cooked a beautiful meal, as she always did, and I felt a bit better for his company. He'd returned from the USA after Wolfgang split up and had written some great songs. He was considering renting a cottage close by. Island Records had offered him a solo deal and he asked me to play bass on a couple of tracks. It was so great to be back with him again after King Crimson. While I'd been screwed up musically, he had only got better, playing with Richie Hayward. I so wanted to impress Bryn. But I was full of

Robert's cranky theories. I damned King Crimson on a daily basis and the longer they avoided paying me any royalties, the angrier I became. There was nothing on paper – I've never considered paperwork necessary between friends – but the verbal agreement with Robert was that my low wages were mere pocket money and would be set against an eventual significant share of royalties. That vote to cut me out was perhaps not strictly illegal . . . but it wasn't fair play either. For a long time, I thought they'd change their minds and give me my dues. Wishful thinking. Not only had they cheated me but they'd damaged my ability as a musician and slowed me down.

Bryn used me for some of the easier tracks but hired Alan Spenner from Joe Cocker's band for the bulk of it. The type of music I'd been playing with King Crimson was actually less demanding than the relaxed laid-back feel in which Bryn and I have specialised over the years. Playing just behind the beat, 'laying back', isn't mathematical at all. It is a special talent few British musicians can master. The secret lies in the drum beat coming a split second later than strict tempo would call for, which has the effect of prolonging the time emphasis within bars of music and giving it a more relaxed feel. Alan Spenner was superb at it. I got there eventually, but it took me another four years and it meant I missed that opportunity with Bryn.

Bryn and his wife were converted to Christianity shortly afterwards and, in the ensuing years, we always had a bond that couldn't be broken. Bryn is now a practising minister and we've remained the very best of friends. In fact, I'm taking a break from this work to meet up with him today.

Sally hated living in Dorset; she considered it too plebeian. Despite my having her back, she hadn't mellowed one little bit and I gradually slipped back under her control and began to agree with her, to follow her lead. She had many good points, certainly more than most people. I'd keep tallying them up each time one of her bad habits drove me nuts; I was certainly learning to be more tolerant. But I still had a low opinion of myself, and felt who was *I* to criticise?

I was commuting to London from Dorset by train and Sally was spending many hours alone with the dogs. She gradually talked me into selling up my dream place and moving to a house owned by an actress friend of hers called Eunice Gayson.

Eunice had starred in the James Bond films and had married Sally's former partner. They had since divorced and she was penniless due to Mr X taking every cent from her. He had previously robbed Sally of over £100,000, leaving her broke too.

When Eunice met Mr X, she'd been living in the most elegant of mansion houses in Eaton Square, one of the most expensive areas of London. Plus she had a house on the seafront in Hove. Mr X, who was suave, sophisticated, a small-time actor and obviously a big-time seducer and embezzler, managed to liquidate the lot, get her pregnant and leave her homeless in the space of one year. I met him once. He called it women's liberation – from their money.

She had rented a caravan when her baby was born and had gone to see her bank manager, who'd known her throughout her successful career. He agreed to give her a 100 per cent mortgage for an apartment in the central wing of a Surrey mansion that had been divided up. She split it up further into self-contained flats that could be rented and make a dent in the mortgage.

As we drove through the gated entrance and up the long, majestic drive, the house came into view. I could see the look on Sally's face. It said it all. I had given up my idyllic Dorset cottage built for farm labourers of the past (with whom I was totally comfortable) to come and shrivel among the pretentious and ostentatious, and Sally felt right at home. It reminded me of Buckingham Palace and I hated it.

I felt myself beginning to categorise people into left boxes and right: Robert and Sally leaned to the right; The Beatles and the Memphis boys leaned to the left. At that moment, I knew what it was all about: selfishness and pomp, or kindness and humility. I also knew which box I was happiest in. I'd have to leave Sally one day if I was ever to be happy and true to myself. A cycle was emerging.

I began to deal with it there and then in what, on first impressions, I thought of as a mausoleum, a heartbreak hotel for the incurably confused. It was a house in Haslemere in Surrey. By sheer coincidence – or another of God's little clues – Haslemere was the name given to Miss Tippetts's little school, the one I had first attended in West Moors, where I had been assessed as being of above average intelligence.

I could hear Miss Tippetts's voice in my head saying, 'How are you doing?'

I didn't reply.

CHAPTER 6

🍃 🍃 🍃

Above My Station

Beyond the woods surrounding the mansion there were two large private lakes, and one of the first things I did after moving in was buy some fishing tackle. The grounds were extensive and very private, so I went fishing. I was an adult, unemployed and living in a building full of actors. As I write this at 57, I can smile; it sounds like bliss to me now, but then I haven't played a King Crimson record lately. I must have been very weird to think it was so awful and to be so discontented.

My first morning there, with the weight of the world on my shoulders, I soaked up the wonders of nature surrounding me and caught two carp. I sat thinking, what am I going to do? Where do I go from here? What's it all about, Alfie? I had left an environment I loved; I had traded my musician friends for Sally and her theatrical acquaintances and, though they had welcomed me with open arms and thought I was 'Divine, darling', I still missed the hipness of Les Fleur de Lys and the company. I would ask myself, how can I find my way out of here and take control of my life again? I wondered if I had ever run my own life, anyway. Hadn't Frank Fenter at Atlantic ruled everyone with an iron fist? I proudly returned to the house to show the ladies that the hunter had food for dinner. I still hoped to be regarded as a man one day.

Sally and Eunice knew many famous actors, who I found to be entertaining, and they distracted me from my stop-start career in the music business. They never mentioned the word 'unemployed'; it came with the territory. They wisely spent their time in the company of like souls, endlessly relating funny stories about all of the plays and films they had done, mimicking brilliantly other famous characters of the theatrical world. They introduced me to a world that seemed more fun, more professional and more mature than the world of music, certainly as talented, and I admired them. As a musician practises, so too can an actor, just by being invited to dinner. I was beginning to study people, and learning to join in and tell my own stories. I became confident in their graceful company, enjoying the subtle ways they would demonstrate kindness and sensitivity by exaggerating my minor success and making me feel good about myself.

I listened in awe to the one-time matinée idol Anthony Steel talk incessantly, barely taking a breath, as one fascinating story segued into another, pausing only to quench his considerable thirst. I wanted to laugh out loud but I didn't want to miss a word. He was to conversation what Jimi Hendrix was to guitar. I was discovering a life outside music, an exclusive world of extreme talent, and I was loving it. It massaged an ego that had taken a battering. I wouldn't have missed it for anything.

I had bought a harmonium after working on the Rick Woolf project back in my Flowerpotmen days and I had loved writing songs on it. But here in the 'Palace of Versailles', I felt awkward and self-conscious and struggled for inspiration. I asked Eunice if we could perhaps switch to another wing and she was more than happy to oblige, so we rented a flat at the rear of the house instead. We moved all the furniture in, with Sally getting angrier all the time at giving up the view, and I felt worse. I wrote a terrible song just to make myself laugh; everybody I played it to thought it was a hit. I took it to Chappell's music publishers and, sure enough, they signed it for £1,500, which was a lot of money for one song. It was called 'Don't Forget the Beer, Dear' and their idea was to get me totally plastered and record it as a joke record.

I am glad to say they buried it, but the money paid the rent and I began thinking of returning to Dorset to buy another house. I longed to be in my own place again with my own slant on life. As I say, the vital new experience at Haselmere, where we were tenants, was invaluable; an enjoyable part of my education. But eventually I realised I was playing a part that wasn't me. I felt I was wasting my time by not writing and playing. Fun and fancy talk in the long periods between high-paying work suited Sally and Eunice; they had been brought up on it and never worried. But I couldn't simply count my blessings and see how beautiful it was. I'd never been that secure and sure of myself. I could rise from a council house to a funky cottage, but this was having ideas above my station. Above my station? Where do we get these ideas from and what good are they to anyone?

I learned a lot from Eunice. I admired her fortitude and courage and business acumen. You could also say I learned a lot from those wonderfully mad days with all those actors. I thought I was wasting my time, but I learned how to struggle with my head held high and see unemployment as an opportunity to rest and contemplate and practise the simple art of being. I was learning to lose the preconceptions I'd held onto about class distinction. I'd felt at home with the earthiness of the Otis crowd at Atlantic Records and now I felt just as comfortable with all these very upper-crust characters. They were real stars, too; they illuminated the darkness of my night. What was apparent was how well they had treated me, and how they respected me not for any talent I might possess but for my humanity. I'll always remember how welcoming they were and how easy it was for me to love them.

Musically, I was mixing with Mike Allison and Peter Sills, a songwriting team I regularly watched playing in the cellar bars in Beauchamp Place in Knightsbridge. German Nico, of the infamous trio, had taken me there after a gig one night. Every move I made was taking me closer to my goal, though I wasn't conscious of this at the time. I was eventually going to get back into the mainstream and score a big deal. The root of that stretched right back to knowing Nico, that oddest and least likely of sources, which proved to me how important every person you meet in life can be. I learned why respect is so valuable.

There was a thriving scene down in Beauchamp Place in the early '70s. Every singer/guitarist was as good as it gets and sang with a lot of soul; they just lived by doing five or six sessions a week. Any one of them could have made it as an original and there they were working right under the noses of record companies, who never saw any of them. They had to pass the hat round to get any money. We called it 'the push'.

Mike Allison and I teamed up with two of these troubadours from the cellars, Geoff Stephenson and George 'the Greek', to back the up-and-coming artist Peter Straker in a Fringe venue at the Edinburgh Festival. We opened up the shows with several of our songs. The idea of three or even four good songwriters in one band appealed to me, as I wasn't that comfortable being on my own. We received favourable reviews, which compared us to Crosby, Stills and Nash, and had a brilliant time. Sally flew up to join us because she was a childhood friend of the financial backer, fellow actor Anthony Andrews.

I had played bass on Mike and Pete's demos, which they had sent to Bruce Welch of The Shadows. I landed a Cliff Richard gig shortly afterwards. Bruce liked the bass playing and had recommended me to Cliff's office. One thing led to another. I traced the source of the break back to Nico's trio.

I had been listening to Little Feat, Crosby, Stills and Nash, the Average White Band and J.J. Cale, who were being ignored by the progressive-rock crowd and radio. I was thinking my American blood was calling me to leave England to try my luck in the USA, but that meant leaving Sally. Had I become strong enough in the last few weeks to do it? At the very least, I was determined to have a test run.

I packed my few possessions, sold what I couldn't carry in a car and drove to my mother's council house at Verwood. Sally had never got on with her, so my mother was glad I had left and by her tone I think she thought she could still exert some influence over me. I don't dispute that both Sally and my mother loved me, but at the time it made me examine why their kind of love was suffocating me. I longed to break away from a lifetime of domination so that I could be my own man and run my life the way I knew I'd have to, if I was ever going to be happy.

It was pointless trying to change anything with words. I had to act. Ultimately, my only course of action was to cut myself off from both of them. One of Sally's friends persuaded me to meet Sally and talk things over and, as I was in the throes of buying a house in Henstridge, by the north Dorset border, I saw no harm in it. She behaved perfectly and I couldn't resist her. We moved to Henstridge together. I was obviously still not strong enough to break away.

While I was at the Edinburgh Festival, I'd met folk musician Tim Hardin and been asked if I would do some gigs and recordings with him. Tim was by far my favourite artist from the days when Johnnie Walker had been plugging him in 1968. His song 'If I Were A

Carpenter' had established him worldwide. It was an honour to play for him and the low wage was irrelevant. He was being given an extremely cold shoulder by the audience and the industry. His songs have outlived more fashionable artists but it takes years in this business for the truth to emerge. After *Sgt Peppers* nobody in the press or record companies knew a good song when they heard one. A *Melody Maker* reviewer wrote of Paul Simon's 'Bridge Over Troubled Water', 'It's just about the worst song I've ever heard.' The magazine eventually went out of business and their reviewers moved to the broadsheets.

It was the start of the decline of the record business; bad taste and ignorance were establishing themselves. It was hard enough to write a great song and now, if you did, they were going to slaughter you. They were kids being perverse for the sake of it.

Malcolm McLaren formed the Sex Pistols right on cue. Package total crap and call it 'punk'. The music press will rave about 'the energy', as they had with King Crimson. It was part of the widespread policy of dumbing down that turned millions away from all forms of media. It undid everything The Beatles had achieved; it turned the clock back to the time when British records sold only in Britain. America and the rest of the world rapidly closed their doors to 'that English shit'. Nobody could get records released in America any more. Venues closed because promoters were getting tired of the damage being done to their property. Hundreds of musicians were thrown out of work. Record shops became places to avoid because the moron count was rising so fast; shopping for records was becoming a threatening experience for the majority of buyers. This led supermarkets to jump into the gap, but they only stocked those products with vast budgets behind them . . . and that is the mess we find ourselves in today. McLaren told the world he'd destroy the record business and he did a pretty good job. What is remarkable is that they gave him the money to do it.

I had met Jim Russell, the drummer of a band called Stretch, while travelling on a train to Maidenhead. He was working on a track called 'Why Did You Do It?', which would become a big hit in 1975. I received a call from him a few months after the song had been in the charts. By that stage, he said he'd also been swindled by the money men and the band had broken up.

This was a normal sequence of events for hundreds of musicians. In my 40 years of being a musician, I have seen hundreds of insulting articles about musicians and artists but I have never seen any journalistic investigation into the countless crooked managers, fraudulent record companies and bent publishers that populate the industry. It takes guts to do that. Artists rarely fight back. When they do – as George Michael did, as Gilbert O'Sullivan did, and as I did to a lesser degree – the business closes ranks and you're history.

I hooked up with the remnants of his band: Hiroshi Kato, the guitarist; Jim, the drummer; and Martin Rushent, their producer. Hiroshi had been a huge rock star in Japan and had turned his back on the whole celebrity thing. He'd come to England to get away from it all. He was a wonderful guitarist and we gelled straight away. For the first time since Les Fleur de Lys had broken up, I felt completely at home. We had studio facilities available at Jackson's in Rickmansworth and several projects were completed, including our own. GTO Records signed us and a single came and went under the name Joe. We were doing recording sessions, so we never took the name seriously; it was just a name to put on a record.

Hiroshi took us to Japan for six weeks of session work with one of the country's leading girl singers. Hiroshi was given the red carpet treatment wherever he went but his humility prevented him from explaining it to us. We began to wonder if he was the President's son. We did our six weeks and I found myself missing Sally, which came as a surprise. We'd spent nearly eight years together, a very difficult eight years, yet the affection ran deep.

Things were looking and feeling good again. In one of my regular calls to Bryn Haworth, I conveyed my enthusiasm for the band, likening them to the old days of sanity and talent, and he took us on the road with him. It was terrific fun and a real buzz to be back onstage with my old buddy. With Bryn on slide guitar, it was a brilliant band. Because most venues had closed since the punk explosion, bands now had to be subsidised by record companies. We had three weeks of subsidised happiness.

Back home, Sally was happier. She had begun to love the solitude of the country. About this time, her mother, whom I truly loved, became ill. She was a Victorian with grace and a sense of humour – a thoroughly beautiful person. I sensed it would please her, so I asked Sally to marry me – I also wanted to believe our troubles were behind us. I had been busy and back in men's company and Sally's domineering nature wasn't affecting my work any more. We had a puncture on the way to Blandford Registry Office. I wondered if it was one of my angels at work but I went through with it anyway. We did it quickly and quietly, with only a handful of friends present. We had a quiet meal together in the evening back at the cottage in Henstridge. Despite our tempestuous times, I still thought we could be happy. Sally had always wanted it. We weren't well off enough to have a honeymoon and Sally was now at her happiest in the country, pottering around at home.

Almost immediately, Sally's mother's health became worse and we had to move to her home in London to look after her. The house in south Hampstead was divided into three flats. We lived on the first floor.

I liked being back in the buzz of London. I was still working with the band and the studio was only a few Tube stops away. Alvin Lee of the band Ten Years After got to hear of what we were doing and tried us out at his spread in Berkshire. He'd made a fortune out of America, where the band had toured regularly. He asked me to join him but I was happier with Jim and Hiroshi. Then I was tried out by Van Morrison, who gave me the nod of approval. But it didn't come to anything. It was always the same with me, wherever I went.

There had to be a spark of something when I was playing that was more than the music. It's hard to define; so hard, in fact, that in our three-piece unit we gave the feeling a name: it was 'the Jah'. And if I didn't feel that in a band, I felt it was a waste of time. It would be boring and soulless. I haven't had cause to adjust my opinion.

The songs that Mike Allison and Pete Sills had sent Bruce Welch had so excited him that he wanted to record them and, because I'd created the bass parts, I got the gig with them and roped in Jim Russell on drums. Hiroshi was tired of the hassles in bands so Joe went into limbo.

We started recording with Bruce at Wembley Studios. Jim had a great sense of humour and didn't realise a remark he made pertaining to the size of Bruce's rear end would hit a raw nerve, but it did, and he was fired. The Shadows' drummer Brian Bennett replaced him. Bruce couldn't get any record companies interested in the album we'd made, so the whole thing went pear-shaped – until we heard that six of the songs were on the new Cliff Richard album, featuring 'Miss You Nights', 'Devil Woman' and 'We Don't Talk Any More'.

I got a call from Cliff's office offering me the bass gig. I was to bring my passport to the office and David, the manager, would talk me through it. I was extremely excited because Cliff's band was still a highly sought after gig, not only in the prestige department but for the high wages which, lest we forget, had eluded me throughout my bass-playing career.

The interview seemed to go well, with David explaining that nobody did drugs or alcohol and Cliff popping in to check me out. David explained that it was a world tour on the back of Cliff's *I'm Nearly Famous*, which Mike and Pete had written, and as Bruce rated me, that was good enough for them. The tour would take in the USA, Japan, Australia, Russia and Europe. I was overjoyed. After all that time on the very edge and all my close brushes with the really big acts of the world, I was finally going to be rewarded. I raced home and I think I probably told everyone I knew. I would have the security of a well-paid job for a year or more. I had never had that luxury.

Three days later, David called again. There had been a mix-up and Cliff had promised the job to a mate of his and felt he couldn't back out. 'We're very sorry. Nothing personal.'

I started writing songs again for the first time in years. They flew out of me and I loved them. I demo'd them, playing all the parts myself, and discovered I had my own original sound and it was decidedly spiritual; it had a mystical flavour. I played what I'd done to a few people I knew from the old days. I was ready to make a great record.

The new breed in record companies were punks, so it was pointless taking something spiritual to them. I was going grey and I was no good at spitting. I didn't have 'attitude'. I thought of pretending I came from Deptford, as so many of those nice little middle-class boys from Surrey were doing, but decided against it. Much as I loved The Police, I smiled at their image. I'd known Andy Summers since our teenage years, when we were both playing around Bournemouth. He was older than I was and there he was, with his hair dyed, all dressed up in leather. Andy had been a great jazz musician all his life. They were all jazz musicians. I could imagine record-company execs having conversations about Sting's songs not being strong enough to make it without marketing. They had to pretend they were punks to get a deal. The public really isn't that gullible, they'll always buy great songs. The Police could have played in their pyjamas and hairnets and still have sold millions of records.

Sally went away to play *Dick Whittington* in pantomime at Birmingham. Ken Dodd was the star and I enjoyed seeing Sally work again. Onstage, she had a wonderful charisma and sang with a lot of heart. Ken Dodd was hilarious. Sally was an inch short of five feet tall; Ken called her the littlest Dick in the business.

Bill Kimber, who'd sung 'Lazy Life' under the name William E., got back in touch and thought he could get me a deal with a major record company, so I left the tapes with him. Then I got another call from Cliff's office. Would I like to join the band, as the job had become available again?

'Yes,' I replied, more cautiously than before, and was given the address for the first rehearsal. It was to be a gospel tour of the UK with a television show in Holland. I got on well with the band and, although I found them unfair at the time, I've learned that management are typically tough on everyone and I understand why they have to be. In the pecking order, real musicians come last.

The band told me that the last time I had been offered the job, the manager was in negotiation with the musician of his first choice, who was holding out for his price. They put me in the frame to show the little upstart if he didn't drop his price, they had somebody else standing by. When they had the player of choice, they dropped me. It was nothing personal.

The management never imagines it'll ever be brought to book, as the people who form its core have no imagination or conscience. It is with enormous pleasure that I bring Cliff's management into this book, as they helped my development enormously and I'd like to thank them. Nine months after letting me down so badly, the manager put his arm around me like a long-lost friend and whispered in my ear, 'If you do this tour for half wages, I'll see you get the next world tour.' He had no intention of giving me anything. It was economics and I agreed to it.

'You fool,' Clem Cattini, the godfather of all drummers, told me. He explained, 'You're here with us because you're the best man for the job. If you don't believe you are and you agree to half wages, you must think you're only half as good.'

He was right but I just couldn't be bothered with it all any longer. It had become too predictable. It was history repeating itself. It was all I had ever known.

I did the tour and I loved the musicians, who complimented me by saying it was the first time the band had ever jammed together at a soundcheck. I would start off a bass figure and it would turn something on in them and they'd run to join in until the whole band was getting off on it. Before that, they had been thinking about going to the pub as usual. They were jazz musicians paying their bills by working for pop stars.

Cliff's gig in Sheffield was fun. The theatre had been designed by a lunatic or a musician-hating vindictive bastard. The dressing-rooms were below the stage. That was OK but there were so many stairs and tunnels and doors leading off down there, it was like trying to find your way out of a rabbit warren. Cliff did two songs on his own to open the show and then introduced the musicians separately as they joined him onstage. I left the dressing-room as my cue was approaching and must have taken a wrong turn early on, as every door I opened led to more and more stairs and more doors. I could hear Cliff begin to introduce the musicians and I was lost in the labyrinth. As I started to panic, I heard him say, 'On bass guitar, Gordon Haskell,' and I pulled open what I was sure must be the last door, which it was. I found myself in the upper circle with the audience, standing with my bass around my neck.

CHAPTER 7

🐚 🐚 🐚

You'll Never Work Again

It was one of my weaknesses as a musician that I felt I had to challenge every manager who came my way. They bored me to death. It was always about the money with them. They were never there for the music. There is nothing funnier to me than a manager or agent who thinks he owns you. When it finally dawns on them that you're willing to jettison everything rather than be subservient to them, it's a little taste of bliss. It takes them only a few seconds to react, but in that time the look in their eyes of total impotence is sheer joy to behold. It's glorious and is worth getting fired for. You leave that arena with your spirit intact and satisfied you've metaphorically kicked some soulless sack of shit firmly in the balls.

Freddie Starr's humour is built around that power and the day he went too far I have no doubt someone told him, 'You'll never work again.' He's still funny and the British public is deprived of a good laugh because of the boring powerbrokers in show business. To the uninitiated, it always looks like the self-destruct button. I had done it with Robert Fripp, then with Ahmet Ertegun and, seven years later, I was doing it again with Cliff Richard. But the very opposite was true. I knew that to stay under the control of these kind of people would eventually destroy my soul, and it was imperative that I continue my journey as a free man regardless of how hard it was going to be.

The guitarist Dave Christopher was of like mind. He had a foot pedal that he forgot to turn off at the end of a number and, as Cliff was introducing the next song, the intro to the previous one restarted as the pedal kicked in. Dave was standing to the right of Cliff, fairly close to the microphone, and said in his wonderful broad Bristol accent, 'Cor, who the fuck's playing that?' I can still see all the puzzled faces of born-again Christians gazing up at Cliff as the entire band quivered with laughter. He even smiled.

I still like Cliff. I loved him as a kid and it was by watching him that I came into this business. It was a thrill to be on the same stage as someone I had once adored and I got a hell of a kick out of it. The new breed of Nazi in the music business has been typically misinformed and Cliff doesn't deserve the vicious battering he has received in recent years. I thank him for making my last professional bass job the one I had dreamed of getting when I was 14 years old. Dreams do come true. Ask and ye shall receive. So many don't think to ask, they're so certain there is no God.

After the Cliff gig, I decided I'd had enough of being a hired hand, which meant I would probably never work as a musician again. If Mr Nice Guy's management is as good as it gets, then I knew I'd never be happy having to negotiate future jobs. Now I understand why Jet Harris got the elbow.

Cliff Richard was a lovely man to work with and his every performance was faultless.

I had to work alone if I was going to stay in the game and I also began to wonder if my American slant on things would ever find a home in Britain. The country still felt so feudal in its outlook and I was tired of being one of the serfs serving my masters with cap in hand. My attitude had been encouraged by the Otis crowd at Stratford Place and whenever I heard American musicians like James Taylor being interviewed, they spoke my language. Something was telling me to go to the States. Years later, I was to learn that the musicians I had met with Otis had also been substantially short-changed by Stax Records. It's the same story the world over.

When I was with Cliff, Sally landed the role of leading lady at the Ambassadors Theatre in the West End with Ruth Madoc. We were doing all right again and success was bringing out people we hadn't seen for years. Susan George had known Sally all her working life. They both had film careers and shared a long history of theatre together. She came to the Ambassadors and invited us to her home in Wraysbury. Susan and I hit it off musically and shared similar tastes in singer-songwriters. Although she was a huge Hollywood movie star, she had been longing to do some recording since her work with Jack Jones. She was soon to go back over to her place in California and insisted I come and stay while I checked out the record companies with my new tapes. Sally didn't object because she knew I was passionate about California. I thought this was what I'd been waiting for and bought my ticket to Los Angeles.

This was my first trip to America and I was going to stay with a movie star. It seemed bizarre but my whole life had been that way. I had never toured there as a musician, even though everyone had assumed I had because King Crimson was a big name in the US. Now I was going to see the film-industry capital of the world on the arm of one of its stars.

Susan George was slightly taken aback that I had accepted her invitation. However, after an evening of playing guitars and singing, she felt I was going to fit in well with the life she was leading and we warmed to each other. I spent the first day in and out of the swimming pool and sunbathing next to Susan, who spent a lot of time on the telephone. The house was beautiful. Situated in the Hollywood Hills, it looked down on Sunset Strip. Susan let me drive her Mercedes sports car to Rodeo Drive, where she showed me all the glamorous shops featured later in *Pretty Woman*. It all looked so luxurious, with convertibles, Rolls-Royces, suntans and successful-looking people wherever we went. It felt like the most positive place on earth. But, hang on, it's me out there. I managed to do $10,000 worth of damage to her Mercedes when a water truck backed into me . . . and that was only my second day. Susan took it in her stride. She didn't know my history and I didn't have the heart to tell her.

There were a lot of visitors each day; Susan loved to entertain and suggest days out for everyone. We went to Malibu beach and saw all the wonderful homes and restaurants there, then popped in to see her friend Olivia Newton-John for tea and a look at her horses.

Susan got free passes for a trip to Disneyland, which I loved. Another day we all went waterskiing. Then there were some evenings when I'd be her escort for a film premiere or an awards ceremony. In the three weeks I was there, I saw America through the eyes of a movie star and had an amazing time meeting all kinds of people involved in the film industry. I had come a long way from the council house in Dorset. I had been on a roller coaster in the record business, with nothing to show for it but a clear picture of how I wanted my life to be; finding myself in Hollywood merely confirmed that my soul had always run my life. I'd dream of being somewhere and eventually

I would find myself in that very place without a clear idea why.

I made a good friend of a young, confident, blond-haired, blue-eyed handsome man who'd come to take Susan out on a date. His name was Bill Gerber.

Bill had been born and raised in Hollywood and his father was the man on whom Neil Simon had based one of the characters in *The Odd Couple*, the tidy but fussy Felix, played by Jack Lemmon. Bill was working for the NEMS agency at the time, Brian Epstein's old company, but he wanted to move on. When he learned my history and heard my tapes, he became very excited and offered to manage me. He put me on at the famous Troubadour club and invited record companies along. It was a good-sized room to play an acoustic set, and the atmosphere was warm and friendly. I did OK, despite knowing that just about every legendary star had played it.

The funniest thing I saw Bill do, which showed the measure of the man, was during an appointment with a guy from CBS Records. Someone from the office had seen the Troubadour gig and thought one of the songs could be a hit. The CBS exec's telephone rang whilst Bill was playing him the tapes and Bill got up, flung open the door and ripped out the phone lines in the reception.

The record-company man in the expensive suit bellowed, 'How have you got the nerve to come in here in tennis shorts and T-shirt, take over my office and tear out my phone lines?'

Bill laughed and replied with utter confidence, 'Because this music demands your attention and you need to learn some manners. Got any juice?'

I loved him and for the next 20 years we would stay close friends.

When I returned to London, there was a deal on the table for me from RCA. My old friend Bill Kimber had landed a top job there and offered me a three-year contract with a healthy advance. I called Bill Gerber to say I'd taken an English offer and to thank him for trying. As the years went by, we'd constantly compare notes.

Bill managed tours that came to England soon afterwards and he thought the country was bizarre. He couldn't find his health food or the right yoghurts and hated the public-telephone system of cramming hundreds of coins into the slot only to get cut off. It all exasperated him. The character Felix often came to mind; Bill had obviously inherited some of his father's traits.

Eventually, Bill wrote and said he was leaving the music business to go to Warner Brothers Pictures, where he quickly rose to vice-president. In the hardest years I had yet to get through, Bill never once stopped trading phone calls. He'd ring at midnight when I had lost everything and was back in the council house in Verwood and say he was depressed. I shook my head in amusement at the wonder of it all and muttered under my breath, 'If only you knew.' But I'd be so thrilled to hear from him and listen to his woes. It was the story of the prince and the pauper all over again. 'Cheer me up, Gordy,' he'd say. 'They've just cast so-and-so in a movie and he's crap.'

I never told him I had hit rock bottom and we continued our friendship based on those three great fun weeks we'd shared at Susan's, when I still had some credibility. I appeared with her at this time on an Anglia Television show, playing guitar for her as she sang one of the many songs she'd written.

One day, Bill's secretary called and said, 'Bill just wanted you to know he made president.' After calling him and congratulating him, I went off to my gig in Christchurch. I couldn't tell anyone in the pub where I was singing for £70 that I had just been speaking to the president of Warner Brothers Pictures.

From 1980 through to the present day, Bill Gerber has been my inspiration. From nowhere he had risen to the very top of the tree and he hadn't done it by kissing someone's rear end.

Back in London, that other Bill in my life, Bill Kimber, wanted to produce my record. We used most of Cliff's musicians, as we'd all had such a good time together on the road, and in a way it was a poke in the eye for Cliff's manager, who had short-changed me.

My demo sound was all me, but when Bill started producing the backing tracks, I could see that the mood was changing. I wasn't too worried at first. I felt that the raw material was strong enough to stand a bit of change, but then I realised that the whole essence was being stripped away. What had previously had my character stamped all over it now sounded sterile and bland. I was beginning to contradict myself. I didn't want punks who couldn't play and I didn't want blandness either. The Americans could do it so well, with acts like James Taylor and Crosby, Stills and Nash. Why couldn't the British?

Bill was over the moon about it but it didn't go down well at the office, which was in the midst of the punk fad and, although they went as far as attempting to put a sleeve together, the album was held back. They put out a single of a song called 'People Don't Care', which received favourable reviews. 'Very laid-back, very Don Williams, very lovely,' ran one in *Melody Maker*, which surprised me, coming as it did from a punk-loving journalist. By the time the second single came out, punk had taken over. Bill was forced to admit defeat and I was dropped.

But I'd had a good year financially. Sally's show was still running, so we moved to Amersham into a lovely cottage. Commuting to London was easy and it seemed like we were becoming stable at long last, but it wasn't to be. My publisher didn't pick up the option, so I began to drain the little capital I had left and then Sally's show closed. She was offered a few weeks in *Side by Side by Sondheim*, and Michael Parkinson, who chaired the show, used to drive with her into the theatre. I was hearing rumours about Sally again when she was on tour, and when she came home our marriage fell to pieces. We sold the house and divided the money equally. Sally took an apartment with Eunice, who was well established in Richmond by this time, and I bought a cheap flat in West Bay, Dorset.

I still had fond memories of Malibu and hadn't got over the euphoria I'd felt during my three weeks in Hollywood. Now that everything was going bad again, I could gaze out to sea from the flat and dream of how things might have been had I stayed with Bill Gerber. I would have made the record with American musicians and everything would have been better.

It took six weeks to buy the flat, in which time Sally had managed to talk me into staying together . . . yet again. We decided we could have two homes with very low outgoings, one near London for work and one by the sea. The flat in Richmond was by the river and, for a while, we had a nicer time together, so much so that I'll always love Richmond for its good memories and its fantastic mixture of town and country living.

Cliff Richard's guitarist, Terry Britten, lived up the road and became a friend. He had done eight years with Cliff's band, writing several hits for him, including one of his best, 'Devil Woman'. He had produced an album for Cliff, recording more of his songs, namely 'Carrie' and 'Wired for Sound'. Cliff had been to dinner with him several times, so Terry was very hurt when he rang the office to ask if he could submit some new songs for the following album only to be told by our mutual friend, 'management', that they were changing producers and all the songs had been chosen. Terry's new tracks brought Tina Turner back with 'What's Love Got To Do With It' and won him a Grammy or two. He no longer needed to worry about being treated ruthlessly by Cliff's management.

The more unpleasantness I witnessed in the profession, the more I needed to be alone, to hang on to my beliefs, or I'd end up so hardened to it all. That's what happens in the end: musicians become old pros, journalists become hacks, politicians become corrupt, we all enter the world of cynicism and spend the rest of our lives telling ourselves it doesn't hurt any more when, of course, it does. It lies deep down in that place where you've buried it, that place called your soul, where it lies festering until it turns into self-disgust and you drink more or you smoke more or do whatever you do to avoid the truth.

Sally and I took a trip to the flat overlooking the sea at West Bay. It was winter and the weather was wild and windy; we loved to watch the waves crashing spectacularly over the harbour entrance. The dogs loved their daily walks along the beach to Burton Bradstock and we'd return by climbing the cliffs and walking along the edge of them, watching the rabbits feeding or looking out to sea. I never longed to be back in London; I never wanted to be anywhere else. But how can you survive in a place that's boarded up most of the winter? Without any royalties or gigs, what were we going to do?

I decided to bury the hatchet with Robert and invited him to West Bay. I suggested a game of squash to try to recapture the spirit of our childhood. He arrived in an old rusty Renault car ready for the scrap heap, play-acting the poor man. He asked me who the simplistic guitarist was I had playing on the stereo – it was the world-renowned Larry Carlton. He saw the view and spoke as the estate agent he might have been. 'You'll pay a lot of money for a view like that.' He left and nothing had been achieved. For all his success, I felt he had learned nothing of any value.

A few days later, I was sitting in an armchair being very quiet and pensive. I was wearing a baseball cap that I'd never worn in my life and it made me look a little odd. Sally was getting worried about me and asked what I was doing.

'I've found the answer to our dilemma,' I said. 'We'll sell all the furniture and take up the carpets, cover the floor with topsoil, plant a forest inside the flat and sit on tree stumps. It'll be great. We could swing from the trees together. I'll be your Tarzan, if you will be my Jane. Dooby dooby do!'

Sally got up from her chair and went to the bedroom. I remember hearing the sounds of the clicks as she opened her suitcase. I couldn't move or bring myself to speak. She packed, called a taxi to take her to Dorchester station and said, 'Sorry, darling. Can't take any more,' and left with the dogs. It was so easy. Act completely bonkers and people will run a mile. It works every time. We had a quickie divorce that cost £12 and we didn't speak to each other again for ten years.

That same week, I received a letter from Athens telling me my father, Harry, had died. His brother George had donated a kidney, which had been successful, but peritonitis had crept in during the operation and killed him. I turned on the news and John Lennon had been shot. I had lost my record deal, my publishing deal, my wife, my dog, my father and my favourite songwriter. Then I pulled a muscle in my back playing squash and I was forced to crawl along the floor for days before I could stand. And when I finally did get up, I realised I'd lost my direction too.

The first thing I did when Sally left was try to contact Amanda, my daughter, who was 12 years old by then. Sally had always discouraged me from attempting to get in touch: any action I might take had always seemed like a threat to her for reasons of her own. Now that I was out from under her control, I freely and curiously made the call. My maintenance cheques had been returned by the court because Amanda's mother had married and her husband had legally adopted my daughter. I found this out when I phoned the court. I was told that they hadn't been able to find me to ask for my approval about her adoption. I said they had found me easily enough once before to arrest me when I was a week late with the payments. They didn't comment on that. Amanda's mother answered the phone when I rang the house and didn't remember me. I don't remember crying; everything was so bleak. I had ceased to expect good news from any quarter.

So I sold the flat at West Bay and moved into a derelict cottage by a railway line in an unattractive town in Dorset called Gillingham. I had friends there and they had that sense of the absurd I was craving. I paid £12,500 cash. It felt great to own something outright. A derelict cottage for a derelict musician. I kept it exclusive and refused entry to movie stars and presidents.

I bravely went to the bank to get an overdraft. I gutted the cottage and pulled in craftsmen as and when they were needed. I went to the council. They gave me a grant for a new bathroom. The locals gibed at me when they saw me covered in plaster dust. I lost count of how many asked with a smile, 'Didn't you used to be in King Crimson and with Cliff Richard?' That question would remain the opening line of any conversation with strangers for 20 years and resentment for non-payment of royalties grew a little with each passing year.

When I'd finished the renovation and had the house exactly as I'd planned it, I felt satisfied. I had been creative in a different direction and it was a success. I was a single man again and managing my affairs on my own. I enjoyed choosing the carpets and furniture and bits and pieces. I thought I might buy a piano . . . but I sat down and looked at the blank television screen instead, asking myself, 'Now what?'

My father Harry had mentioned in his annual and brief letters that he had a wonderful brother living in Las Vegas. I picked up the telephone and dialled international enquiries.

'There's only one, sir. G. Hionides at 1575 Van Patten Place.'

She read me the number, which I dialled. A man's voice answered and I asked him if Harry had ever mentioned a Gordon to him.

'No, I don't think so,' came the reply.

The following day, I tried again and George introduced himself. He said he knew who I was; he'd spoken to his sister, Mary, after I'd called and they remembered Harry mentioning me. 'When ya coming over?' he asked. I said there wasn't much happening here, and he replied, 'Whatta ya gotta lose? Bring some cheese and baloney, we're out. I told Mary we've got mice in the fridge.'

And he laughed the same laugh as mine. I bought a ticket to Vegas and I didn't have to ask anyone. It had taken me nearly 40 years, but I had got my parole.

CHAPTER 8

≋ ≋ ≋

The FBI is Raiding Us

As the plane approached Las Vegas, I could see the incredible glittering array of skyscrapers built in the middle of the Nevada desert. I had seen it in a dozen movies but its boldness and sheer size still took me by surprise. As the plane was landing, I went back in time to what it must have been like in the '20s at the time of Al Capone. Names like Humphrey Bogart and Edward G. Robinson sprang to mind as I relived the movies I had seen of gangsters and cheap broads. The ghosts of Marilyn Monroe and the Kennedys, Frank Sinatra and the Rat Pack, Bob Hope and George Burns were all here. I could smell the intrigue, the capers, the murders and the racketeering all going on, while the biggest stars in the world performed their immaculate shows full of style with no expense spared. Millions of ordinary people had fun here. Hell, there might even be a living for a 37-year-old musician.

Vegas is the American Dream and you either love it or loathe it, call it vulgar or a place where you can live a little. It had to be more interesting than Gillingham. Mary met me at the airport with a friend who looked like Lauren Bacall: worldly wise, tough and sassy. With arms outstretched, Mary greeted me in a sing-song voice, 'Oh, Gordon. Hello, dear. Oh, Gordon. Oh, my, how wonderful that you came.'

Mary was about 65 years old, very slim and with a Vegas-weathered tan covering every wrinkle. She wore a thin cotton dress and kept kicking off her shoes, revealing her swollen feet. She introduced me to her friend and we walked to the car. Between the airport lounge and the car, Mary lost about $5 in the slot machines. 'All this change makes holes in my pockets, dear. This dress is very precious.'

As we drove down past the endless casinos, Mary spoke of all the shows that were going on and how her friends had managed to get us both some complimentary tickets.

'Is George here?' I asked eagerly.

'No, dear. He's sorry. Georgey had to be in Miami. He's in sports.'

'Oh, what kind?'

Mary said, 'Racehorses.' I guessed he might be a sports columnist or connected to the media in some way.

Mary continued, 'You'll meet him, dear. One of Georgey's friends is getting you a ticket so you can go see him in Miami. George is longing to see you. You'll love Miami. Alfie will see to it you do.'

Mary shared a home with George. It was a ground-floor one-bedroom apartment, part of a condominium with a communal pool. The Hilton was across the road and the Sands Casino could be seen to the right of it, marking the start of the Strip, the stretch of casinos that run for about a mile up the street. Mary slept on the sofa in the lounge. George had the bedroom. There was a shower next to it and the kitchen was built into one side of the lounge.

Mary said that I must have George's room and showed me into the bedroom, where there was a double bed. 'I'll make us both some nice coffee while you unpack, dear.'

I hadn't realised that midsummer would be a crazy time to visit Vegas. It was 110 degrees in the shade, humid and I'd brought all the wrong clothes. People were in shorts and T-shirts and sneakers. I called out to Mary asking if I could have a swim to freshen myself up.

'Of course, dear, and there's a shower next to Georgey's room.'

I threw off my clothes, walked out and jumped into the pool immediately outside the front door. The desert sun burned down mercilessly each time I pulled myself out of the water and within 20 minutes I was deep fried. I knew already from the warmth of Mary's smile and by her sweet, gentle voice that my instinct to make the long journey hadn't let me down.

Mary sat on a chair by the door, smoking a cigarette and sipping her coffee as I swam. 'Georgey always takes a dip every day when he's here,' she said. 'He likes to go in with all his clothes on. He always calls out to me, "Mary, I've done my laundry." I miss him so much when he's in Miami.'

I felt enormous relief knowing I'd found like souls in my family at last. I'd heard that people of Greek extraction were warm and loving and she proved this correct.

'George says you must fly to Miami in a few days' time. But first we're going to show you the Strip,' Mary said as she smoked another cigarette. She showed me old photographs of Harry from when they had all lived in New York. I got the feeling she wanted me to stay for good.

She seemed so poor by the way she was living on a meagre state pension but so rich in spirit and she was obviously connected with somebody who could fix things. She was given free tickets to several shows so that I was assured of a good time and every day, wherever she went, she gambled in the slots. She'd buy some milk from the 7-Eleven and always put the change in the slots there.

After the first day of resting, swimming and long conversations with Mary, I went for a walk on my own to the Strip to see the casinos for myself. Mary had gone to clean someone's house. I noticed Kenny Rogers was appearing at the MGM, so thought it was a good place to start. In the movies, you see the rows and rows of slot machines but you don't hear them like you do when you walk through the doors. The outside of the buildings are so glamorous and extravagant it comes as a shock when you enter. The sound of hundreds of machines tinkling out their winnings is quite deafening. Everybody's waiting to hear the extra loud one when somebody wins a million in the casino's specially made $100 pieces. And somebody always does, which is why everybody is so totally absorbed with each machine. The guards stand by ready for the light to shine above the head of that lucky person. I liked the poker machines, especially after Mary had taught me to play when her friends called round for their regular game at the apartment. I don't think I could get hooked like so many people do, but it's better value than a motorway café breakfast back home. In Vegas, they throw in breakfast for a dollar, giving you a chance to win some money or lose some money. I felt I had been more cheated in England.

I got into the soundcheck of the Kenny Rogers gig at the MGM casino the same way I got into King Crimson . . . by pretending to be a musician. I talked with a few members of the band, who wanted to swap places with me in England. I didn't have the heart to disillusion them. The concert room looked like those of the Bailey nightclubs I had so often played in the '60s in the north of England (they had been based on Vegas) but the stage was huge – big stars look like bigger stars on big stages. I've been squeezed onto so many tiny stages in England and it always makes me feel apologetic for taking up so much room. Vegas booked the top acts to pull in the punters to gamble. Singers and musicians were valued for a sound economic reason, so they always looked after them.

Mary had lived in New York with Harry and George, and then George decided to go to Vegas one day and he took her along. They never went home.

Vegas was full of transients, lost souls and con artists. They'd come, lose everything and be stuck. They found jobs and ended up staying there for the rest of their lives. Mary made hats. 'Do you know the group Kiss?' she asked. She made their hats. She did a bit of cleaning for a nice woman over near the Hilton. I got the picture. All manner of people called round every day to sit, have coffee and play some hands of poker. I was taught a variety of games by five little old ladies who chain-smoked the whole time and caught up on the gossip: who was caught skimming at the Sands last night, which casino boss was shot this morning in his car in his driveway.

Someone would say something like, 'His wife wanted to get rid of him anyway. He was a loser.' That kind of extraordinary event was everyday stuff here.

One of them would interject with, 'Who hasn't put in their *annie*?', meaning the bet.

Some of them were real hard cases, with faces to match. I saw some of them as the old broads of yesteryear, all washed up on the scrap heap, each with a tale to tell but knowing it could never be told.

A 75-year-old Welshman called Jock came over most days. He'd come to America in the '30s as a jockey and spent most of his professional life riding for Al Capone. Of course, Capone didn't just buy horses, he bought jockeys as well, and Jock had been particularly reliable. He showed me the gold pocket watch he carried and asked me to read the inscription on the back of it. 'To Jock. Thanks for everything. Al Capone.'

'Never rode a straight race in my life,' he said with a half smile.

'Why don't you write a book?' I asked, naively.

'Because there's too many people paying me not to.'

I met one guy I wasn't keen on – Lou, an unsavoury character who called round some days to scrounge off Mary. She was broke but always gave him $5, if she had it. He had lost his house at the tables and had come up with a novel idea. He was going to hang around the elevator in the Hilton until someone mugged him. It took him a year and it happened just like he said it would. He sued the Hilton for $100,000 and left town without paying Mary back a dime.

His friend Jason was more likable but clearly going down the same road. He was a young, energetic, good-looking lad with similar ideas. Jason had the job of putting $20,000 on a particular horse at a specific time for New Yorker Joey the Fish. Jason did this efficiently for a while, always winning and handing it over to a nice-looking guy called Michael, who popped into Mary's occasionally. I went to Caesar's Palace with Jason one night and we won at the craps table. The following morning, he came round and said he'd woken up feeling lucky again and had found a dead cert running at noon. He rang George in Miami and talked about it.

'Don't do anything dumb, Jason,' George had said simply. 'None of us can lose, remember?'

Then one day Jason did do something dumb. He used Joey's money to bet his own race in the morning, believing in his heart he'd win the big one and still be able to do Joey's bet at 2 p.m. He lost Joey's $20,000 and came running into the flat in a sweat at about one o'clock and rang George. After about ten minutes, we had a visitor. Michael, the friendly man I had briefly met the day before, burst into Mary's without knocking and there, in front of Mary and me, pulled out a .44 Magnum, walked calmly over to Jason, stuck the barrel up his nose and cocked the gun.

'The money has to be in New York by tomorrow morning or we're both dead,' he said, quietly and calmly. He apologised to Mary, nodded to me and left. Nobody said anything and I never saw Jason again. The desert around Vegas is full of missing persons.

Then there was Mary Alexander, the psychic lady. She did readings and healings for various customers around town. I asked a topical question. 'How do you cope with guys you know have murdered people?'

Her answer was surprising. 'Oh, murder is understood on the other side.'

I'd already picked up on the vagaries of Vegas and the only law that seemed to apply was 'Thou shall not be dumb'. She gave me Shirley Maclaine's book, *Out on a Limb*, which had just been released at the time, and said there was something in it I should read.

Mary and I went to dinner at one of the casinos, gambled for a while and saw the Carl Perkins show. We gained more than we lost and I wasn't bored for a second. The casinos' attitude was that, if by some oversight of theirs you do have money left in your pocket, then they'll try again to take it from you tomorrow. Muggers didn't dare rob you. They understood what would happen to them if they did. The money belonged to the casinos. What was in your pocket tonight, you'd lose tomorrow. Mary and I walked home with confidence.

After three or four more nights in the casinos, I had reached the conclusion that, much as I was having a fascinating time in Vegas, I couldn't see me settling there or working there as a musician. It's a playground for visitors and home for those who can't escape. I caught the plane to Miami to see George.

I was met by a well-dressed, educated and charming man who introduced himself as Alfie. He said George was waiting for me in arrivals. George threw his arms around me and gave me a huge bear-like hug. He had a half-smoked cigar in his mouth and was dressed in a T-shirt, shorts and trainers. His stomach was enormous. We all got into Alfie's Town and Country shooting brake and he dropped us at an apartment by the waterway while he went on to his travel agent's office in the main street.

George took my bag. 'There's a rat that lives here somewhere,' he said, 'but he was here first, so I can't ask him to leave.' The place was clean and smart, with the minimum of furniture. In the lounge there was one huge work table with a vast array of telephones. Calls came in from New York as far as I could gather, bets were taken and for the rest of the story I had to wait until I read about it in the newspapers.

I was a tourist and Miami Beach was on the doorstep. I went to the stylish and beautiful Fontainebleau Hotel, where they welcomed non-residents. I swam in their magnificent pool, which is so large it has an island in the middle. The Florida sun shone brightly, the pina coladas kept coming and all the beautiful girls around the pool made me wonder, with all this, if Dorset was the place for me. As the drinks kicked in, I forgot all about home and felt on top of the world.

I was impressed with George, his humour and his obvious humanity, and couldn't wait to see him at dinner. I didn't expect to get much out of him about Harry: he joked all the time and Mary had said how sad he still felt about their brother's premature death. I didn't want to bring the subject up and, besides, George's personality suited me better. The life I was living was much closer to that of a gambler than the academic one Harry had lived after the war. I felt George was on the same wavelength and his brand of humour fitted my own perfectly. We both woke up each morning with absolutely nothing left to lose.

I went to meet George at a restaurant where Alfie held court and was treating us to dinner. They were gentlemen; they were men of the world. They were the kind you see in movies, the kind little girls and boys in England had told me don't exist (it's only a movie, Gordon). I was smart enough to know you don't ask too many questions of these nice people. They were good to me. I was family. The kind Frank Sinatra had around him when a critic stepped out of line. I considered hiring these friends of the family to collect my missing royalties. I also had the feeling every word was being monitored somewhere, which, as I was to learn a little later, it was.

George was very funny and always making wisecracks. He didn't take anything seriously but apparently he was a genius at remembering numbers, the kind it's wiser not to write down. He was invaluable to Alfie, who paid him enough to get by.

One night as we went to bed, George leaned over to me and said, 'You'll have to make yourself scarce tomorrow. The FBI is raiding us.'

'How do you know?' I enquired, thinking it was one of his jokes.

'Because the cops have told us,' he laughed.

It's no wonder he didn't worry about a thing. Nothing was serious. I asked him if he'd ever won the big one.

'Sure,' he replied. 'I won $12,000 one night and put it under my pillow. It was such a big lump, it was uncomfortable and I couldn't sleep. I tossed and turned all night. So I got up and took it down to the casino and lost the lot, then came home and slept like a log. We're a family of chemists, Gordon. We turn money into shit.'

His Brooklyn accent added authenticity to his story. It was like there was a movie happening all around me. He made me feel that whatever losses I'd had in my life weren't serious either; he taught me in those few minutes how much fun he thought it all was, the way he laughed it off, just as I remember Harry laughing. I can't imagine he ever had to seek any kind of therapy or spend one minute searching his soul. He really didn't give a damn. I hope he loved his life. If it was an act, he was one hell of an actor.

When Mary told me he was in sports, I'd imagined him to be a columnist, but he had been a gambler all his life. He'd wound up working for Alfie's operation out of Miami, their customers being the big boys of New York. They all had fictitious Damon Runyon-style names like 'Sammy the Squid' or 'Bill the Hook' and wherever I went in Vegas, George was known as the only man anyone could ever trust. You could give George a suitcase stuffed full with $100 bills and it would always reach its destination. He'd get on a plane in Vegas, go to New York and hand it over, and return immediately down the escalator as the pilots of the incoming flight were just coming up. 'I forgot something,' he'd say to them, and they'd nod and shake their heads and smile. Everybody knew George and everybody loved him, and that was good enough for me.

He started gambling at the age of 12 on the New York streets and had built a reputation for being good with numbers. He kept his money in the sides of his shoes. My father was the scholar and the family all rallied behind him to get him through university. Their parents emigrated from Greece in 1900 and were dirt poor. Mary was glamorous and loved the nightlife, but never married. They worshipped Harry and were very proud of his achievements and his 'wonderful' dictionaries. The famous director Elia Kazan had once asked him to feature in one of his movies when they were all kids in New York, so my childhood dreams of him being a film star weren't that cock-eyed. Kazan used Gregory Peck instead.

My six weeks in Vegas and Miami had passed quickly. At the end of it, George and Alfie took me to the airport. On the way, we passed Alfie's office. It looked like any small-town travel agency but I doubt if there was another one quite like it – especially in Dorset.

On the plane home, I read Shirley Maclaine's book and was spooked. I had written three songs before I left Dorset to go to Vegas entitled 'The Other Side', 'Breathing In' and 'Mumbo Jumbo'. I found all three song titles within her story.

I had learned something of my father, but I felt I'd learned a lot more besides and George became another of my role models. Nothing and nobody was ever going to bother me again. I viewed all my past adversaries as naive amateurs compared with the characters I'd met and enjoyed in Vegas.

I also felt I knew who I was a lot better than I had just six weeks before.

CHAPTER 9

☙ ☙ ☙

Of All the Garden Sheds
in All the Arctic Circle

Back at my newly restored cottage in Gillingham, I started writing songs. I was still charged with tons of positive Vegas energy and the results filled me with optimism. To record the new songs would cost money, so I had the house valued, got a pleasant surprise and put it on the market. I had made £8,000 clear profit in six months and I figured I could do up another house, make another profit and not only would it sustain my writing, but it would cover the cost of recording. I found a studio that was highly recommended and bought another derelict cottage five miles away in Shaftesbury.

The recordings turned out sounding like demos. Although the studio owner shared the same musical tastes, the accent was on his obsession with drum sounds. I soon learned that nobody made records in Dorset but a lot of people made tapes. It's not the same thing. However, because of the quality of the material, I landed a publishing deal with CBS in New York, with a £10,000 advance less commission, so my gamble had paid off.

I restored the cottage in Shaftesbury and put it up for sale. There was always a waiting period of three or four months during selling, which was perfect for writing without stress, knowing my financial position was solid.

About this time, I had been reading David Nobbs's books on *The Fall and Rise of Reginald Perrin* and, noticing so many coincidences in locations where Reggie had gone on his travels, I felt compelled to contact the author. The books and the TV series had been such a joy and such a confirmation of my sanity that I wrote as a fan, mentioning a wacky novel I had written at West Bay. I received such a helpful reply that we struck up a pen-pal relationship that has endured for 20 years.

When my success came with *Harry's Bar*, and I was appearing at a club near to his home, it was a unique experience to finally meet the man who had always found the time and patience to exchange views on politics and attitudes in Britain as they changed over the years, as well as commenting on the many adventures I was having. In lots of ways, David got me through Thatcherism. I didn't get where I am today without having to endure Margaret as well. Reggie had been a great comforter. As Uncle George kept me laughing, so did David Nobbs; unbeknown to him, he played a significant role during the most challenging time of my life.

I found Thatcherism distasteful in the extreme. If I have to accept she changed the face of Britain and modernised it, then so be it. But the sheer greed and selfishness borne of that period has had dreadful repercussions. I can only comment on the music business, as that is the subject that I pride myself on knowing well.

The Sex Pistols were Malcolm McLaren's puppets and for Thatcherism, you can read McLarenism. Entrepreneurial, yes; Union Jacks, yes; God Save the Queen, yes; Divide and Rule, *definitely* yes. Anti-'60s, yes. Unmusical, yes. Instead of making love, it was now sex. 'Safe Sex' screamed the government slogan in its crass barbarianism, introducing any six year old to the concept that love had nothing to do with any of it. Whole generations of children were brutalised and desensitised at an early, impressionable age. Their first chat-up line was no doubt, 'Do you want to have sex?' which, for the next generation, graduated to 'Fancy a shag?'

Traditional, classy love songs that had seen us through two world wars and Vietnam were called soppy or drippy by generations that had never seen the business end of a gun, yet firmly believed they were *hard* in their naive, cowardly little minds. The voices of the ignorant and inexperienced were deafening and I couldn't wait to leave the country again.

The publishing deal with CBS led into a cul-de-sac and the new songs were rejected, so no advance was forthcoming for the second year.

* * *

At the start of 1984, I began putting together a live set and did my first solo gig for years in the South Western Hotel at Tisbury. It went well and I was given a slot every Friday. I soon realised I had amassed a wealth of knowledge over 20 years of playing and was always reminded of Donnie Elbert's ability to sound good with just one guitar. I was developing a style quickly, keeping in mind that on early rock 'n' roll tracks the main thing you heard was the voice and the acoustic guitar. On an Eddie Cochran record, you feel the rest of the band but you can barely hear the bass and drums. I was on to a winner as my timing, the natural feel that had served me so well on bass, was turning on the audiences wherever I went. I soon had four nights a week, all within thirty miles of my home. I was finding it tedious getting gigs, so foolishly took on an agent for a short period. Every single one he arranged was the kind that no musician wants to play, which was why those venues were forced to get acts through agents.

Typical of one of these gigs was a large, old seaside hotel/public house on its last legs in Southbourne, the residential side of Bournemouth, generally chosen as a place to retire. The agent called and said, 'What it is [pause for fabrication], is they want to get rid of the few old regulars that patronise the place and attract more young people. Your job is to bring in the new and get rid of the old.'

'Great,' I lied, thinking, 'What a turd.'

During one of these gigs, I set up the gear and there were about 12 old people around the edges of the huge bar room that resembled a barn. I started with 'Nature Boy', as it crosses two generations, Nat King Cole's and George Benson's, and it sounds great on one guitar. It's a beautiful song. An old man with a stick started waving at me and shouting, 'Too loud.' I turned down immediately but he got up and came towards me, shouting, 'You're still too loud. I've been to Wembley and they're not that loud.'

'OK,' I said. 'I'll turn it off.' It was already as low as it could go, so I cut the power – but still he wouldn't lay off.

'Now you're being ridiculous,' he bellowed.

'Tell you what I'll do,' I said. 'I'll stop altogether.' Which I did. Before he said another word, I threw myself at his feet, turned over and did an impression of an upside-down beetle I'd studied earlier in my boredom, shaking my arms and legs at him. He raised his walking stick above his head, brought it down as hard as he could across my neck and walked away.

The manager ran across and ordered me out, screaming, 'I've never seen anything so unprofessional in all my life. I'm calling your agent in the morning. You'll never work in Bournemouth again.'

I bawled back at him, 'Unprofessional? Where's the stage? Where's the dressing-room? Where's the audience? . . . You're an idiot.'

I got a letter a few days later confirming I would never work in Bournemouth again. And I never did. They had to bulldoze the pub six months later. My fault, I suppose.

I was then offered a job in Norway for three months, doing six nights a week, to which I agreed. I was promised paperwork but it didn't arrive. By this time, I was used to the flaky way things were done in Dorset, so I accepted it.

I reached Oslo and no one was waiting for me, so I called the Norwegian agent, who told me to go to the airline desk, where I could pick up a ticket to Vadso, a town right up in the Arctic Circle.

The first part of the journey took me halfway up the country to Trondheim, where I changed planes. The next plane was a bit smaller and went as far as Hammerfest. It was snowing by now, and the pilots were getting younger and the planes smaller. By the time I got to the last leg of the journey, we were on what I considered a shorter-than-your-average grass airfield surrounded by mountains and the plane was a single-engine 12-seater. The snow was getting thicker on the ground with every passing minute and the luggage went into the nose cone. The pilot was the last to board. He was about 18 and carried a map and a torch. He asked three of us to move to the back of the plane to help balance it for take-off because the prevailing wind was against us. The music playing was Buddy Holly's 'I Guess It Doesn't Matter Any More'. Buddy and his band had died in a plane crash. We took off as the snowstorm intensified and I thought back over the last few years of my life and wondered how I had been so easily convinced that this was a good job.

We landed safely and I was met by a friendly Norwegian whose first words were, 'The club was burned down last night, but it's OK, we've sold you to another one.'

We drove to a campsite under blue skies and through the whitest, brightest snow I'd ever seen. There were two shivering magpies perched on the perimeter fence and a few pine huts.

'This is where you stay, the bath and shower building is over there.' He pointed to a block a hundred yards away through three-foot-high snowdrifts. 'I'll leave you to sleep and pick you up tomorrow.' It reminded me of a concentration camp.

'Fame at last,' I thought. Great. The alternative was the dole queue along with 2.5 million others.

The hut had four bunks and a wall heater made in Kristiansund. I know it was made in Kristiansund because that was all there was to read and I studied it many times. Rearranging the letters, it read stink, insane, mad and arid. After using all the facilities, I went to bed. Dreams were free.

As I was dropping off to sleep, somebody banged on the door. It was the DJ from the club, along with his latest conquest. 'Hope you don't mind,' he said.

'Of course, be my guest,' I replied. I lay in my bunk and had to listen to them copulating five feet away from me. Nice girl.

When she left, he introduced himself and told me there was nothing to do up there. 'People do two things – get drunk and fuck.'

He cheered me up no end after all the excitement of my trip so far.

In the morning, I looked out of the window to see if I had imagined the whole thing. The contrast of the pure-white virgin snow and the deep-blue sky took my breath away again. There was something fabulous about it and for a split second I wondered if I was developing masochism. I dreaded going out in it. It was minus 25 degrees according to the thermometer on the wall outside and the shower block was some distance. But I wrapped up and set off with my towel and sponge bag. Trudging through the deep snow, I said hello to the two magpies, who asked where I'd come from. They knew Verwood and Reg the milkman; they used to peck the silver tops off the milk bottles. They weren't that keen on the Jersey milk but sometimes that was all they could get. They found it easier up here in the Arctic because so many humans dropped dead in the snow from hypothermia and were never found; one human could keep them in food for six months.

'Didn't you used be in King Crimson?' said the uglier one as they flew away.

As soon as I was washed and dressed, I headed for the nearest travel agent but the cheapest fare home was £1,100 and I had £120 on me. That was before I had credit cards. There was no way out. I went back to the shack and the DJ was just getting up. He looked a bit like Otis Redding and I was grateful to him for demonstrating so clearly what a female orgasm should sound like. I have to admit I felt a degree of envy, for in that bleakest of bleak mornings I had still managed to meet someone to bring me down even further . . .

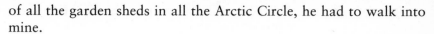
of all the garden sheds in all the Arctic Circle, he had to walk into mine.

* * *

There was an attractive Norwegian girl sitting in the front, paying me a lot of attention, during the first afternoon show. Blonde and blue-eyed, she was the original design for that breed that became the California girls. She invited me to her place, a beautiful flat overlooking the harbour, and told me I could stay. She turned me on to Tom Waits, gave me roses and I had the most amazing four weeks of my life, considering it had all seemed so hopeless the day before I met her.

The audiences were fantastic. I played better than I had ever played and I was in love for the first time since my divorce three years previously. Isn't it good, Norwegian Wood? Lennon hadn't lied.

I was sad to leave Vadso after it had shown me the power of positive thinking. It is situated relatively close to the Russian border and on any night in the club I could meet Russians (KGB), Americans (CIA) or the British (RAC). I used the microphone to good avail to send up the whole Cold War situation, as the men supposedly fighting it got drunk together. It all confirmed my suspicions about 'the Big Lie' sold to us by politicians.

My next venue was further south in a steel town called Mo i Rana. I remember it for two reasons. First, I broke the attendance record and second, for Charlie. He was the bouncer, barman and assistant manager all in one, and he demonstrated to me how to deal with persistent drunks. Charlie looked like Sean Connery and the girls loved him, the drunks were scared of him and the owner could trust him. He was an ex-seaman and had a Dirty Harry approach to life. Any trouble was dealt with swiftly and firmly. One night a drunk was bothering me while I was singing and Charlie rushed over and grounded him with one blow. Lifting him up by the ankles like he was merely carrying a turkey, Charlie transported the drunk to the exit. The unfortunate's head hit every one of the twelve steps on the way down. Miraculously, ten minutes later, he re-emerged at the top of the stairs on all fours, only to be met by Charlie's boot in his backside. That time he reached the exit even quicker. Charlie was the captain of his ship and, though I hate violence, part of me wished I had some of Charlie's fighting skills. He was every girl's ultimate hero. Everybody felt safe around Charlie and he wasn't the slightest bit arrogant about it. He was always grinning with that big smile of his behind the bar and I still miss him 20 years on.

The boss was so keen for me to stay that he offered me the job of running the café during the day, with Charlie doing the nights. It could have been a very decent life up there in Mo i Rana. They'd adopted me and I felt a great warmth from those people. I had no other plans but something in me was telling me to move on.

My last month of that first trip to Norway was in Spielkavik, a beautifully placed town near Alesund. Its surroundings are a mass of waterways weaving in and around the mountains, with little villages all along the winding roads of the valleys. To get there, I had to travel by plane, train, ferry and bus. The scenery was spectacular all the way, so the digs came as an awful contrast. Musicians aren't known for their tidiness and I was getting used to the contemptible treatment that troubadours had to accept. At the end of the day, all the bosses cared about was whether or not I could shift more crates of beer than the act they'd had the week before. If I could, I would be sure to be re-booked. I liked the clarity of it all and for the next 12 years I managed to get re-booked at every place I ever played.

The room I was given was marginally more welcoming than a cell on death row but not as well appointed. The double bed was a flimsy affair of a mattress vaguely supported by a selection of loose slats on legs. The sheets were revolting and covered in stains. Under the bed were piles of dog-eared skin magazines; on the bedside table, three ashtrays all overflowing with dog-ends, bottle tops and sweet wrappers. Empty beer bottles were scattered all over the floor. I was beginning to hate Heineken and the whole culture of drinking. It screamed out that the previous occupant had spent his whole fortnight in the darkest depression and he'd left his imprint of despair on the place.

Here was I having to face one more job, one more time, smiley-smiley to everybody, just to make friends quickly, just to please everyone, while living in this filthy, disgusting mess. A plate with the remains of a meal had been left on the bedside table and used as an extra ashtray; it had been a lamb chop with fried egg and chips in a previous life. The carpet was a light enough colour to be able to count the hairs on it and in my boredom during the long days waiting to play I had the time to count them all. Seven pubic and eight long black ones were scattered evenly amongst the beer stains. The stench was of all human life rolled into one. The bathroom was on the floor below. I'd creep down half-naked in my snow boots, hoping I wouldn't pass anyone on the stairs. The shower had more pubic hairs in it and had been ripped off the wall. The window wouldn't shut but the cold, minus-20-degrees breeze was refreshing by comparison. I had to stay there for two of the lousiest weeks of my life. I managed to get the sheets changed and took a shower by standing on the side of the bath with my boots on, washing my feet separately after I'd dressed.

On the only occasion I took a girl home, my side of the bed gave way, casting me to the floor, the most dramatic instance of coitus interruptus I'd ever encountered. It was the romantic equivalent of chatting to someone from the inside of a coffin with the lid off, as I tried nonchalantly to carry on the conversation from under the bed. I seem to remember asking, 'Have you got any biscuits?'

However many bad moments visited me, I was learning how to make the most of it and I have to say that Norway is by far the most stunningly beautiful country I have ever seen. The mountains, the fjords, the rivers and forests, those bright-blue skies in the morning and the amazing aurora borealis at night all contribute to make the perfect example of mother nature at her most majestic. Norwegians were also the most friendly people I'd come across for a long time. Men like Charlie were tough but lovable and the women were beautiful. I was booked back everywhere and, all in all, it was better than playing in Bournemouth . . . and twice the money.

I hated the loneliness of touring and living alone. As fast as I made friends, it was time to move on, but it was making me sing with much more feeling. I *was* the drifter in the song, I *was* the gambler in 'House of the Rising Sun', and the audience could feel the genuine aching of my heart and responded accordingly. I went home feeling good and knowing I'd made a lot of progress, both musically and spiritually. It had been a toughening-up process and I was good at my job. Suddenly, I had a good living, independent of the morons in the record business, who would never know how songs like 'House of the Rising Sun' had been written.

The work in Norway came thick and fast and I regularly did a month in Oslo at a notorious rough house called The Scotsman. The bonus of being in Oslo was the number of great musicians I met, all of whom became my friends; we were all in the same boat. Some would say the boat had sunk long ago and we were all in the lifeboats. Michael Moore was one step further. He was in the water and swimming for his life. Once voted the best guitarist in the UK by a leading folk magazine, he did one trip to Oslo and never went home. I met him on arrival at The Scotsman at three in the afternoon; he was drunk and tripped over, tipping a litre of beer over me. We struck up an instant rapport of mutual shipwrecks in the first sentence. You get to recognise and respect each other in that world, like ex-cons do. Each survivor has a knowing look. We could write each other's memoirs. We had become the people our parents had warned us about.

I did five sets of forty-five minutes, by which time my soaked jeans had dried out, but on meeting him at three in the morning, he did it again. He couldn't stand up, but his sense of humour was outstanding. He was a wild, talented, tortured soul and he'd been ruined by the business. The tragedy was that he had been banned from playing most places because of his antics. The sort of behaviour that in England would get you signed to a cutting-edge record company got you fired in the real world. He had married one of the waitresses from The Scotsman and occasionally he'd get to sing when the act didn't turn up. He'd done it for years, to the point where he'd get so bored with the drunks, he'd push his luck a little further every night. One night he bet someone he could sing 'Proud Mary' for two hours without anyone noticing. He won the bet. I had made my mark there and I always got him up to do two or three songs just to bug the management, who had used him, abused him and finally refused him.

After The Scotsman closed at 3.30 a.m., we'd go to another bar and, at 6 a.m., on the way home, Michael and I would say goodnight to the girl in the doorway of McDonald's as she gave her boyfriend a blow job. Oslo was out of control years before England went the same way. Girls were being serviced across the bonnets of cars in broad daylight.

One day, Michael left me a note on the stage at The Scotsman. It read, 'I've gone to the mountains and I don't know if I'll ever come back.' It was the first time I'd cried for years. I loved Michael for the same reasons I had loved Tim Hardin. They were both crucified in their lifetime for feeling deeply for their music and their fellow man. I miss both of them terribly.

CHAPTER 10

⬟ ⬟ ⬟

Has McCartney Signed the Cheque?

Each time I returned to England, things had changed. The right to buy my mother's council house arose and I bought it. The second house I had renovated was sold and I bought a terrace at £26,000, then sold it the following month for £30,000 after sleeping in it for three days and hating it. I couldn't settle, yet I was bored with the constant slog of Norway. Four hours a night for six nights a week eventually wears a man down. No amount of applause can remove the aching in your bones from the constant travelling, the sadness in your heart from the loneliness and the degradation one feels having to live in disgusting accommodation. I was never just singing the blues – any fool can copy that from a record – I was living them. I had become the real thing.

I was now wondering if, having achieved a high standard for my live performance, I would no longer have any fascination for it. I had neglected my writing mainly because the gigs were so exhausting, so one cancelled out the other. I wondered if maybe playing the housing market was the best support system I had devised. The builder who had helped me encouraged me to buy another house in Shaftesbury at £26,000. 'It's just a paint job,' he'd said. But the roof had to be renewed and the property market slumped. I worked on it for months in conjunction with local gigs and sold it but made nothing. Then the slump spread to Norway, so I no longer had that safety net. Even though I had grown tired of the whole caper, it had acted as a kind of security. I knew I had to keep up the payments on my mother's house because evicting her wasn't an option. Nothing seemed to be leading anywhere. I longed to have a home life in Dorset but it seemed elusive and, with property in the doldrums and Thatcher driving me crazy, I was vulnerable to persuasion.

My girlfriend in Dorset was a divorced girl of 32 called Lesley. She had a wonderful four-year-old daughter called Faye and I had grown very fond of them both. I would see them between my trips to Norway and, though I couldn't envisage settling down with them, we saw a lot of each other. Lesley had suffered a very rough time with a messy divorce and a disproportionate amount of public humiliation: her husband had been unfaithful and, as is often the case, she had been the last to know. Lesley had a wonderfully ridiculous sense of humour and an equally ridiculous temper. When she found out about her husband, she scrawled the girl's name all over his car in red paint so he could share some of the embarrassment. Not content with that, she took all his clothes to the high street and publicly cut them to shreds on the pavement outside the shop in which he was working.

Dorset was dull at this time and I felt starved of good company, as indeed did she. Lesley loved me to death and life had been tough enough on her already without me adding rejection to her baggage. She thought it was time I gave up music and jettisoned any hope of my success because I was approaching 40. She wanted me to live with her – and I must admit I was tempted; I was so tired of the constant struggle. Thankfully, Bill Gerber was still in touch from Hollywood and, bearing in mind that he never lost faith in himself during his own struggle to the top, I decided to follow his admirable lead and not give up the ghost. I sold all my possessions so that I could get everything I owned into an estate car and moved into Lesley's flat in Gillingham. But I felt very detached. The constant travelling in Norway had turned me into an unemotional drifter. I still wanted to feel free and be able to go anywhere I pleased at a moment's notice. I should have recorded 'Wherever I Lay My Hat'.

This may have been the subconscious reason I was attracted to the job I saw advertised in the local press: 'Barkers Removals require casual labour. Driving experience of seven-ton removal lorry an advantage.' With three gigs and the driving job, we could have a life. Lesley was pleased to think I was, at last, settling down. I smiled back at her, partly because of the idea of having a removal truck at my disposal. She kissed me and said she had found the man she had waited for all her life. I kissed her and thought, 'I hope you're wrong.'

On the fourth week of the job, I was notified that I had reached the top 10 in the Paul McCartney Song Contest. This was an occasional event staged to help promote Paul's business interests in the late Buddy Holly's music. I had recorded the song 'Almost Certainly' live – straight into a cassette recorder – and hadn't expected to be in the running. The other entrants had submitted quality productions. The winners would be announced on the day of the prize-giving, which was taking place in a hotel in London, where a whole day had been set aside with Paul and Linda providing us all with food, drink and a live band.

I was being encouraged back into the music business and left the removal firm. I had lasted four weeks – good going for me. I had only reduced one person's garden to rubble when trying to turn the lorry around in their drive, so my work record was improving slowly but surely.

I took Lesley to the McCartney bash in the hope that it would convince her that anything is possible in this life and each and every one of us has the potential to achieve the life of which we dream. A day with the McCartneys was just what I needed. Jonathan Ross was the master of ceremonies. I came second and was presented with a cheque for £500. In my inebriated state, I said, 'Has McCartney signed the cheque?' Nobody thought it was funny.

Linda came across to our table and encouraged us to go and meet Paul.

'He doesn't want to be bothered right now,' I said sheepishly. 'Let it be.'

But she was insistent and said, 'You must push yourself. I did. I met him in a club and went right up to him.'

I really liked her honesty, and Lesley and I went over to meet the man. He was Paul McCartney, star. He sang the first line of my song and said I should get it to Charlie Rich.

'It would mean more coming from you,' I said. I figured he could have the publishing rights and that it could be an earner for him now he was unemployed. Nobody thought that was funny either.

We had our photograph taken with Paul and the only bit of him that came out was his ear. He had a good ear, but I was disappointed with the picture. It was the last shot on Lesley's roll of film. I hung his ear in her living room for months after that. Nobody believed it was McCartney's ear, but it was.

* * *

I arranged to do a month at The Scotsman in Oslo to get back to where I once belonged. I saw all the old faces and met two buskers who played in the main street outside The Scotsman. Don't imagine buskers are all poor. One of them, the more successful of the two, spent six months playing in Oslo and lived off the proceeds in Hawaii for the other six. He was as brown as a berry and a very happy man. The other had some kind of death wish and had to have the water in his lungs pumped out every year from playing in the cold. I couldn't see myself busking; to me, it still feels like begging. It takes a great man to rise above that notion and beat the system as they do. They are free men.

On my return to England, I decided I couldn't lead Lesley on any more. She understood and let me go. I moved to my mother's while I looked for a place to rent. There was only one solution to my predicament and that was to earn a lot of money. I had no idea how I was going to do it. Norway was no longer an option.

To keep my performance up to scratch, I took some local gigs to tide me over. I knew if I didn't gig, I'd be undoing all the good work I had achieved in Norway. The England I'd known was slowly being demolished by Thatcher as she lined the pockets of big business and bulldozed anyone in her way. Rows of shops were boarded up in every town as supermarkets put everyone out of business. The north of the country was a graveyard and the south was a shark-infested ocean of opportunists.

I tried to avoid listening to new successful bands like The Smiths because they depressed me even further. I had experienced 24 hours of darkness in northern Norway in the winter and was hoping for some sunshine and light in England, but what I saw was a man-made kind of darkness. I noticed people had divided into two distinct camps: the smug and ruthless were having the time of their lives while the rest grew more frustrated and angry.

I looked for another record deal. John Sherry had been my agent in 1972 and he still rated me. He thought there might be a deal out there still, so I gave him some tapes and mooched around Dorset, meeting up with old friends. It was on one of these days that I met a woman I'll call Mrs B. She was blonde, beautiful, sensitive, extremely attractive and, at 25, too young for me at 41. She was visiting a mutual friend at a small village nestling under Hambledon Hill, a historic hill fort near Shaftesbury in Dorset. She was easy to talk to and, over the next three days, we shared life stories and liked each other enough to want to help each other. We agreed to look for a place where we could go 50–50 on the rent, which would benefit us both as rents were so high.

My previous girlfriend, Lesley, spotted us in the neighbourhood and delivered a painting I had left hanging on her wall, by air. It struck me on the head and she walked away. She had thrown a bucket of white paint over it and it was suffering from multiple stab wounds. The song that had come second in the McCartney contest was almost certainly about her:

> *Almost certainly I loved you,*
> *And almost certainly was true,*
> *But you had your doubts,*
> *And you found me out,*
> *Now almost certainly, we're through.*

Neither Mrs B nor I were working now, so we spent most of our time together, visiting the coast, seeing friends or just being at home. I felt sure of her and she wanted another baby. I took pleasure in helping her with her existing child, taking turns to change his nappy. It wasn't difficult and it only took a minute. His crap was easier to deal with than that of the music business. I crawled around with him on the sitting-room floor and made a makeshift tent for us to sit in and play together. Occasionally, we'd scream at the world from that tent. Occasionally, we'd cry. We both felt safe in there. I enjoyed being six months old again, with Mrs B doing the cooking for us both. I could have been a good father – and I knew then what I had walked away from in 1968 and the fun I had missed. The cottage was full of love and laughter, and men could be little boys again. The world could go to hell.

Things went very well for the first few months until my overdraft reached its limit and no deal was forthcoming from John Sherry. I suggested we could make do with one car, but it didn't go down well. One of the many downsides of having been associated with King Crimson or Cliff Richard is that people assume you must be loaded. Anybody in the game knows better, but the moment you associate with those outside the profession you can spend half the day persuading them of the reality. Mrs B had wrongly guessed that I was well-off. She left.

I decided to remortgage the house my mother was in and cut the record I had always wanted to make. I raised enough on the deal to fit a new kitchen and bathroom for Ma and put aside the rest for recording costs. I would start my own label, call it Wilderness Records and use all the knowledge I had gained over 25 years. If I expected a record company to invest in me, why couldn't *I* invest in me? The song that started the whole half-crazed notion was 'Hambledon Hill', which I wrote when Mrs B walked out of my life. We'd walked up the hill the day we met.

The song practically wrote itself. In 1645, during the English Civil War, the locals, who held no allegiance to either side, fought with Cromwell because they were tired of the continual thieving of their cattle and the destruction of their crops. They were outnumbered 4–1. Some were killed and the rest were held in the local church. Legend has it that on the field where they died there is never a bird to be heard. It was originally a Middle Neolithic campsite – skeletons have been found with arrows still embedded in them. It's ironic that Mrs B and I should choose such an ancient battleground to attempt the love of a lifetime, and for it to end.

I have learned over years of writing songs that my higher self always takes over, eclipsing my negativity. The lyric encapsulates all the love and beauty of the experience without showing a trace of anger or bitterness. There was always a mysterious invisible editor standing next to me as I wrote. There have been many occasions when I have descended into my darker side, mystifying those close to me. 'How can you write such beautiful songs,' some have said, 'yet have so much anger inside you?'

I recorded 'Hambledon Hill' at A Room with a View studios and I was determined that nobody was going to screw it up for me this time. The two musicians I used wanted to redo it and overdub, and I firmly said no. It was the first record I truly produced and it was given exactly the right treatment; the whole atmosphere is captured in the recording. It gave people tingles down their spines. It knocked everybody out. When I mastered the record in Soho (transferring tape to record), the engineer, who had cut many a hit record, suggested I talk to a new record plugger in London who was making a name for himself. I played it to him and he took it on. When he came back from Radio 1 and Radio 2, he was ecstatic. The radio folks were mightily impressed and reckoned it could well make the playlist.

All the signs were that I had made a hit record. We decided there and then to do an album and a video, and I thought to hell with the money; I'd borrow some more and do the whole thing properly. I was insane. Emotionally, I still wanted to die and now I was going to have a hit and parade my stupidity in front of the world. I went ahead and recorded in two different studios, retaining a spiritual feel throughout the album. The distributor was an old friend, who had since gone on to sell millions of records for various artists with his partner, who was involved at Immediate Records where I had started with Les Fleur de Lys and my song 'Circles'. They were my only contacts in distribution; I knew very little about that side of things. They charged me £2,000 to distribute and press 1,000 records, 1,000 CDs and 1,000 cassettes, which in retrospect wasn't a bad deal.

However, the artwork got screwed up so badly the plugger was too embarrassed to carry the single and we waited for the CDs that never came because the bill hadn't been paid at the factory. As the album hit the airwaves and was getting a terrific reception everywhere, they had to plug with the vinyl LP disc, making us look completely incompetent up against the competition, who were by now fully entering the CD age. The popular BBC Radio 2 DJ Bob Harris was the first to play tracks and he appeared to genuinely love it.

Just as the interest was building, my distributor went bankrupt, leaving me with a record on the radio that nobody could buy and an overdraft that had grown to £31,000. The timing was immaculate. With the mortgage on top, I needed to remortgage for a total of £65,000. As the house was now worth £120,000, I could still salvage my life and start again. I drove up to the distributor's office and grabbed all the stock. Nobody tried to stop me. If I could sell the 3,000 units, I could recoup my costs and if I could sell more, I might even clear the entire debt. I found another distributor to take it on and I began to get calls at my home from companies dealing with export. I was being thrown into the very inner workings of the record business, meeting people doing jobs in warehouses I never knew existed as a musician. It was strange but fascinating and it took my mind off affairs of the heart. I sent a letter to Dave Lee Travis's Saturday show and he played the song. Anne Robinson followed suit. I made the video in three locations: Hambledon Hill itself, the famous Gold Hill in Shaftesbury and in the town's little theatre. I assumed, as it was a song about Dorset, I'd be sure to get spots on Southern Television for the video and figure prominently on the radio stations within a 50-mile radius, creating local sales through local record shops. I wasn't that lucky. Hambledon Hill itself was a local geographical feature with a fascinating history, but nobody in the local media seemed aware of this and ignored the record named after it. The irony is that I made national radio from London and the song was BBC record of the week as far away as Scotland and Wales. In my own backyard, they had me down as 'some old local act' and ignored it.

I met up with Johnnie Walker at this time. He was working at GLR, the London radio station, and all the disc jockeys there supported the record. I hadn't seen him for ten years and we went out and played pool. He said two things I remember: that he couldn't stand the bullshit of the music business and, after we'd spent the entire evening laughing, that I should become a comedian.

It had been an inspired song and those good souls that loved it enough to buy it still claim in their letters to me that it remains up there with my best work. I managed to sell 11,000 copies from a former council house in Verwood. For me, a beautiful, spiritual moment is captured in the grooves. The story behind it is something else. It is surrounded by doom and gloom and death and romance and broken hearts and was a huge burden to have to carry debtwise. The flaw in the entire project was not the distributors being typically incompetent but that I was supposed to die.

I wasn't supposed to have to face what came next. In my temporary madness, I hadn't cared about the consequences but now I had to pay it all back to the bank, plus the interest that accrued daily. Dear Mrs Thatcher and her banker buddies encouraged everyone to borrow up to their necks. 'Be brave. We need you worthy entrepreneurs.' Once they'd baited their hooks with a 7 per cent rate for suckers like me, they jacked the rate up to 16 per cent in a matter of weeks, reeling us all in and destroying thousands of people's livelihoods. Ordinary, sensible people, not just idiots like me: shops, small businesses and farmers who had believed in their individual talents enough to start up their own company in the first place. Some used their redundancy money to 'have a go'. What choice had they? They were cast into the unemployment lines and told they were either too old to retrain or that there simply weren't any jobs. They were tricked into remortgaging the homes they had lived in and paid for through years of drudgery and a misplaced sense of loyalty to their employers. When they finally plucked up the courage to do something and fight for their independence, they were screwed by the very people who had encouraged them. They lost everything. People committed suicide or simply died of a broken spirit during this period of Thatcherism. My immediate problem was paying back the £65,000 debt I'd secured by remortgaging the house. If I failed, not only would I be homeless, my mother would be too.

House prices took a nosedive and I had murder in my heart for Thatcher for persuading me it was a sound idea to buy the council house. Little did I know all these events would be the making of me. If this disaster had not happened, I believe I would never have developed in the way I did over the next ten years. I literally had to sing seven nights a week for five hours a night after that just to prevent the bank from repossessing the house and rendering my mother homeless. By singing and playing to that extreme, I created a voice and guitar style that would eventually earn me a fortune. So maybe I have to thank Thatcher, after all. Hearing myself say that to myself, I can confirm that God certainly does move in mysterious ways.

It was 1989 and I was financially ruined, completely heartbroken over Mrs B and still stuck with not only having to house my mother but living with her, doing her shopping and occasionally taking her out. I had built the perfect prison and torture chamber for myself.

Somehow, I managed to maintain the mortgage so my mother was safe. The stroke of luck that came my way was getting an order for 1,000 *Hambledon Hill* albums from a friend of mine called John Lee working for the K-Tel label in Switzerland. I pressed CDs to order, paying as I went. I licensed it to Warner Bros. in South Africa and received a further £1,000. It also attracted a lot of revenue from airplay. Considering the disappointing distribution, it had generated a lot of renewed interest in Gordon 'we thought you were dead' Haskell.

At this point, John Sherry, my former agent from the Atlantic Records days, came back into the frame. He signed me to a publishing deal and paid me £300 a week, which wasn't bad; enough to service the debt. He sent down a photographer to do some publicity shots. He was going to manage my affairs and he carried some weight in the business. Things were looking brighter and it was still a relatively new record. I had inadvertently put my career back on track.

The photographer John had sent to Dorset to take pictures alighted from the train at Bournemouth Central. She was tall and had all the telltale signs of the ex-model. The platform became a catwalk as she strolled toward my gaping mouth. She had a hint of the Oriental about her. I closed my mouth and waved to her as she approached.

She looked out from beneath a mass of black curls and, with angelic eyes that looked straight into my soul, she said, 'I'm Sarah

Cheesbrough. Are you Gordon Haskell?' Her voice was gentle and calming like a warm breeze.

'I used to be,' was the best I could do. I didn't expect to meet a girl I liked instantly so soon after my last disaster. I figured I would be a misogynist for at least two more lifetimes. Sarah was 32. My taste was maturing.

I took her bags and put them into the boot of the Mini I was driving. I asked if she had any preconceived ideas of the shoot and she said she had some but she particularly wanted to experiment with some night shots.

I took her to my favourite stretch of coast. We parked in the village of Worth Matravers and took the 20-minute walk down through the hills to Winspit, a fairly deserted cove that at one time had been a quarry for the stone that built large parts of London. The influence of Dorset shaped a lot of that city, hence Portland Place, Shaftesbury Avenue, Dorset Square, The Dorchester, Weymouth Street and so on. The caves that were created when they quarried at Winspit are huge and Sarah was fascinated.

We walked back to the village and had tea in the garden of the little teashop where the sparrows are so tame they peck the crumbs from your plate. I was nearly 46 and sick of being a sparrow. We had to pass through Wareham to get back to the Bournemouth area and we stopped by the river for a drink at the inn. Sarah decided to stay overnight, so I booked a room for her. She had an idea for a night shoot using lit candles down on the beach at the well-known rock arches of Durdle Door, so we stayed for a meal and waited for the sun to go down.

When we reached Durdle Door, the moon was shining on the water, creating a shimmering effect, and she handed me two long burning candles. She was going to use a technique involving a long exposure and asked me to wave my arms about to make a fiery patterned effect. I wanted to say there was a man in the village who did that to frighten the old ladies and shouldn't I be wearing a raincoat, but she was too lovely.

Having done all that, I knew our day was ending and I didn't want it to. I decided to take a room at the same inn because I couldn't bear to leave her for a night in with my mother. We drove back to Wareham, checked in, had a quick drink and went to our rooms.

* * *

My newlywed mother just as war
broke out in 1939

My father, Harry

With my cat Bubbles
(accidentally run over by
my mother!) in the
garden at Verwood,
Dorset, 1955

Les Fleur de Lys in Soho, London, 1967: (from left) me,
Pete Sears, Chris Andrews, Phil Sawyer and Keith Guster

Les Fleur de Lys (mark two) at the Polydor building on Stratford
Place: (from left) me, Bryn Haworth and Keith Guster

My long-suffering wife, Sally Smith. We are now reunited after 25 years

Lazing at the poolside with Susan George
at her Hollywood mansion in 1979

Post-'Hambledon Hill' days in Chelsea, 1990, just before leaving for Norway again (photo by Sarah Cheesbrough)

Jamming at Mill Valley, San Francisco, in December 2000

At the Brook, Southampton, in 2002,
with McCartney guitarist Robbie McIntosh

My perfect paradise in Ashmore, Dorset, before the 'hit'

Cover of *Harry's Bar* (photo by Mike Innes)

Wearing the gorilla suit that kept me warm in the unheated London flat the night before the £2.8 million deal with Warner

Martin Smith, my best friend, to whom I dedicated 'Someone I Knew'

With sax player Paul Yeung, who featured on 'How Wonderful You Are', *Harry's Bar* and many other Haskell recordings (photo by Michael Head, courtesy of *Blackmore Vale* magazine)

Johnnie Walker and me after the
invasion of the charts against all odds

Two days later she rang and I could tell she was excited. 'You'll never guess what's in the fire shot,' she said. 'Did you know what you drew when I asked you to wave your arms about with those candles? You drew a perfectly shaped heart, and it's golden. It looks fantastic. I knew it would work.'

'Wow, when can I see it?' I asked, and we made the date for the following day.

I drove up to her flat in Chelsea in the morning. It was in a mansion block just off Sloane Square.

She leaned out from the second-floor window. 'Come on up,' she cried and pressed the buzzer to open the door. She was all smiles. She was halfway down the stairs as I was walking up. She made some tea as I looked around the sparseness of her bedsitting room; I no longer felt like a poor relation in her presence. She was obviously skint like me, although art critics would call it minimalist. I saw the photographs and we hugged each other for the first time, which led to our first serious kiss.

'Oh, dear,' said Sarah. 'How did that happen? You're nothing that I want.'

Within a fortnight, I was living in Chelsea. It was a strange mixed feeling of not belonging yet wanting so hard to adapt and forget the past. It was easy to say that, but could I really? Memories of Les Fleur de Lys came flooding back and now, having a manager and a publisher, I was feeling more optimistic careerwise. I knew London like the back of my hand and it was great having the Mini to whizz about in. I rang all my London friends to let everyone know I was back and picked up where I'd left off in 1977.

Sarah's building was on four floors. An estate agency had the ground floor, the fashion editor of *Cosmopolitan* had the first floor, Sarah shared the second floor with a gay couple in the opposite room and the top flat was occupied by Chris White, the bass player of The Zombies and writer of Argent's big hit 'Hold Your Head Up'. Chris was Sarah's previous boyfriend and they had remained good friends. We met almost immediately and I liked him instantly. I wasn't bothered that they had once been close.

I had many good times with Chris, who is a great songwriter, and listened to the musical he was writing taking shape. It was a good feeling to be able to nip out to places on Sloane Square or the Kings Road to eat or for a bottle of wine with a fellow professional. I was catching on to the general London lifestyle again, but I was disillusioned more than enlightened. The Kings Road had changed beyond all recognition. Instead of the individualism of shops like Granny Takes A Trip, there were the chains that Bournemouth had, and instead of music cafés featuring John Martyn, there was karaoke. In brief, it had become 'Straightland', a place for the rich and tasteless. It bored me.

Chris and Sarah were paying very low rent to an Irishman who, it turned out, didn't own the building at all, and had discovered that the real landlord had forgotten its existence. The Irishman acted with authority and collected the money every week. Uncle George would have been greatly amused. Sarah was paying £30 a week to some bum off the street to live just off Sloane Square.

The pair of them had many visitors, mostly connected with spiritual matters, reincarnation and spirit guides, and I regularly met mediums and trance channellers. If we weren't writing songs or hustling gigs, we were all in one room trading spooky stories. Time passed quickly.

Something came up about the blue curtains in Sarah's room and she casually said that an actress had made them for her. The actress turned out to be my ex-wife, Sally. Strange coincidence, I thought, there of all places. A shudder went through me and I was reminded of all those paranoid days I spent trying to make sense of everything in the mid-'70s. Had I progressed? Had Sally?

I wanted to help Sarah get work as a photographer, so we plundered my telephone book and called every contact I had ever made in the record business. Within three months of our relationship starting, she had landed the Cliff Richard at Wembley programme, an RCA shoot for a girl band and one of the Stock Aitken Waterman acts. She also photographed the reformed Zombies, featuring Colin Blunstone, because John was managing them. We were doing all right. *Hambledon Hill* was attracting licences in Europe and I was asked to play The Scotsman again in Oslo.

Sarah wanted to go with me and try to contact the group A-ha to take pictures. She managed to land a fashion shoot as well, so it seemed a good idea at the time. Her brother-in-law was working at the British Embassy there and had a lovely house, so she wouldn't have to stay with me in the squalid little dump provided for us low-life musicians. When we did get there, I was invited to the house after playing The Scotsman but Sarah forgot to leave the door unlocked and I very nearly froze to death in minus 20 degrees in the garage at 3.30 a.m. The family returned just in time to thaw me out.

* * *

John Sherry was furious at me working when he was paying me to write songs. He stopped my wages for the month, so it was all a complete waste of my time. Did he say wages? Funny, I thought it was for the publishing rights to my songs. Before we left for Oslo, I called the people responsible for paying Sarah on the Cliff Richard job and asked if the guy writing the cheque had broken his arm. The payment of the bill was eight weeks overdue. John went stark raving mad and eventually fired me for interfering. No musician is ever allowed to play the businessman. No artists are allowed to chase their money and start getting tough with the cretins who think they can take as much time as they like to pay the bills. What about our bills? When you cross that line as a musician, the doors all shut together. The music business belongs to them; it's their private little club where they all meet and smarm, and to which membership does not, nor ever will, extend to artists or musicians. The well-known adage rings true: 'This would be a great business if it wasn't for the artists.'

It is why there is such a huge turnover of performers. They call them one-hit-wonders and the public believe them because nobody is that interested in the truth. They're disposable items to the businessmen. The artists they feed off are like matches to them: strike once, ignite, blow out and throw away.

I was out of a job and it upset Sarah a lot because, since she was being managed by John, she was caught in the middle. She didn't need an unemployed 45 year old under her feet, particularly as we were living in only one room. It had a lot to do with why we broke up.

The John Sherry management had turned into a fiasco. Just another tyrant really, no great surprise; he'd been a drummer before he became an agent, so why he felt he was my commanding officer I'll never know. I felt it was time to leave. I returned, somewhat relieved, to Verwood.

I'd written some fantastic songs during this period, one of which was 'Go Tell Sarah'. It was about second-hand people surplus to requirements. It's about selling oneself cheap, about having a pimp to sell you, and it is a personal favourite of mine.

CHAPTER 11

❦ ❦ ❦
Someone I Knew

My feelings of relief at being back in Verwood didn't last long. I soon found it depressing there after Sarah and that whole fantastic period of enlightenment, perhaps because my mother never seemed to have a good word to say about anything at that time. Every idea I aired was a bad one. I was holding a bad hand.

In 1990, 'Almost Certainly', the song that had come second in the McCartney contest, went to No. 1 in South Africa, performed by Judy Boucher. It was the title track of her album which sold 45,000 copies and I picked up the £600 it had earned me. I found myself thinking about Uncle George again. I thought about Vegas. I thought about placing the measly £600 on the 2.30 at Kempton Park. Maybe backing horses was more lucrative than music; the odds looked better from where I was standing. I didn't dwell on the fact that I'd obviously been short-changed again.

I rang Las Vegas and Mary answered the phone. She told me Alfie and George had been arrested in New York. Despite this, George was still making everybody laugh, including the FBI and the Las Vegas Police Department. Mary had spoken to him at the time of his arrest and he'd said, 'It's free board and lodging, Mary. What have I got to lose?' The whole operation was being broken up.

Alfie had been accused of running a $500 million illegal gambling operation from 1491 Lincoln Terrace, Miami. George's joke about the rat that I had taken literally was for the benefit of the bugs the

FBI had planted in the rooms. They were trying very hard to link Alfie to the Colombo crime family in New York, but it was never proven because it wasn't true. Somebody had twice bombed Alfie's travel agency in Miami and succeeded in destroying it on the second attempt. He was just about to announce his retirement on his 73rd birthday, but the cops were determined to get him. It was in all the papers. By all accounts, Alfie was a very popular man; he was a gentleman. He never hurt anyone who owed him money after losing a bet, and because of this the Mafia was losing valuable customers to him. It was rumoured that the organisation was working with the FBI to put Alfie out of business.

Mary was laughing as she told me the story of what George asked the arresting officers. As they were putting the cuffs on, he said, 'Promise me you'll look after my sister and my dog, Sherman. If you can't afford both, just look after Sherman.'

The cops were laughing too. They eventually dropped the charges against George, though Alfie paid dearly. It was estimated he was skimming $5 million a year out of the operation. That's a lot for the Mob to lose. The FBI could be seen to have been successful by breaking it up. Mary said George had taken Alfie's arrest badly and was bored out of his mind hanging around the apartment all the time.

Mary added, 'You know what, honey? Alfie is still paying George from the prison. He was always good to George, so we're both managing OK. Are you coming over? We'd love to see you.'

So I made a quick trip to see Aunt Mary and Uncle George in Vegas. This time, though, I'd go from there to San Francisco and meet Harry's widow, Alexandria, and their three daughters, my half-sisters. The four of them were all getting together for Thanksgiving. America filled me with positive energy that I badly needed and it was money well borrowed.

George was quieter than before but still very funny. He stayed in his room a lot and slept or watched the television. He'd get up early and walk downtown, place the odd dead cert and return for coffee and a hand of poker. He was a brilliant card player, with an incredible memory. Sometimes we played gin rummy and I swear he knew every card I was holding in my hand. Needless to say, he won every game and I must have merely added to his new-found boredom. He had lost his brother Harry and now Alfie was in prison. George's world was slowly dying.

Mary was still gambling on the slots at the local store but we found plenty to talk about. She briefed me about Harry's family before I flew up to 'Frisco a few days later. Harry had married a fellow New Yorker, also of Greek extraction, in 1950, and they'd had three girls in swift succession.

Artemis, the eldest at 43, was an archaeologist but had since worked as an interpreter for Reuters. She now works at Harvard and lives in Boston. Christina is a year younger and was hit hard by the early death of Harry at just 55. She passed all her exams but chose to live within a spiritual community in Iowa. She is still looking for an inspiring occupation that will engage her vivid imagination. Dee-Dee, the youngest at 40, rose to become a highly qualified aeronautical engineer. She lives in Oakland, California, with her girlfriend, drives a pick-up truck and is learning to play the piano.

They spoke of Harry's innate love of mankind. They said Harry had a spiritual intellect that influenced every decision he ever made. It all rang true with me and explained why I had always felt so different to the English side of my family. I enjoyed meeting them and felt at ease. They are all strong individuals going along totally individual paths.

Occasionally, Harry's learned friends would talk him up to me and I put them at ease by showing no sign of resentment for having never known him. On the contrary, I think I was given the better hand – I was glad I'd been brought up by my mother and not the woman Harry eventually married.

Harry's wife was a scientist and everybody in that family had to be an academic regardless of their dreams or aspirations. Christina had longed to be an actress. In her 40s, she is only just about to blossom into who she really is. She was forced to study subjects at school with which she had zero affinity. I was glad I'd been raised in England. I'd had a lot more fun and, having committed myself to a lifetime in music, my mother was now not only supportive, but quite a fan as well. After meeting Harry's widow and his other children, I came away appreciating my mother more and, when I returned to England, I thanked her for keeping me. I told her I loved her, which was something I'd had enormous difficulty with in the past.

But I was always meant to meet Uncle George. It was he who left such a lasting impression. He made everybody laugh; he was a player, a man of the world, second to none. He had become my new role model.

One year later, when I was back home after playing gigs at The Scotsman in Scandinavia again, Mary rang from Vegas to tell me George had collapsed and died in the shower at home, naked and

penniless, the same way he'd entered this world. I tell a lie; he was
one kidney short. He'd given it to Harry. All he said about that was,
'What did I need two for?'

Mary told me that on the day he died some guy had called round and
asked George to lend him some money. Mary's voice was trembling as
she spoke but she managed to say, 'George gave him his last $10.'

George had said, 'You're welcome to it. Go on, take it. I won't
need it where I'm going. There's no charge in the shower. Try Alfie's
Revenge in the four o'clock at Belmont.' Mary said he must have
known he was going to die. He just wanted a last laugh.

With the death of Uncle George in 1993, I felt the soul searching
come to an end. I was 47 years old. It was time now to put all the
family mysteries to bed and get on with living my life.

The music business was making me harder with each passing day. I
had reached the point of no return. I still lived and loved music, but
couldn't square it with the sort of cold-blooded heartless swines with
whom I had to negotiate deals. When somebody said something
insensitive to me – something which might have upset me once – my
response would be to identify them as the type that causes all the
misery in the world and laugh in their cowardly faces. I'd ask them
why, when they looked in the mirror, they believed that they were
seeing this marvellous person when all I could see in their face was
the image of a complete idiot. I'd ask them how long they'd been
doing cockroach impressions. I was a little too trigger-happy, really.
I'd goad people into saying something nasty. None of it was very
clever. Being kind and caring was considered a weakness by
Thatcher's followers. The Dalai Lama says, 'All that is asked of us is
to be kind to one another.' I needed to decide once and for all what I
stood for and, what's more, to be proud of it. I enjoyed hitting them
back twice as hard as they were hitting me, but it wasn't the right
way. I still had to learn about balance.

Harry had done what a lot of us do at some time in our lives –
celebrate and throw caution to the wind. He wasn't a villain. He was
intelligent, a war hero and a much-loved man. He had a wonderful
nature but he made a woman pregnant. It happened to be my mother.
It could have been any pretty girl. It's the most natural thing in the
world and why we all make such a fuss about it is beyond me. It was
about to happen to me in Dorset. You meet someone, you're attracted
to her, you have a drink or two and the girl gets pregnant either by
accident or design.

In my case, as before in 1967, the girl had big ideas. Along with Thatcherism in the '80s, there came an attitude among certain young women that led them to believe that if you got pregnant, you could get a free house and live on 'the Soc', as they mockingly called it. Thatcher had created a scarcity of jobs and the unemployment lines were getting longer and longer. It shouldn't surprise any of us that some women found a way out that they misguidedly thought would be easier. The trouble is that raising children on your own isn't the easy way out; the girl I made love to just thought it was at the time. She knows better now, though I know for a fact she'd have never given up her baby, not for anything. She went through hell on her own but she never stopped loving Jasper for a minute.

I was just back from Scandinavia, where none of the women want to get pregnant and they make damn sure they don't. I was so used to *them* taking the precautions I had become careless. The night I visited a guitarist friend, the lady in question had moved into the flat upstairs and came down to say 'hello' – identical to the scenario I'd faced in 1967. She was attractive, well-spoken and seductive. I was glad to be among friends again after a gruelling tour of Norway and everyone was relaxed and in a party mood. I stayed the night and thought no more about it. We, like Harry and my mother before us, had celebrated life that night . . . and created a life in the process. I left England almost immediately for another tour of Scandinavia and on my return three months later received a call from her friend saying I was going to be a father again. The girl who'd come to say 'hello' gave birth to a beautiful boy and he's unmistakably mine.

I never had a father and, apart from loving a child and giving him or her advice, I see children as individual souls, not as possessions. Our relationship seems to be working exceedingly well. Jasper shows no signs of psychological damage and has a highly developed sense of humour. His mother has done a damn fine job in difficult circumstances. I've had no end of squabbles with her but one day I hope it will be different and we'll be able to laugh at ourselves and each other good-naturedly.

Jasper and I laugh a lot. We're both exceedingly childish. He's 11 and I'm 57. We are getting scooters for Christmas and we're going to dress up in gorilla suits and ride down the road together. The world can think what it likes.

* * *

There was nothing much else happening in Dorset but I met up with guitarists I admired and landed a well-paid gig on a ferry travelling between Helsinki and Stockholm. The SS *Cinderella* carried 3,000 passengers and was a floating first-class hotel. The job was playing in its pub for forty-five minutes, five times a night, seven days a week for five weeks. The last spot ended at 3.30 a.m. It took a further 30 minutes to count the tips that had been stuffed into a large beer tankard.

I was glad I'd experienced something similar in Norway. This wasn't a gig I could have done as a novice. It was extremely demanding and full-on energywise – the crowd loved you just that little bit too much sometimes. Women go crazy when they go to sea and I was never alone for a minute. Scandinavian women just don't want to get pregnant. It's a hell of a problem for the authorities in Norway, Denmark, Sweden and Finland. I tried to help, but I failed.

The ship was beautiful and every meal was a banquet. The staff canteen offered the same food as the guests enjoyed and it was open all hours. My cabin was tiny but there was plenty to do on board. It was July and to sit on the deck on a sunny day while sailing into Stockholm, looking at the beautiful homes and gardens either side of the estuary, was relaxing and put a smile on my face. I went for a daily swim in the indoor pool, had a sauna and went to the casino. Occasionally, if the weather was rough, I went to the ship's cinema.

After the first week, I had made £500 in tips and sold about a hundred *Hambledon Hill* albums at £10 each, on top of my £500 wage – three times what I would make when 'How Wonderful You Are' was in the charts. There was a main band on board playing in the ballroom and it was great to be a part of something again. All the musicians were top pros. My favourite companion was an English ventriloquist called Paul Zerdin. He went on to do very well, including performing on the Royal Variety Show. On this trip, however, he kept me laughing offstage for hours with his brilliant impressions of Bruce Forsyth, Jimmy Savile, Frankie Howerd and Kenneth Williams. He would string them all together in rapid-fire delivery, changing from one to the other without taking a breath. We had a great busman's holiday and it remains one of the highlights of my working life.

The air conditioning was notorious for adversely affecting performers' voices, but with the help of a steam machine in my cabin, laid on by the management to protect their investment in me, my vocal cords were rescued.

There was a good recording facility on board and I made demo tapes as I wrote between distractions. I decided this kind of job could fund another album, only this time I'd be less reckless. *Hambledon Hill* had more than recouped its recording costs and the new songs were much more upbeat and reflected my time with Sarah. The spiritual theme that had emerged on *Hambledon Hill* was still there but I had benefited from playing live so much; the batch of songs were easier to programme into a set. *Hambledon Hill* didn't cut through in a noisy bar situation, it was more suited to a monastery, and I'd written more up-tempo songs since I'd been playing in bars. Three trips on the ship would pay the recording costs. I signed up for another three months with Viking Line; one hundred and ten days, to be accurate. I remember because it became the worst nightmare of my life, the toughest job I would ever do; but it would produce *Butterfly in China*, my strongest album to date. By then, I'd have a powerful voice with bags of grit and the strongest, gutsiest songs I'd ever written. I felt it had to be just a matter of time before I got a break from the hard slog.

'You're doing the SS *Isabella* next time – God help you,' said the entertainments manager as I left the *Cinderella* for the flight home.

I shrugged it off and thought, 'I'm a tough guy now. I can do this job blindfolded.' In a few weeks' time I would realise what he meant. I was tough but I was going to need to get tougher.

I was getting the debt down now and wasn't afraid of losing any more. As well as allowing me to be my own man, I was looking at recording as an investment. Finding that I could sell records on my own label had empowered me. I had attained the confidence level that Robert Fripp had been born with – and it had only taken me 47 years. I loved it because the world had written me off and it had no idea I was going to prove everyone wrong. I knew it and it made me smile every time I was treated with contempt by agents and some of the little Hitlers that ran pubs. At last, I was at ease with myself and I could also handle my mother with more care. I didn't need a relationship. I didn't need anybody. I was becoming more like an American act, both in the nature of the material and the grittiness of its character. Willie Nelson is the way he is because of the life he's led and I was becoming the same. I would no longer fit into a trendy place in London or the provinces, but I'd be right at home in Nashville or New Orleans. It made life easier to be that removed from so-called 'normal' British life, as so little of it interested me. Suddenly,

London seemed naive. I no longer missed it, but I missed me. I was going to have to wear the suit of armour for some time yet and I was certainly going to need it in a month's time for the SS *Isabella*.

While I was home, Robert Fripp and I were invited to a reunion in Bournemouth by members of The League of Gentlemen, the group we'd been in as schoolboys. I had mixed feelings about going, but the drummer, Stan Lawford, wanted Robert and me to make friends again so badly that I agreed. Robert gave my new records a lot of praise and we hugged each other. 'This is great,' I said. 'This is how it was when we were kids together.'

'Did you ever grow up?' he replied.

He just had to be cute and, of course, brutally accurate. Well, at least we were both trying. He was in his 20th successful year as a world-renowned musician; I was in my 30th successive year as a complete screw-up – we had both worked diligently all our lives to achieve this. But after knowing people like Uncle George and Alfie, it all felt a little flat. I couldn't kid myself into thinking otherwise. I no longer had anything in common with any of them. We all tried, but it achieved nothing.

I went to see a new studio in Yeovil, in Somerset, run by Jon Sweet. He'd had success with the song 'Ocean Deep', which Cliff Richard had recorded, and had used the money to develop a digital studio. He was very up-to-date and was determined to make records that were radio friendly. I felt fairly detached from the modern technology that was advancing so quickly, so I decided I needed a producer to break me into the digital world. I had avoided drum programmers like the plague but when Quincy Jones embraced them I wondered if I was being a Luddite. My favourite recordings up to then were those I had done in the old-fashioned way, with a live rhythm section, because programming never sounded as if there was a spirit present in the grooves. Every musician had suddenly become obsessed with perfect time. Having a great groove is perfect time to me and the human spirit adds its own light and shade in the dynamic. Computers can't do that convincingly. It's contrived. There is no human touch. Every record was sounding like that to please radio stations that wanted a contemporary sound to impress their advertisers. My favourite artists, Joni Mitchell and Michael Franks, had gone that way under pressure from record companies, so I caved in and left Jon to programme all the drums, which took three times as long as a real drummer.

We made a start on the basic tracks and then I had to leave to go to the Baltic. As I was going to be away for so long, Jon carried on without me, which is not the way to make records. I flew out to Helsinki to pick up the ship in all innocence and my mind was mainly occupied with the new record.

The SS *Isabella* was the *Cinderella*'s poor relation: older, rustier, smaller and with fewer luxuries. It had a foreboding look about it, from the dozens of cigarette burns and stains on the carpets to the depressed-looking crew. I was shown to my cabin and wondered why the numbers to the cabins were all at the bottom of the doors.

I asked the entertainments manager if the routine was the same as on board the *Cinderella* and he said, 'These are very special people. These are 24-hour cruises and everybody who comes on board only comes to drink and buy the duty free. So we sail out of Finnish waters and stop for a few hours, then turn the ship around and go back to Helsinki. These people aren't interested in going anywhere. Give them plenty of rock 'n' roll. I'll show you the pub and you can test the equipment.'

The playing area was actually larger than on the *Cinderella* but there was no stage or the usual balustrade around it to protect the singers from would-be Frank Sinatras. I missed Paul Zerdin, my only English companion on the *Cinderella*. This time I was the only Brit on board and I felt like the alien I was. I had a good look around the ship and could see its typical passenger was akin to a drunken football thug and I began to mentally prepare for a set similar to those of The Scotsman in Oslo. Nothing of a sensitive nature would be feasible. If I did all the rocking stuff, I'd be fine.

It was October and it stayed dark and gloomy all day. I wanted to get on with the job just to start ticking off the days. I was scheduled for 110 nights, with no days off. And of those 110 nights, I can only remember the bad ones. There were 110 of them.

The noise the crowd made was the same as in any football stadium, which I had accurately predicted, so I was prepared to play louder to get heard and to hear myself. When people went to the bar, they were ordering eight litres of lager at a time. The bar staff had specially made wooden frames so eight glasses could be carried by each customer. There were drinking competitions going on everywhere. The women weren't noticeably different, but I found myself thinking of Crufts, which I'd seen once. They were all desperate to be loved in any form they could find. I welcomed everyone to the Ugly Bugs Ball.

There were some advantages to nobody speaking English. Nobody would get hurt, no matter what I said. The Finnish Government obviously wasn't concerned that thousands of its citizens were permanently depressed or drunk, or both. I told myself to stay focused, keep my cool and do what I was being paid to do. I could see through their pretence and learned from Norway how music comforts these tortured souls and I was happy to help. I was still shrugging my shoulders in the first week, though I counted every minute of every passing day. The temperature outside was minus 20 degrees; you could hear the ship breaking the ice as it entered the frozen harbour of Helsinki and you knew you'd made it through another night. Then 2,500 drunks would leave the ship as another 2,500 excited passengers boarded. There was no let up.

I soon found out why the door numbers were where they were. When I finished the gig at 3.30 a.m., I'd step over bodies sprawled along every corridor. They were crawling back to their cabins and the numbers were at eye level so they could find their way back through the confusing maze of passages. Some were totally naked outside their cabins, after their wife or girl had kicked them out.

I had my share of Finnish women. The ladies' chat-up line was, 'I take what I want.' I didn't have the strength at the end of a night to argue. I felt cheap but I no longer cared. I was merely an observer, a reporter doing research on the human race.

I began writing songs in my cabin. Self-imposed solitude became a necessity if I was to survive the trip. I wrote 'Someone I Knew' then. Over the years that followed, it became one of my most requested songs. I had written it about Sarah and those days in Chelsea that seemed such a lifetime away. In about three years' time, someone in a pub in the New Forest would ask me if it was about me and subconsciously it may well have been, for the person I had become was a long way from the someone I had known.

Someone I Knew

These are sunny days in many ways,
I'm sailing on through a smoky haze.
I still believe that love was true
When I think about
Someone I knew.

I sing to folks I feel I know,
In all the places where the lonely people go,
They smile and say 'We've been there too'
When I think about
Someone I knew.

We taste the wine and it feels all right,
And somebody's always there to take me home each night.
And the hardest thing is knowing what to do
When I think about
Someone I knew.

I treat them well and it's too bad,
Cos they love me just the way I wish you had.
And peace of mind is long overdue
When I think about
Someone I knew.

But these are early days, and you can bet,
Though it's been over for so long, it still ain't over yet,
I still believe that love was true,
When I think about
Someone I knew.

In seven years' time, the song that was written in such dire circumstances and abject misery would be dismissed as 'fabricated world-weariness' by those who call themselves music critics.

CHAPTER 12

It's Not My Problem, You're the Monkey

I had only experienced the sea in the summer in the Baltic. Now there were regular storms and rough seas and very little daylight. I was singing and playing standing up and was constantly being thrown off balance as the ship rolled. It was only a matter of time before the crowd would be thrown too.

One night, about 40 drunken morons, including myself, were all-dancing all-singing and were thrown by a huge wave that hit the ship. It resulted in me being buried beneath them all as they fell over on top of me and my guitar being crushed. You could say rain stopped play that night.

I called the purser and the entertainments manager to show them that I no longer had an instrument, so I was going to bed if it was OK with them. By this time, I'd stopped caring about anything. There had already been several nights when the speakers and their stands had been knocked over and I'd stopped bothering to pick them up. Now that the guitar I loved was broken, I was going to start demanding some changes. I wrote a list of demands and handed it to the bosses as I went ashore to a music shop in Helsinki to try for a part-exchange deal on another guitar.

A new guitar was £750. I bought it and handed the bill to the Viking Line management for reimbursement. They refused to pay, so I went on strike. They needed me and I had them by the balls. I also insisted they build a stage with a protective barrier to prevent it happening again. My strike lasted three days, and they gave in and paid up and built the stage. I knew I wouldn't be getting rebooked, so the gloves were off for the remainder of the cruises. When the agent visited the management to remedy the situation, I grabbed hold of his balls and squeezed, looking him straight in the eye. I told him I'd only just started, so if he didn't like it he could fire me. Nobody in their right mind wants those jobs, so he kept me on. In fact, the entertainments manager once hit a customer and they couldn't get rid of him either. Such was the strength of the unofficial union. You soon learn when you're doing a job like this that you got it because nobody else would accept the conditions. You were taken for a mug. That gives you the bargaining power to call some shots because you know you can't be easily replaced.

I was earning the respect of the other musicians on board. They were all communists hired by the agent to keep costs down. While they had to pay me £500 a week, the Yugoslavian musicians in the bands were only getting £100 for doing the same hours. I began to hang around with them and enjoyed learning about their lives in the Eastern Bloc. Most of them had worked in Norway, as I had done. The Scandinavians were the only people in Europe who could offer musicians seven nights a week; they do like their music. Without them, there would be far more ex-musicians driving vans for a living.

On the first day of every month the top brass and their wives came on board for a night to see the latest entertainment. I wanted them to remember not to book me again and had planned a few pranks. When my spot was announced, I would come onto the ballroom stage in bandages, looking as if I'd had a serious road accident. The first-aid department cooperated with glee and did the costume. I looked like the Invisible Man and the wives became quite concerned, while their management husbands visibly fumed. Then I put on a long, brown overall, took a stepladder and acted as if I was a maintenance man, repairing the lights above the stage during the band's performance. When I was bored with that, I fetched the ironing board and brought all my ironing to the front of stage among the customers on the dance floor. The band loved it; the management didn't. It was my last week. They got their own back by making me help with the karaoke in the middle of my set. I hate karaoke. It was an apt ending to my days working for Viking Line.

When I went home, the overdraft and mortgage took up all the money from that 110 days. I asked myself why I didn't just declare myself bankrupt and keep all this cash to start afresh. It would have been the smart thing to do, but how would it feel knowing I'd evicted my own mother? There was no easy option. The right business move would be to trade down, settle everything and restart with a small deposit and a much smaller overhead. I didn't have that luxury. I had inadvertently bought a property with an intransigent sitting tenant. The establishment had become no better than loan sharks by lending at 7 per cent and raising it to 16 per cent. It was immoral, but I had to go on.

I got a call from Norway almost immediately. It was for five weeks' work touring Denmark. They'd heard I was good, so I don't think it came from the Viking Line connection. I went to see Jon Sweet, to see what progress he'd made with the tracks for my album. I suggested I do the vocals before I left for Denmark, so he could work around the general vibe of my singing. I did all the tracks without any problem. Recording was a piece of cake after playing in hell. I went off to Denmark knowing this trip would cover the recording costs. I had never recorded an album like this before but I was making a conscious choice to be more flexible. 'Be more easygoing,' I told myself. 'Be more laid-back.'

The Denmark trip was different to earlier ones in Scandinavia because I had to take my own car and carry my own equipment. I drove an old Renault 5 and used the ferry that runs from Harwich to Esbjerg. It was a different venue every night and the agent was very pleased to see me because I had more gigs than anyone he'd ever booked before. He'd got me 44 gigs over 36 days.

It was November and it rained and snowed and I worried that the car would let me down. 'It's not my problem, you're the monkey,' he said in his broken English. He gave me the telephone number of a breakdown service. His nickname for me was 'Youfuckingoldman', but I got used to it. I'd get home from the nightly slog of another packed, rowdy bar, identical to the one the night before, at five or six in the morning and the agency telephone would start ringing at 9.30 a.m. It wasn't possible to get a good night's sleep. Each week, by doing afternoon sessions as well, I could earn an average of £1,200. The simple fact that I did it without blinking an eye restored my self-respect and convinced me that I could work anywhere for the rest of my life.

The travelling was dangerous. Most of the roads ran through great long stretches of farmland, with very few roadhouses or cafés along the way. The cocktail of driving through snowstorms, dense fog or pelting rain under the influence after an exhausting performance was a recipe for a disaster. I caught myself falling asleep at the wheel on many occasions and soon learned to take a nap in a lay-by. The bars sent back glowing reports to the agent, with requests for more acts like Gordon Haskell.

It felt good to be pleasing the listener, the agent and the guy running the joint. The pain I had gone through in the past ten years had crept into my vocal delivery and there was nothing fabricated about it. It may have all begun with the need for high earnings but it made me what I am. My music gives the impression that I'm laid-back and soft around the edges but there was nothing remotely soft about the life I was living.

I felt if I kept going, I could make a successful record one day. In a way, making records is similar to cooking. My constant mistake had been supplying all the right ingredients but allowing someone else to prepare the food itself.

By working in Denmark, I was able to service all my debts and have enough money left over to produce my own records. In retrospect, I had a very good business: efficient, profitable, independent and with the built-in potential of a hit record.

Rather than rest between my five-weeks-on, five-weeks-off skirmishes in Denmark, I began playing in Southampton. I had no other interests to distract me. I was totally focused.

I had become an athlete and taking a rest would only lessen my fitness for the job in hand. I was rebooked on every single occasion but it still wasn't cutting any ice with London. I sent the acoustic demo to ten record companies and Rondor Publishing. Six of them telephoned to say they would come to a gig in the Mean Fiddler, if I arranged it. I was surprised by their enthusiasm but gave them the benefit of the doubt. I hadn't received a phone call from a record company in twenty years and now there had been six in a row. China Records was raving on the phone, saying, 'This is the type of act we're looking for.' I think the caller was either on cocaine or his boss knew my name and talked him out of it. Who knows? Not one music company showed up at the gig, which was one of my best ever.

The letter from Rondor Music had said, 'If I can't be there, I will definitely send along my assistant. We at Rondor are very impressed.'

My letter was equally absurd. I wrote:

Dear Stuart,

Thank you for your letter regarding the Mean Fiddler gig.

I am currently looking for a Hornby-Dublo Signal Box No. 3846 in the 1958 catalogue. With your contacts in the Kings Road, I feel sure you would be able to locate the item either in bric-a-brac shops or in the many karaoke bars in your hip neighbourhood. Since my accident playing bowls, I have not been able to move around so easily as the wooden leg they fitted has a spike on the end of it and it keeps getting stuck in the drains. I have ordered a castor but there is a long waiting list for them. If you should happen to be in my area, I shall be playing at the local village fête on Saturday and I'm sure the vicar will make you most welcome. His wife, Doris, does make the most marvellous sponge cakes with raspberry filling. I will be performing with my band, The Inbred, and doing the Alma Cogan songbook, and I believe some of the songs have been bought by your company in a recent spree of catalogue buying. You'll feel right at home.

Yours sincerely,

Gordon Haskell

I received the reply:

Dear Gordon,

I don't understand your letter about the Hornby-Dublo at all.

The reason I wasn't at the Mean Fiddler was because my assistant got on the wrong bus.

Best wishes,

Stuart

During my second trip to Denmark, Jon Sweet sent me the mixes of the new album and I thought they were awful. In an attempt to sound fashionable, he'd overcooked it. I couldn't believe I'd spent so much time working in a Danish torture chamber to pay for something so unpalatable. I told Jon it hadn't worked and I took the project back to another Dorset studio where I could do it in the traditional way. I spent £1,800 on the studio and the musicians, and it was going the way I wanted. Then the district council decided the studio owner was in breach of the by-laws and we had to sit on the tapes awaiting appeals. They never were completed and for the second time in a row I had worked the hellholes of Denmark to put money into studio owners' pockets. I had wasted my time and my hard-earned money.

Jurgen, my agent in Denmark, only had one video I liked. I had hours to kill at his flat before leaving for a gig, so I watched it again and again. It was *Havana*, starring Robert Redford. It resembled my own life, and the more I saw it the more I became obsessed with every detail. It depicts the life of a poker player, and the people in his life are similar to those I had known in Vegas, like Alfie and Uncle George. Redford's character becomes cynical and worldly, and the odds of him falling in love are compared to the old theory that a butterfly fluttering its wings over China can cause a hurricane in the Caribbean. I had been through many a hurricane. I felt emotionally bankrupt and I was looking for the big one to get me out of a hole. I watched that movie 49 times in Denmark and continue to watch it now whenever I need reminding of the odds.

As soon as I was back home, I went to see Jon Sweet and he understood what he had done wrong. I believed in him; he was great to work with and I'm glad I persevered because on the third attempt the songs were recorded without the technology destroying them. Jon and I were a blend of the ancient and modern, and it eventually worked very well.

I also met a guitarist known as Damage, who reckoned, after seeing me work at The Brook in Southampton, that I could do even better in the south of England than I had previously. I said I'd give it a go, on the understanding that we'd be a duo and the money would be shared. I couldn't see how I'd ever make ends meet but we got our first regular gig at The Thomas Tripp in Christchurch and became a big hit with the audience there. I was committed to Denmark for another year but it was a good sign of things to come. For two years, Damage and I built a strong following working five nights a week. He is, without question, a world-class guitarist and as tortured as the rest of us. Great players generally live in perpetual pain and he was no exception, but our circumstances set us apart. He had a comfortable home, but I didn't. He could manage on the little money he earned, but I had to earn a lot more. I had to improve my life or I'd go crazy.

I had become a gambler from the moment I had mortgaged the house to make a record. My only way out, like a lot of gamblers believe, was to gamble some more. This was misunderstood by many friends and associates, who thought I was overly ambitious. I wasn't. I simply hated the debt because it made me a prisoner. I despaired at the thought of working for the rest of my life just to pay it off, with no real future at all. The odds of winning were all against me because

I was too old to interest the music business, the music press or any would-be managers, but I had no choice. I couldn't afford to throw in the towel even if I'd wanted to. It wasn't ambition, it was my destiny at work.

Damage's relationship with his girlfriend had changed into a platonic one and one night I received a call from her saying she had a problem. I was her problem. I explained nothing was going to make me betray my friend but she talked me into having a little chat. I turned down her offers but she was obsessed. Eventually, after seeing me with another girl, she became enraged. Damage called me to let me know she had put an axe in her car and it had been sharpened. She had also taken the superglue to fix my car doors. I saw her waiting outside my mother's house as I left for work. She chased me and I eventually gave her the slip. On arrival at a wine bar in Lyndhurst, where I was doing a gig, I saw her staring into her glass of beer at a nearby table. As I was setting up my equipment, she came across and grabbed my cigarette, stubbed it out on my forehead and threw her pint over me. The barman threw her out and I never saw her again.

Damage and I managed to get through it all without falling out. The music just kept getting better and the more entangled our personal lives became, the more we expressed it through our music. We became close for a while as a result.

We had started laying the tracks of what would finally become the album *Butterfly in China*. But, this time, I had finished with Denmark and was focused on making a great record. We had the makings of a classic album and we completed it despite the girl. Damage was in love and he suffered.

One night in Southampton I bumped into an old friend from 1965. Martin Smith was drinking in what he had named the 'Old Farts Corner' at the Talking Heads. He had enjoyed success with Simon Dupree and the Big Sound and the progressive-rock group Gentle Giant in the '70s.

My opener was 'How are you? What have you been up to lately?'

'You're a bit nosey, aren't you?' he replied. 'I don't know what it's got to do with you.'

Our conversations became a joyful three hours of total gibberish and pure escapism. He had an amazing imagination and listening to his surreal ramblings was like having Peter Cook as a close friend. Whenever he telephoned, an absurd squeaky voice on the line would begin a sales pitch for something or other. This is one I remember: 'I represent a small family firm of wholesalers established in 1910 in the Outer Orkney Islands. Your name was given to me by a bugler serving in the Territorial Army Reserve Corps Military Band. He said you might be interested in a box of 24 Second World War gas masks in mint condition. For every order received, we will send you a free ticket to Worm World, the new theme park opening up on the A303. You may have seen the recent advertising campaign on Lundy Television, "See worms in their natural habitat." Are you interested?

'Tell you what I'll do to help you along with your decision, I'll throw in an oil filter for a 1959 Morris 1000 and John Lennon's penknife. The penknives come in a choice of six colours. All genuine.'

Martin had loved *Hambledon Hill* and he got me five gigs a week in Southampton and the New Forest. They were all his regular watering holes, where musicians of a high calibre worked. He introduced me to the legendary Roger Pope, one of the best drummers in the world, who had made his name with Elton John. Occasionally, I'd play with Roger and a great rock singer called Bruce Roberts. Everything was in a spur-of-the-moment way. Nobody had any plans. Roger suffered with similar girlfriend problems to those I'd had – his girl had thrown his entire drum kit into the River Test. He made me feel fortunate.

Martin Smith and I were inseparable. Martin was funny, bizarre and bordering on the totally ridiculous. He walked into one of my gigs wearing a cricket jersey and umpired the performance, raising his hand at the end of each song and shouting 'Bye', 'LBW' or 'Howzat'.

What I never knew was that he was an alcoholic. One night he asked me to take him to Southampton General Hospital. He said he'd eaten a bad burger. The nursing staff informed me of his condition. All Martin said was that his favourite song was Paul Simon's 'Fifty Ways To Lose Your Liver'.

Things carried on much as before. I went back and forth to Denmark, began to get bored with it, stuck it out and returned for more gigs that Martin had found for me.

On my last tour of Denmark, I had food poisoning. Jurgen put me on bread and water but I didn't get better. I performed for six weeks with the runs and lost three stone in weight. I came home and was diagnosed as having a rare bug that can kill you. I took it as a sign to call it a day. I was now able to earn enough on my own in England. It had taken from 1984 to 1996, but during that time I had never been unemployed, and I was independent.

Martin was living in a tiny bedsit, he had a heart of gold and one day, when I wasn't expecting it, he died on me.

Just before he died, he threw a party at the Talking Heads to celebrate his 50th birthday. All the money he raised went to the lifeboatmen, those brave souls who have to rely on people like Martin to collect their wages, something he had done regularly for years. I knew he had gone on a special diet to help his condition but he was always so cheerful when I saw him that it had never crossed my mind he was close to death.

I drove up to the Talking Heads and saw him as usual after my Saturday gig at The Bent Brief. He was in the 'Old Farts Corner' and we went into our routine of nonsense. He died the following day. I'd have liked to have been with him till he drew his last breath. I would have liked to have been the one at his bedside, holding his hand and thanking him for being the greatest friend I ever had.

Martin's funeral was a total embarrassment to his rich property developer brother, who paid for it. Thinking everybody shared the same low opinion of Martin as he did, he booked a small remembrance chapel that only held 25. Over 600 people turned up and most of them had to stand outside in the grounds and overflow into the street. I wrote the obituary.

On the wall of the 'Old Farts Corner' in the Talking Heads hangs a plaque that reads, 'Martin Smith Acres 1946 to 1997'. The obituary underneath says, 'He enjoyed life and pitied the tyrants that seem hell-bent on destroying it. He didn't charge for cheering me up. It was free. I pay for my house, my car, my food, but it doesn't make me happy. Martin did.'

On subsequent visits, I'd look over to that corner where we had spent hundreds of inspired hours laughing the night away and my heart would break all over again. I can't go in there any more.

CHAPTER 13

❧ ❧ ❧

The Truth is Boring

always dedicated 'Someone I Knew' to Martin after he died, and the more I sang it, the more convincing it became. The record was finally finished and I released it on my own label, as I had with *Hambledon Hill*. I couldn't get it reviewed in any papers. When *Harry's Bar* was reviewed by every publication in the country, they said I hadn't made a record for 30 years. Only three years previously, they had all refused to review *Butterfly in China*.

Two highly respected promotion men took *Butterfly in China* on board. Don Gallacher, who managed P.J. Harvey, said I was his favourite writer and signed up the publishing rights for movies, and Don Percival, who was strong at radio, felt it was a winner and was willing to give it a shot in return for the publishing rights elsewhere. They really tried hard but it wasn't to be. We drew a blank. Radio 2 played one track once. But direct sales were strong at gigs and it soon paid for itself. I then analysed it critically and felt all the tracks were too long for radio and that I still preferred real drums to the computerised kind.

I was naturally disappointed that it had sunk without a trace, but the enthusiasm from fans who bought it was some compensation. I broke even on it and that was OK. I had become happier within. I loved my job and I'd made a record that had been highly regarded by the few who had heard it. Even Robert Fripp praised it.

I loved the regular support I was getting everywhere and if I could make 300 people happy every week, I felt that I wasn't wasting my life after all. People poured their hearts out to me in the bars. They felt my pain and I felt theirs. We were all equal in those places. None of us knew where we were going but we drew comfort from a certain camaraderie that existed between us. We were all refugees from war-torn, post-Thatcher Britain. An ex-con who had done serious time in penitentiaries in America read his poetry to me. It was terrible what he'd been through and his whole face was wracked with pain. He always came to see me play and there were often tears in his eyes during my half-hour break as we talked about his life. I've lost count of the number of tough guys who have shared their life stories with me, men who'd lost everything in business or had their marriages and families torn apart. Hardened criminals would warm to someone like me, expressing the same emotions they felt but couldn't put into words. It was the very opposite of a church congregation, yet to me it was deeply religious because the lost souls were uplifted by the company and their lives were a little less desolate because of it.

It was a unique scene and it meant a lot to me. It took away the notion that I was doing it to pay debts. It gave me back a dignity that had been trampled on for years. I felt appreciated and understood, and I paid the audience the same respect and gratitude they paid me. It was what music was designed for: to heal, to comfort and to spread happiness. It was a million miles away from egotism and yearning for fame or fortune. I was still playing to those people, when that came to me. Calling me a 'pub singer' was accurate, but misleading. No one in the press would ever know the real story because my audience wasn't the kind the media would want to talk about. I was light entertainment to journalists and they all assumed the demographic, as they like to call it, was just ladies of a certain age. One day in the future even my own manager would say, 'The truth is boring.'

The places that became my second homes were The Bent Brief and The Platform Tavern in Southampton, The Thomas Tripp in Christchurch and The Inn on the Furlong in Ringwood. They were packed with familiar faces and I always did well with them. By 1997, my set consisted entirely of songs requested by the audience. I'd written 90 per cent of them. From their popularity, I felt I had at least ten potential hit songs but the record business didn't need me and I didn't need them. I had achieved what I had set out to do. I was my own man and no one could take that away from me. I could do no wrong. My reputation grew rapidly in the three counties surrounding me. I worked five nights a week at £100 a time, all within thirty-five miles of home, and by selling thirty CDs a week I soon paid the studio bills. The publicans made money, I made money and the audience went home happy. I had all day to write and life was getting better all the time.

At long last I was feeling like a professional writer. Other musicians hid away to write but I had never been able to afford such a luxury. Faith in my own abilities would unlock the door to the prison I had built for myself. I'd served my time. Now that I was adopting a more confident air, though, I decided to get away from the negativity of my surroundings and take a cottage specifically to write the next album.

The cottage was in the hamlet of Acton, near Swanage, and it had a view across the Downs all the way to the sea. Every morning I walked for two hours and collected my thoughts in preparation for a day's writing. It had the same effect as meditation. It was such a relief from years of slogging away in the rough neighbourhoods of the world, with their squalor and posturing.

The area known as the Purbecks is my favourite part of Dorset. The coastline from Studland in the east through to Swanage, Dancing Ledge, Winspit and beyond to Lulworth and Durdle Door is stunning, and the hills and hidden coves are ideal for an old dreamer like me. Added to the natural beauty of the entire area is the preserved steam railway that runs up through the valleys to Corfe Castle from the terminus at Swanage, and on my daily two-hour hikes I could mentally transport myself back to the '50s when I was a boy. I was in heaven, whichever way I walked. There were hills to climb, rocks to negotiate and woods to wander through, and the air was as pure as it could be. Whether walking by the sea along the top of the cliffs, hearing the seagulls and watching the fishing boats, or hearing the steam trains in the distance as they chugged out of Swanage, I could have stayed there forever in complete contentment. The natural stone cottages, with their heavy, thick slate roofs, surrounded by the lush green fields with their dry-stone walls, summed up my idea of the perfect world, created as it is out of natural local materials dragged out of the very ground they stood on. No concrete was to be seen.

I thought of the long, arduous journey I had chosen to take back in 1965, when the world had seemed so beautifully innocent and when I was innocent too. On my travels around the world I had seen nothing but the rapid decline of everything I treasured. The stupidity of man had filled me with despair. Yet here I was; looking around me, nothing had changed. The small corner of the world I chose to be in was still as beautiful as it was on the day I was born and it wasn't any less real than an inner-city slum. I imagined being asked how I felt about rap music and whether my music had any relevance. My answer to those kids moaning about their lives and adding more ugliness to an already ugly world was simple, 'If you hate your neighbourhood, get on a bus and leave. If you love the cut and thrust of drug dealers, violence, pimps, whores and a concrete wilderness, stay where you are. But do shut up about it. It's become excruciatingly boring.'

I had finally accepted the world as it was and not how I wanted it to be. All I had to do was stay focused and do my job, which I had become good at. Songs from now on would be designed to uplift the listeners and not have them reaching for a razor blade. I wanted to heal and be healed.

Domineering people had delayed me greatly; debts had forced me to work twice as hard, but I had benefited. The endless pain of broken relationships, betrayal and wars declared, both political and private, were all predestined. It had been in the scheme of things, as the song that came to me that day in the Purbecks was telling me. The entire lyric and its music wrote itself in my mind as I walked back to the rented cottage. Songs flew out of me for the two weeks I was there; I had enough material for two albums and there wasn't a negative thought in any of them.

England had proved problematic for recording and a dear friend in Denmark, Michael Wedgwood, whom I had met in Dorset, had a studio there and offered me generous rates. He had quite a history, similar to my own. After leaving the bands Caravan and Curved Air, he'd wound up as a bandleader for a 12-year slog in America, ending up in Alaska. He had returned to the UK to start his life again and I'd taken him with me on my last tour of Denmark to introduce him to Jurgen, my agent, and the work on offer there. Within a week he'd fallen in love, become engaged and decided to put down roots there.

It would feel like a holiday to record at his house and I wanted the album to be very relaxed and cool, in the same vibe as a J.J. Cale album. I took my friend Jim – who used to hide in his attic rather than face an audience – as the main guitarist and we flew out to Denmark.

The first day was fantastic and everyone celebrated. Unfortunately, the drummer and Jim got so drunk that night they were no longer up to the task in hand and I wasted the rest of the week battling against the demons of alcohol and picking up the bill. I had something I could use, but it had to be finished off back in England and, although the songs were strong, something told me not to publish to the world at large just yet.

I pressed 1,000 CDs and sold them just to cover my costs. I wasn't that disappointed, strange as it may seem. It was as if I had built one component for an aircraft and was quite content to wait until I had the wings.

Something was going on that I had no control over and it was something incredible. I seemed to be at ease with the world, with little money or home of my own, yet I felt as if I were walking on air, being guided by a benevolent wind. I had no clear reason to go to America at that time but I felt compelled to do so. I think it was to test my gut feeling that I had finally reached the high standard of my American counterparts and I wanted to prove it by showing myself in the country whose music had inspired me for 50 years. It was to be a dummy run for something of which I had no inkling.

I called an old friend in LA to say I was thinking of coming over and he'd soon arranged a string of dates for me to play. They were all proper music venues of various sizes, where well-known artists regularly appeared. If I wasn't in the running, I'd soon find out.

America would lose me three weeks' wages plus the cost of the trip, so I found a day job to fund it. I hadn't done an ordinary job for years but I felt I could do anything now. If I could handle myself in the roughest joints across the world, everything, by comparison, would be a breeze.

The advert read: 'Driver wanted with knowledge of London.' I was perfect for it and the pay was fair. The firm made furniture using the highest quality craftsmen. Their clients would typically live in Belgravia or Chelsea and be related to royalty. Someone would pay £3 million for a flat and then gut it and have a new kitchen designed. Specially made panelled doors were built traditionally with carvings that took weeks to do. My job was to deliver them.

I turned up smartly dressed to suit the type of customer with whom I would be mixing, but there was no delivery that day. Instead, the boss put me inside a room where all the sawdust was delivered by a chute from the workshops. The room was eight feet square and the sawdust filled every inch of it from floor to ceiling. It was my job to squeeze the compacted sawdust using an industrial vacuum cleaner and transfer it to a farm trailer standing alongside. I had to wear a mask because the dust came from the MDF used on the carcasses of the kitchen units. There were warning signs in the office about it being carcinogenic. By the time I had finished the job, I was covered with sawdust from head to toe: in my eyes, ears and up my nose, despite the mask.

I went into the workshop, where all the carpenters were busy at their benches, to use the small sink there. As I had been hired as a driver, I felt I still needed to be clean and smart, so I brushed my clothes and stripped naked by the sink to get myself thoroughly clean. This action brought the boss out of his office to see what was distracting his workforce. When he asked me what I thought I was doing, I explained, 'I can't very well go to Belgravia with sawdust in my crutch, can I? Either you want a driver or a dogsbody. Which is it to be, sir? . . . With respect.'

He showed no signs of a sense of humour but probably felt he had to maintain some kind of protocol and discipline. Dodgy chemical sawdust in my lungs and throat wouldn't help my singing career and I had to find some amusement in my predicament. I had the luxury of knowing that this job was temporary for me and I felt duty bound to express what my fellow workers were surely feeling about their employer but were too afraid to say.

I repainted the outside of the workshops, I washed the vehicles, I generally tidied the yard and, once a week, I'd willingly go back into the sawdust chamber of horrors. This sort of boss likes to get his full shilling and I was perfectly happy with that. I had my air fare; I'd done four weeks; I'd worked well and delivered efficiently and obeyed every command. I had even been popular with everyone.

Once, the boss called me over to his elegantly appointed office far away from the pollution he was creating. Barely looking up at me, he pointed to his fireplace and said, 'Make up my fire, Gordon. I'm cold.'

I dutifully obeyed but I longed to start a decent conversation with him, like any normal human being does when sharing the same small space with another. I was a friend of the president of Warner Bros. Pictures, of movie stars and West End actors and actresses, of rock legends, and I was a pretty fine writer myself. I was intelligent. He mixed with royalty and London's high society. But who cares who anybody knows? Isn't it about who you *are* that counts? I enjoyed making up the fire as I had enjoyed washing up with the kitchen help at Susan George's in Hollywood.

I was clocking up every experience at this time and preparing myself for something that was in the air. I was flying at a higher altitude than ever before and I was loving the feeling of being on top of the world, even when I was covered in sawdust. I had already achieved a good position in life. It just wasn't what anyone would regard as a 'good position'. George and Martin were smiling down on me and saying, '*Now*, you understand. *Now*, you're ready for what you are about to receive.'

I left the company and bought my ticket to Los Angeles.

When I did my first pub gig in 1984, a young university student had caught the act and we'd become friends. His name was Aidan Pickering. I discovered a few years later that his father was Sir Edward Pickering, one of the greatest newspapermen of all time, who'd risen to be chairman of many national companies, finally being appointed to the Press Complaints Commission. Aidan was a budding lead guitarist but was following in his father's footsteps to become a journalist. He landed a job with a Southampton radio station, where he had helped me with the *Hambledon Hill* project, and moved on to a Southern Television station as an outside-broadcast reporter. During my time abroad, he had moved to Los Angeles to work as a reporter for Fox Television news, where he had been for ten years now. I called to say I was coming over without any real plan in mind and he invited me to stay at his apartment. By the time I arrived, he had fixed a series of gigs in and around Hollywood. These caught the eye of King Crimson fanatics, who quickly arranged more shows in San Francisco, Kansas City and Chicago. I had a total of 15 dates. Aidan was still playing guitar in his spare time and had an eccentric friend Mike staying with him. Mike is a great fiddle player and we did some of the LA gigs together. On a free weekend, Aidan took us to Palm Springs. It felt more like a holiday than a tour and we gambled in the casino and acted like boys on the town.

Aidan was on television every day, reporting the latest shootings in South Central, the darker side of Los Angeles, while Mike dabbled on the stock exchange. These guys were full of courage, extremely intelligent and great company.

I went to San Francisco to do two nights in a small music venue. American musicians joined me onstage and I felt up there with the best of them. My dummy run was working well.

I loved San Francisco and could see the attraction of living there. The whole setting around the bay is beautiful. As I crossed the magnificent bridge into the city, what struck me was its elegance. I didn't expect to find that in an American city after Vegas and LA. The colourful trams that trundle up and down the steep streets that the city strides and the parks that surround it reminded me of the beauty I had found in Dorset. Like Vegas, I had only ever seen the city in the movies. Unlike Vegas, I could have settled down there quite easily. It is, after all, the birthplace of the 'Love Generation'.

I stayed overnight with Harry's youngest daughter, Dee-Dee. I had met her during my Vegas excursions but had never been to her home. She is a sweet girl, quiet, intelligent and diminutive. Her girlfriend was bigger, bossier and wore the trousers. We all travelled together to the gig in their huge pick-up truck.

As an aeronautical engineer at Oakland Airport, Dee-Dee has an impressive job. She checks aeroplanes for their airworthiness and is often called out in emergencies. Apparently, grounding aircraft is quite a common occurrence. I flew back to LA trying not to think about dodgy aircraft and domineering women. I then called up Bill Gerber, who was now the ex-president at Warner, and was invited to a dinner party with the actor Greg Kinnear. I had recently seen him in *As Good As It Gets*, the Jack Nicholson movie. After my recent experience of making up the fire for His Royalness, it seemed poetic justice to be spending an evening with movie stars.

Bill gave me a warm welcome and explained to the gathered company that his latest way of keeping fit was to swim to Alcatraz, right across the San Francisco Bay. I asked, 'Do you get to wear the chains?'

'Good line,' Greg said. Bill smiled but didn't offer me a writing job.

We moved to the private cinema in his garden and watched a new movie Bill had produced. It was extremely violent and set in a district of LA. I asked him if he was ever scared living so close to such violence. 'It's just a film,' he answered.

Bill had always inspired me and I found myself comparing our journeys in my mind. Twenty-two years had passed since we first met. He'd become a millionaire and I was still a pauper, but he continued to graciously welcome me into his home. He didn't typify the

Hollywood depicted by so many. He respected me and appeared to be extremely happy.

At one gig in LA, I said to a black guy in the audience, 'It's great to see you out of prison.' Aidan had heard me use the line in bars in England, where it went down well, but quietly explained it was dangerous to use it here, especially to blacks. However, the man laughed and said afterwards it was rare to hear a white guy with so much guts and soul. I kept using the gag.

One of Frank Fenter's old friends from the Stratford Place days, Selwyn Miller, was also in the audience. He is now managing David Gates, the writer in the group Bread. He thought I shouldn't be funny onstage because no one would take my music seriously. I took this advice on board and cut the comedy, remaining serious and detached throughout and creating an atmosphere to match. No one signed either version of the act. I thanked Aidan and Mike for a fabulous time and left. By the time I got to Kansas City, I was myself again.

The Crimson fan who had arranged my gig there was Rick Chafen. He had once visited me in England and I liked him. It was good to see him again and after picking me up from the airport in his old beat-up Datsun, he drove us to his apartment in a heavily built-up area filled with tower blocks.

He'd had his own radio show called *The Best Music You've Never Heard* and had been plugging my music since the Crimson days. Demos of mine had found their way onto an album called *It's Just a Plot to Drive You Crazy*. It had been amazingly popular with the purer kind of fans, who still rate it as their favourite Gordon Haskell album, some even choosing it as their Desert Island Disc. It sold better than *Butterfly in China* and cost nothing to produce. People sometimes prefer raw food to the overcooked kind. I took notice and began thinking about the next record. Overproduction had obviously been burying the real me and it was clear that I needed to avoid that mistake in any future recordings. I worked so much because I was popular. The voice and the guitar were my appeal and anything else would need to be added to the pie very sensitively.

I can best describe Rick as being close to real madness – and I know he'd take it as a compliment. He showed me my room and then asked me if I'd like a drink.

'I don't drink coffee or tea,' he added.

'Anything will do,' I replied and I saw him go to the fridge. When he opened the door, it was full to capacity with Coca-Cola's distant relative, Dr Pepper. No food or milk, just Dr Pepper, stacked neatly in rows.

'Uh, I'll have a Dr Pepper,' I said. My spirits dropped a degree as he removed his teeth and placed them on the table separating us. Now he not only sounded insane, he looked insane, with a harrowed face and long, grey wispy hair.

I shuddered when he said, 'By the way, I don't advise you to step outside the apartment. This is an unsafe neighbourhood.'

I was this guy's pet canary for the next three days.

He went to his record collection and put on some masterpiece by an avant-garde band that Dan Cairns of the *Sunday Times* had recommended and I was reminded of John Lennon's description of avant-garde as being French for bullshit.

'Have you tried The Bong?' asked my friend Rick, he of the glazed eye, hunched back, toothless grin and Dr Pepper.

'No, I haven't,' said I, looking at the hubble-bubble pipe he had placed between us. We tried it and Rick began to reveal that he was in the throes of talking with the education authorities in America about a new way of speed-reading he had invented. He had even written to the Pentagon about it.

'It could revolutionise the education of a whole new generation.' He reckoned he could read a book in five minutes using his new technique. That would mean a child could read 160 books a day, 800 a week, and be ready and qualified to work at NASA by the age of 10. He reached for his notepad and began drawing a diagram of the brain with wires coming out of it, criss-crossing from one side to the other. I tried to follow as best I could but he was too clever for me, though it sounded more convincing after he passed The Bong for the third time.

I told him of my theories on how best to recycle contaminated sawdust and democracy in the Western world by loading it onto airliners and sprinkling it all over Eastern Europe mixed with cocaine. He said the CIA had already done it as part of their anti-Communism programme, and I nodded and listened with interest. Such was the inspiration of The Bong. He looked forward with excitement to a song being written about it and hoped I'd be able to include it in the next album. I respected him for that, nodding wisely. He changed the record.

I longed for the comfort and security of the sawdust shed; I wondered why dope-heads are so convinced that drugs do them no harm, and if they ever saw how ridiculous they all are; I missed Tommy Cooper and Max Wall, smiled at the memory of them then went to sleep happy. It was good to know what kind of customer bought King Crimson records. The Ecstasy drug scene at the time wasn't going to be any different. Millions of records were being sold on the basis that they sounded great if you took the right drug to alter your perception of musical merit. It is an age-old con-trick that pseudo-intellectuals fall for every time. It was obvious that if I made a great record with a great song based on the ideals of the '50s, I was never going to cut it with the drug scene. But I was going to make a record and turn the clock back to 1958. It was fun then and I wanted to have fun again. I was feeling on top of the world. I was going to do it my way or not at all.

My next American date was in Chicago. Skyscrapers, like rows of giant polished glasses all lined up on a bar, glistened in the winter sun as the taxi took me downtown to the club I was booked to play. Signs that read 'This Is The Home Of The Blues' made me feel proud to be playing in a tiny part of it.

Christina, my half-sister, was driving from Iowa to stay with me for two days and we had arranged to meet in a good hotel in the centre of the city. The hotel lobby was plush and full of leather furniture, and it felt good to be meeting Harry's little girl there. If Christina had been born into an age of polite society when ladies had escorts, dressed soberly and were respected wherever they went, she would have fitted right in. She looked and sounded vulnerable and I welcomed her with open arms. We had both struggled all our lives and I was glad to see her. We met and rested from our journeys in the temporary splendour that two wanderers like us would appreciate, simply by each being served with a cup of coffee and a piece of cake in a five-star hotel.

The concert was a double-bill featuring me and a singer-songwriter from the band Wigwam. I had always refused to sing King Crimson songs because they didn't mean anything to me. In Chicago, the audience demanded that I sing 'Cadence and Cascade' and I finally gave in. They loved it and I have no idea why. When I finished my set, the main act refused to appear because the piano wasn't right for him, so I did the second half as well. I played for a total of three hours and met dozens of Crimson fanatics, who confirmed my hunch the previous night with Rick – Crimson fans are *special* people, just as the purser on the SS *Isabella* had described

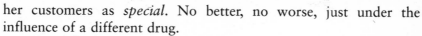

her customers as *special*. No better, no worse, just under the influence of a different drug.

I loved Chicago, enjoyed seeing Christina and flew to London fairly pleased with myself. I picked up my five nights a week as soon as I was back. I felt privileged and totally confident that I was finally on the home straight.

CHAPTER 14

◉ ◉ ◉

How Wonderful You Are

The ambition to have a hit record had vanished from my mind. I'd accepted the general consensus that I was too old for fame and fortune. I was left with the pure desire to make people happy, to help them through the night and enjoy the beauty of just being. Recording was to be a pleasure as it had been in 1967. Now that the business of music was no longer of any interest to me, the whole process of creation could be entirely natural and driven by my higher self.

I went looking for a cottage to rent. I wasn't sure if I could afford to pay the mortgage on Ma's and rent my own place but the experience of Jack's Cottage in the Purbecks had been such a success I wanted to repeat it. I'd written so many songs in a fortnight there it was false economy to stay where I was. I only needed one more gig a week to cover the rent and it fell into my lap as soon as I made the decision to take the risk.

It was while I was looking for a place to live that I met Dee again. She had been a fan at my Friday gig in Lyndhurst in the New Forest in the years when I was working with Damage. I remembered her as the girl who had come into the wine bar looking pretty wild. Grabbing a box of my CDs, she had enthusiastically taken them around the room . . . and sold the lot. I liked her for that.

She was 25 years old then and going through her rave stage with an equally wild partner. This had ended and after a six-month stint backpacking in Thailand, exploring her mind and enjoying the sunshine, she had moved to Shaftesbury. She had always preferred living in the country but hadn't expected to find me living there. After getting over the shock of bumping into each other, she invited me up to her flat for a cup of tea. There had been an instant mutual attraction but because I'd been about to go to America we hadn't taken it any further, agreeing to call each other when I returned.

I combined a visit to the letting agency with a date for the evening with Dee. It was one of those days when everything went right. I asked myself what kind of place I wanted to rent and decided it needed to be on top of a hill surrounded by open rolling countryside similar to the Purbecks. A cottage answering the description was available in Ashmore, a tiny, unspoilt village resting on top of the highest hill in Dorset.

Dee and I went to see the place together and I didn't hesitate to take it. It was perfect. Dee ran across the fields in her excitement, calling out to me, 'It's beautiful.' As we approached the cottage, I knew I was going to fall in love with this place and this wonderful, beautiful person who was so at one with nature and who didn't have a pretentious bone in her body. She looked as if she had never lived anywhere else.

I couldn't quite believe she would stay for long because I was 53 and she was still 25, but she had no such doubts. She said when she'd first seen me at the gig in Lyndhurst she knew I was the one for her.

Ashmore was our natural home, the ideal nesting place for two like souls living on top of the world. Having moved into a new area, Dee was unemployed and keen to find a job in life where she could 'make a difference'. It was difficult for her and she thought I was so lucky doing something that made people happy.

My extra gig had come from the other side of Dorset in Weymouth, an area I hadn't explored. That soon led to several more in the town and I met Ken Watkins, a fellow troubadour, who reminded me of my old buddy Martin Smith. I was still missing Martin badly. Ken had the humour and the talent, and, as a Buddhist, he had a very wise head on his shoulders. An occasional conversation with Ken was like being in the same room with the Dalai Lama.

Like Martin before him, Ken recommended me to more venues and suggested I get together with Robbie McIntosh, who often played in Weymouth. He thought it would work well because our combined popularity would be a draw. He was right and we filled a 200-seater. It was the first time I had done a pay-at-the-door gig since the Rainbow in 1972. I started doing more with Robbie, who had been in the Pretenders and had spent six years in Paul McCartney's band. Now he was launching his own album, *Emotional Bends*. I landed the support gig at Winchester, where I met his manager, Ian Brown, who would eventually be instrumental in changing my life forever.

I only spoke a few words to Ian that night. He said he had seen me at the Kashmir Club in London and assumed I was a successful American act just visiting. He'd been very impressed but didn't think I was approachable.

'I am the gherkin of the record business,' I replied. 'If you go into any supermarket anywhere in the world, you'll always see the gherkins there – but when did you ever see an advertising campaign for them?' For good measure, I added, 'Steady sellers, gherkins.'

I continued doing my five or six nights solo, slowly reducing my debts while my good reputation showed no signs of fading. I had more work than I could handle. It had become a joy to go to work in the evening and come home at 1 a.m. and look up, high on that hill in Dorset, to the night sky, at the hundreds of stars shining down on Dee and me. I never tired of that journey home.

I was at ease. Away from Verwood and the unforgiving years of Scandinavia, Ashmore was heaven on earth. When the bluebells came out in the woods in April, there was acre upon acre of blue carpet to walk through. Sometimes we'd lie down among them, breathing in their scent and looking up through all the beautiful old oak, ash and silver birch trees to the blue skies.

In the shops, there were old sepia postcards for sale, showing how it had all looked in 1910. Nothing much had changed. The village pond had survived, as had most of the cottages, and I felt a sense of time standing still. As each season came and went, I was tuning myself to be at one with nature. I planted daffodil bulbs in the garden and saw the first snowdrops push themselves through the frostbitten, rock-hard, chalky soil and marvelled at their delicacy and immense strength. They were determined to bloom against all odds in those brutal conditions.

I steered clear of falling into the age-difference trap with Dee and let her be her age as much as I was able to. She couldn't bear the pain that I was carrying from the past and, on some occasions, I made her cry if the unwelcome subject of the music business crept back into our conversations. Dee stuck it out and we were determined to go forward together. She had a past she was trying to resolve too. Together we thought we might just do it.

My next-door neighbour was still working as a farmhand, and he and his brother and sister had lived in Ashmore all their lives. John, the eldest at 82, rode his bicycle for miles every day up and down all the hills and was fitter than I was at 54. On Sundays, he'd turn the radio up full and sing along as loud as he could to *Songs of Praise*. The city incomers who'd bought up most of the property around him complained bitterly about the racket, but, at his age, he wasn't impressed. When they spoke to him, he pretended to be deaf – with a smile on his face so they would write him off as simple and leave him alone, which they did. The new neighbours had lots of money but they seemed to be plagued with problems. Not so John. He was ungovernable and a menace to the new world order.

I felt as if the cottage I was renting was mine for life, with John next door and his brother, Nigel, on the other side. They were comforting bookends and I could go to sleep at night knowing I had Dee and the salt of the earth around me.

Dee and I were crazy about each other and she continued to accompany me to gigs. I loved her wild enthusiasm and I was guaranteed to have a good night just by having her around. Once, when we walked into The Bent Brief in Southampton, a character known as Jimmy the Hat, who was 65, turned to her and said, 'What do you want to go out with that old git for?' as he was taking a phone call at the bar. We heard him say, 'No, not the cling film, the black stockings.' He turned to us and said, 'That was my club.' Dee asked him the name of his club and he said 'Call Lonely'.

He asked me to buy him a drink and then began telling us his life story. He had been a silver-service waiter on the big ocean liners sailing out of Southampton in the late '40s and had served the Hollywood stars. Edward G. Robinson and James Stewart were his regulars. He was a great feed to have in the audience and I'd let him sing the occasional standard to keep him happy. I loved his zest for life and his ability to fascinate all ages with his stories.

There was no ageism at The Brief. It was a massive jumble of colourful characters drawn from all walks of life. Along with a few ex-cons was an ex-hooker, well over six feet tall, who always arrived drunk. She spent most of the night hollering out obscenities. 'Anybody want yellow rain?' was what I'd hear halfway through 'Rainy Night in Georgia'. In Scandinavia, I hadn't enjoyed this type of character but in my new persona I loved them all and they loved the music. The hooker would get up in the break sometimes and sing 'Falling in Love Again', substituting the original words with:

Gonorrhoea, gonorrhoea,
Never wanted to,
Give it all to you,
I can't help it.

The sad fact is that she had a divine voice, like Julie London's. I could have listened to her all night. Despite the shocking language she used, it struck me that deep down she clearly had a beautiful soul which only ever revealed itself through her singing. Somewhere along the way, a long time ago, she had traded her hopes and dreams and her body to make ends meet, yet there at the very core of her was a soul crying out in anguish. It made me think of her true potential, despite everything she had become. The great singers of the past all had this quality and the lives they'd led were what had made them so great. You won't ever learn that at fame school.

I have never revealed this before, because it was unpalatable for radio, but it was that hooker who inspired me to say to myself, 'How wonderful you are.' And I hung on to the thought until I was safely back at Ashmore in my own romance, where I could carry the idea through to mean absolutely everybody in this world; a universal love song that could inspire each and every person who'd ever had any doubts about themselves or the power they possessed.

If Dee believed how wonderful she was, all her problems might disappear. I sang out the first original line of the song while she was making breakfast, 'Dee-Dee cooks the eggs, with her skinny legs.' I still have the tape of it as the song was being written. I completed it later when I was alone, starting with 'I go out most nights', as I was doing at that time . . . but I'll get to that later.

Another crazy character who made his mark with me was a man who came to my weekly Thomas Tripp gig in Christchurch dressed in a full RAF squadron leader's uniform. He requested the same two songs every week, 'First We Take Manhattan' by Leonard Cohen and my own song, 'Country Gold'. I spoke with him every week because he could bring me up to date with the politics at No. 10. He was Tony Blair's personal pilot, you see, and had also been Maggie's before that. He told me one day he'd had to fly Tony Blair's dog up to Chequers, as Cherie was missing him so much. Another day, he'd been training the SAS to fly helicopters low over the Thames in preparation for Bosnia and was worried he would miss the gig. That was the reason he'd arrived a little later than usual.

He remained serious as he spoke and, although I wanted to laugh at times, I let him carry on because he was convincing and he had a kind face. One Wednesday he arrived in a sweater and slacks, so I asked him where his uniform was.

'Well, Tony's in China, isn't he?' he responded without hesitation. 'He's given me the week off.' That night I checked the newspaper and he was right. Tony Blair had gone to China that morning.

We were all living on the same plane as Spike Milligan – and for the same reasons. Our greatest comics were dying off. Without Tommy Cooper, Les Dawson, Max Wall and Reggie Perrin, the country was struggling to laugh. Even the media had to call it by another name. But comedy is comedy. You can't have *alternative* comedy. The alternative to comedy is tragedy. But the wheel is turning and young people are again looking for quality. A new model is emerging. As the punk generation reaches middle age, it's being spooned out the same medicine as it prescribed so unmercifully. My faith in the future has returned.

The more so-called crazy people I met, the more I enjoyed the gigs. They seemed to be on the increase, as if attracted by something in the music or in the plain fact that I was a friendly face in an unfriendly world, and I always made a point of talking to them. Most people walk away from perceived crackpots but I felt an affinity with them. They were the sole reason I never played on autopilot, which can happen with a lot of musicians I've seen who do regular gigs. The average person these days has a short attention span. These people studied every move and every word I sang, and listened intently to the repartee between songs.

I began to love my audience because half of them felt more alienated than even I did. I could see the world through their eyes and we understood each other's pain; the love in the room could be felt not only from the oddballs but from the whole audience as it spread. I had ceased to care about me. I cared for them all and I loved them all and I began to write for them all. The vibe, as they say, was truly beautiful. I'd reached the place where Uncle George had lived in his mind when I'd first met him in Vegas. The world was totally absurd and everything was a tragicomedy, but the love in that room was real enough. I *was* Reggie Perrin and the characters around me were the supporting cast. We were in this thing together and the world outside could continue to go to hell in its ignorance. We had found a way to be happy.

* * *

There were absurd elements in my relationship with my mother too. The more frail she became, the slower she was at shopping. She began checking the price of every item each week and if a penny had been added to the cost, she'd put it back on the shelf. It drove me mad. It was taking an hour to do a simple ten-minute job. I wanted to get back to my work. I voiced my concerns to her as gently as I could in the queue at the delicatessen section, but she swung round and shouted, 'Oh, shut up or you won't get a doughnut.'

My old friend from Switzerland, John Lee, showed up one night to see why I was getting more gigs than anyone in the neighbourhood. He was still working on the fringes of the record business and had moved back home to Poole to take care of his sick mother. John bought the council house she was in and after she died ran his business from there. He'd been a musician in the '60s in Edison Lighthouse but was clearly making a lot more money working for a record company. They specialised in back catalogues. I was curious. He was amusing . . . and who knows? He might have been interested in managing me. He invited myself and Dee to his house the following day.

As a record executive, he had made a few changes to the house. He claimed he'd spent £60,000 in the bathroom alone, with every modern gadget imaginable and the most expensive suite on the market. The kitchen resembled a medieval castle, with iron grids on all the cabinets and heavy oak furniture around the dining area. The larder door had to be lifted in by a crane and had come out of a dungeon in Europe. He'd had to remove the windows to get it in. We sat in the lounge looking at the largest television set we'd ever seen and I played him some recent recordings. He said he had a studio upstairs in the bedroom. I went up and I could see that he had bought the most expensive state-of-the-art equipment possible. He played me his own songs and they all sounded like hits. But he wasn't interested in releasing anything. 'What's the point?' he said.

The next time we visited, we couldn't get up the drive and had to park outside. The entire garden area was occupied by six covered wagons forming a circle like a scene from a John Wayne movie. In the centre was a small marquee where he'd put his garden furniture, and which he was using as his main office. He'd bought the wagons because he liked the look of them. I did too. The neighbours avoided him.

Much as I loved being around John, I decided against recording with him for the time being. We would have spent the whole time laughing.

I began to write in earnest in October 2000. 'Voodoo Dance' came first and it coincided with meeting Ian Brown again. He was still promoting Robbie and I was doing a couple of duo gigs a month for him. Robbie and I alternated with songs and we were having a great time in 'proper' concert situations. Ian Brown took the demo away with him because he was on his way to London. He called me the day after to say that Gut Records loved it and wanted it for a new Tom Jones record being made. I was surprised and delighted, of course, and it spurred me on. Nothing came of it, though, as there was a legal dispute going on. Surprise, surprise; where's there's a hit, there's a writ.

During the next three months, I wrote most of the songs that would become my best-selling album, *Harry's Bar*. I had kept to my ideal, only reaching for the highest in me. Writing had become the absolute joy I had aimed for. There isn't one word or one musical note I would wish to change. I can't fault it because it seems so spiritually perfect in a world filled with hostility and hatred . . . and every thought was drawn from a lifetime of learning.

Dee had found a job but she hated it. The money gave her independence and each day she came home from work, I would have another song to play her. Her yearning to be a free spirit and her love for me were tearing her apart, and I wrote 'Freeway To Her Dreams' about her dilemma. When I played that and 'Voodoo Dance' at gigs, it was patently obvious to anyone with half a brain that they were both hit songs. No sooner had I played them than the requests to play them again came in thick and fast. And then I wrote 'How Wonderful You Are'. The audience loved it immediately. I knew it was the best song of the latest batch but I carried on writing in perfect harmony and contentment.

'All The Time In The World' was inspired partly by Dee's impatience to find a direction and partly by a line from *The Shawshank Redemption*: 'When they closed that [prison] door, all you had was all the time in the world.' It suited my own experience of the prison life I had been forced to live for years in Scandinavia. I rested from writing and played all of them in public for the next three weeks. There wasn't a dud among them. The scene was set to record a beautiful album whenever I felt inclined. I could have made appointments in London to try for a deal, but the thought never crossed my mind. I was deliriously happy just playing them directly to the public each night.

During this time I had a cancer scare. A growth had appeared just above my lip and I had to have a minor operation. Dee was terribly worried and I didn't want her life spoiled by the prospect of nursing an old man, so I pushed her away and that made things worse. We went through our drama fairly rapidly but it shook us up badly. It brought forth 'There Goes My Heart Again', yet another song inspired entirely by my love for Dee.

In December, I had a call from Nigel Slater, who had created a website for me when I'd released *Butterfly in China*. We had been friends for years and he was good enough to handle all the emails. He rang to say he'd received one asking me if I knew of an Amanda Armitage.

Did I know an Amanda Armitage! This was my daughter, born 32 years ago and whom I had never seen. After getting confirmation from Nigel that I had been expecting to hear from her, she wrote a carefully worded letter. She realised that I might be married with children. She wrote that she was married to Trevor Bath, a sergeant major in the British Army, and had two children, Charlie and Craig, and they lived near Gosport, barely 40 miles away. I wrote the most encouraging, loving letter of my life and she rang the following day. She was businesslike on the phone but something in her tone gave her excitement away. I could imagine her biting her bottom lip and I felt warm inside as we discussed the arrangements calmly.

The pub/restaurant Amanda chose for our meeting was The Old Mill near Fareham, one of her favourite haunts. It was a very attractive, tile-hung, eighteenth-century watermill sitting alongside a pretty stretch of the river. I had been to the pub only a year before with Dee, when I had done a radio spot for Wave FM.

It was 23 December 2000. The place was in full swing when I arrived at midday, half an hour early. Of course, all the decorations were for the Christmas celebrations but my first thought as I entered was, 'How nice of them to decorate the place for our reunion.' I wasn't sure if giving presents at our first meeting in so long would be appropriate, so I decided to save them for Christmas Day.

Amanda's story is full of coincidences and near misses. This time, though, any minute now, it was going to happen. Amanda would walk through the door and find her father. She had waited a lifetime. Exactly one year later to the day, I would enter the singles chart with 'How Wonderful You Are'. I'd written it two weeks before we met. As long as we live, neither of us will ever forget the significance of the

23rd day of December. The two colossal events are forever entwined and the song title is so apt.

I don't think either of us knew what to expect. She might be hostile. I might be defensive. But suddenly I didn't feel nervous any more. I felt God was directing this picture and was on our side.

She walked in smiling and looked very similar to my sister, Heather. We met, we hugged and our eyes did all the serious talking. It was as easy as if we'd never been apart. We took our table and ordered lunch like old friends. I assured her everything was going to be lovely and that I'd been an ignoramus at 24. I said I wasn't going to dress things up to make any excuses. I asked her to tell me her life story from the beginning and what she had learned from her mother.

Just after Amanda was born, her mother had nearly died in a head-on collision. She was in a coma for months and her boyfriend had died in the crash. She had severe memory loss, so Amanda went to her grandmother's to live. A few years later, Mum married and her husband legally adopted Amanda. They had a further two children but Amanda suffered as the odd one out. She wanted to find me at eight years old but didn't know how. She only knew she had to and was determined, even if it took her a lifetime. She certainly was my daughter.

She had joined the army at 16 to get away from Liverpool and she was posted to Woolwich. A clairvoyant had told her I lived in Dorset. She found out through social services that I had married and it had made her angry. She met Trevor and fell in love and they were soon married. Their first child was born in the same hospital as my niece. Ten years later in 1997, having left the army and become a midwife, she was working opposite where Martin had died at Southampton General in the city where I was appearing regularly. We must have passed each other more than once on the daily commute. Her best friend now was a woman who was raised in Verwood. I would have delivered milk to her house as a boy and known her parents well.

Amanda visited Verwood on many occasions, not knowing I was living three miles away. Craig and Charlie always looked forward to visiting the Moors Valley children's park. Trevor had been Arctic training in northern Norway at the same time as I'd been there. I'd met many British soldiers and may have even talked to him in a bar.

At a lecture that was given on absent fathers, she followed the advice given and searched for an address, but with no luck. In November 2000, she then decided to buy a computer and found my website with Nigel Slater's email address. It was a happy ending to a long, painful journey for us both. She is extremely bright and has a wonderful attitude to life. She has a marriage made in heaven, two perfectly adjusted children full of personality and no hang-ups. She is a highly qualified midwife, with so many letters after her name it begs the question: who needs parents?

I would like to have been there for her as she was growing up but it wasn't meant to be and we have a beautiful relationship now. *C'est la vie.*

The day I was reunited with Amanda, I had to go on to The Bent Brief, the gig in Southampton. At the end of the night, I was selling CDs as usual and a man bought one and argued that he'd given me a £20 note. I emptied my pocket and there were only tens. He was a con artist, which wasn't unusual for The Bent Brief, and I laughed at him and looked him straight in the eyes. He punched me in the mouth and loosened one of my teeth. I reeled backwards and said, 'That's a strange thing to do on the evening before the birth of Christ.' Even for me, that was a strange thing to say. He ran out of the door. I had a delayed anger attack and packed up the gear and swore to myself that that was the last time anybody was going to hit me and get away with it. I was going to have a hit of another kind and never set foot in a bar again.

I'd overreacted, of course, and I carried on the following night much the same as ever but I believe that night was the turning point. It knocked some sense into me, literally, and I should write and thank him . . . especially as I later found the £20 note in my other pocket. The gig paid £100 and the dentist cost me £99. Congratulations, you have made a whole pound.

After the punch in the mouth, which also remains tied to the magic date of 23 December, there were a lot of people who said, 'It's a shame he turned his back on the pubs, isn't it?' Every bar I ever played in made a profit on me. So you're darned right; I don't want to play bars for £1 . . . I don't have the teeth for it. The publicans were the ones taking holidays in Barbados, not me. I sang my guts out, I felt every note I sang, I was sincere and I got paid. That's it. Working bars is shite and anybody with a grain of sense knows it. You use a lot more courage and energy than you do playing the Albert Hall. I take my hat off to all the guys out there still doing it. They've got more true grit than all the spoilt rock stars on the planet. May a miracle happen for them, too. After 18 years of it, I was glad it was over. I do miss the crazy people, however, and I'm richer for the experience. For all their particularities, they were the only ones who knew what it was really like out there in the wilderness.

Ian Brown, having seen me with Robbie McIntosh as a duo, had the idea of adding Hamish Stuart and making it a super-group of three singer-songwriters. Robbie and Hamish had been together for six years in the McCartney band.

We got together at Steve Smith's studio and recorded a song each. The sound we made was fantastic and I was pretty thrilled to be a part of it. They'd always had status and respect, something I felt I'd only ever had with King Crimson, which was spurious because I had no respect for that band. Hamish's pedigree is second to none and includes the Average White Band, Chaka Khan, Quincy Jones and Diana Ross. Need I go on? The English record companies weren't interested in him, Robbie or me. Michael McDonald and Hall and Oates can invite Hamish Stuart up onstage at Hammersmith Odeon when spotted in the audience but he can be refused entry at the Larmer Tree Festival for having no ID. That's the England we know and love. Hamish could count Marvin Gaye as having been a close friend and admirer of his talent but the music industry remained ignorant or hostile, or both.

We attracted big crowds wherever we gigged because the public *do* know their music and we did a successful tour of Germany. A German record company sat up and took notice but it was slow coming together. Had they moved quicker, there wouldn't have been a Gordon Haskell record because I really was honoured to be a part of that line-up and had no desire to be a star. It was enough to share the same stage with two giants of the game.

CHAPTER 15

Harry's Bar

I carried on much as before after Christmas that year. I was happy, too. On one of my few nights off, Dee dragged me out of my cosy nest. She wanted to spend an evening with me watching someone else play for a change. She loved to dance. We went to see an American blues singer, the excellent Bill Thomas, who was appearing in the back room of a pub in Salisbury. As I watched the drummer, Sam Kelly, setting up his kit, I leaned over to Dee and said, 'This drummer is going to be good.' Seeing the way he tapped his drums had reminded me of my days with Les Fleur de Lys. As soon as Bill Thomas started the groove, the volume and the dynamics were perfect. Sam was my man and I couldn't wait to talk to him. I thanked Dee for knowing a good thing and getting me out of the house.

At eleven o'clock, I said hello to Sam and asked him if he was recording anywhere. He told me about Steve Watkins, a 32-year-old engineer who was working at Warehouse Studios near Oxford, and I went home knowing I'd found the answer to my recording problems.

I booked Sam, Peter Stroud, who was his bass player, and my saxophonist, Paul Yeung, and we went into Warehouse the following week on my credit cards. Paul is from Southampton and often accompanied me at The Bent Brief and the Talking Heads. He is, without a shred of doubt, the most soulful player I've ever heard in my life. It was the perfect band for what I wanted to do.

It's not modern rock 'n' roll, but it uses the same principles as the original rock 'n' roll records. They played with the swing that they still carried from the jazz era, at the same volume as jazz and with the same subtleties. Modern rock is crude in comparison. Whole generations have grown up believing that volume is equated with dynamism. With no exceptions, volume is just volume. The very best rock 'n' roll was played by jazz musicians in a much lighter way. It's no coincidence that Charlie Watts is a jazz drummer. Listen to Little Richard, Jerry Lee Lewis, Chuck Berry, Fats Domino, Ray Charles or Elvis Presley and then imagine them with a heavy rock drummer. It wouldn't have worked. The Beatles and the Stones understood that.

I was now only interested in making records if they could begin to sound remotely like the records I had bought as a teenager. Music back then had been so much fun and I missed the good-natured spirit of it all. Jerry Lee Lewis, Little Richard and Chuck Berry always made everyone so happy.

I arrived at Warehouse Studios early and waited for the band to arrive. I made a cup of coffee and read the *Sunday Times*. In the music section, there was a review by Dan Cairns of the artist Roni Size's new album. Dan had written, 'testament to his famous unremitting beats, staccato runs and slamming bass lines over and around which weave those curlicues of sinister sonic allusion both energising and unsettling'.

I smiled and felt joyous that I had no part to play in that world of total drivel that is the music business. These were *my* credit cards I was using. I had created my own world and was living by my own rules now. I didn't have to answer to anybody, let alone Dan Cairns, with his fascination for 'curlicues'.

So I acted as if we were all back in 1957 and routined the band and recorded them just as Sam Phillips would have done at Sun Studios with Elvis or Jerry Lee.

The familiarity in previous studios had often degenerated into an attitude of 'It's only Gordon and he's easy.' But Sam and Pete were strangers to me and they had a quiet respect. I had my hat with me and all I said to the band was, 'When I take my hat off, I'm a nice guy,' placing my hat back on my head as I spoke. 'How Wonderful You Are' was the first song we recorded. I knew it was the ace and I couldn't wait to get it down and hear how it sounded with a band. It had felt great doing it, but had we captured it on tape?

We all agreed we had. It sounded so relaxed, warm and soulful. We moved swiftly on to 'Al Capone', which captured a unique atmosphere created by Sam's unusual drum part. It was all so effortless. This was how it must have been to record in America. Nobody was uptight and, with Sam's Jamaican roots, he played like an American drummer, just behind the beat, not on top of it. And what a difference it made to my music.

It was heaven to listen to and a joy to produce. Everyone was happy. Steve Watkins, at 32, was having the time of his life. His favourite music was heavy metal but he was exactly the right man technically for the job and he loved the stuff.

Sam had been right. Dee had been right. I had been right. Steve reminded me of the same kind of man Glyn Johns had been on my first record in 1966. Some time in the future, the whole world will be after Steve Watkins. His laid-back state of mind couldn't have been a better match for the material.

We had a ball recording and laughing all day in the most relaxed place on earth. The combination of Ashmore and Oxford was magical, spiritual and mind-blowing. England has never been able to produce the J.J. Cales and the James Taylors but here was a situation where it was possible to get the feel and the sound. I wasn't copying the artists, I was simply determined to create the same environment they had always enjoyed so that the songs weren't destroyed as they had been before.

I realised after it was all done that Harry, my father, had spent years in Oxford and I wanted to call it *Harry's Bar* there and then. But Ian Brown had other ideas. At the time, I wasn't thinking of the renowned Harry's Bar in Venice, where Hemingway famously drank. I have no idea how the name Harry slipped into 'How Wonderful You Are'. The subconscious is a strange beast. I completed the album in ten days and I gave it to Ian Brown for his label, Flying Sparks. He called the album *Look Out*. I had become so laid-back and pleased with myself, I let him. *Look Out* was a rock 'n' roll song. I didn't want to be seen as a rock singer when I had a jazz classic in the bag and, at 55, it seemed obvious to me to push 'How Wonderful You Are'. But I was no longer involved in any of the decisions of the music business. I was enjoying myself too much.

The total cost of recording was £7,000 and Ian Brown's offer was to give me the equivalent amount in his time as a PR man and split any earnings 50–50. I'd had 100 per cent of nothing for so long it seemed like a good idea. He would tell the press he lent me £200 to make the record and I would go along with the deception. It's called public relations and it costs a fortune. It is totally absurd that something as sacred as music cannot reach the public's attention without a lot of lies being told.

He sent me, Hamish and Robbie off to Germany while he prepared to release it. The tour in Germany was such a refreshing change for me; we had first-class hotels for a start. Hamish and Robbie took it all as read but I loved the cleanliness and class of it all after those diabolical years in Scandinavia. Being with them and hearing their stories of all the big names they'd worked with, and still associated with, made me feel I had entered the inner sanctum of the rock 'n' roll elite.

Ian Brown had sent the record out for review and I made the front cover of a couple of roots-music magazines, but none of the major publications would support it. Bob Harris and Paul Jones played a track on Radio 2. Then the distributor went into liquidation, taking the £3,000 he owed Ian and me along with him. According to Ian, the distributor was paying himself £100,000 a year at the time and drove a Jaguar XJ6 but he couldn't afford to pay me. Ian was promoting Thea Gilmore and wrote my album off as a non-starter, which was normal, going by my track record of the past five years. We might have left it there. It was only my anger that kept the ball rolling.

My anger, partly with myself for re-entering this stupid business and it bringing me down, was too much for Dee. I had written the best songs of my life and traded them, lock, stock and barrel, with Ian Brown for a bit of PR that had led nowhere. I decided not to let him bury 'How Wonderful You Are' and started ranting to Dee about it. She ran upstairs to avoid the bear-with-a-sore-head routine and to cry her heart out. She wanted to remind me just how happy we had been only a few weeks earlier. She was right. We still had Ashmore, I still made hundreds of people happy every week in bars and I was extremely lucky to have a beautiful girlfriend as well. 'Can't you see how lucky you are?' cried Dee. 'I stare at walls all day, *every* day.'

It made her ill and her stomach pains became so acute I had to take her to Shaftesbury Hospital, from where she was transferred by ambulance to Salisbury. They found nothing wrong with her, as they had found nothing wrong with me when I'd had a similar complaint at nine years old. I had made her ill with my anger at the music business. If only I'd had the sense to direct my anger at those responsible.

After a fortnight, she suffered another attack and I bought some painkillers from an all-night garage. She sat on the bed crying while I sat in the lounge drinking coffee. All I needed to do was put my arms around her and tell her I loved her. But I didn't and she cried all night long, wishing she could reach me and feeling she wasn't of any use to me any more. I had disappeared into my cave to recover and rethink. All her low self-esteem returned and, after trying to repair the damage I had done, we reached an impasse at which point we both gave up. She went to her mother's to think it over.

To add to our woes, my landlord served me notice to quit. The farm labourer was retiring and our cottage, being the smallest on the estate, was required by him. He was living next door in a larger property which could attract a greater rent. I had not foreseen this happening. My anger went through the roof. I had to face the fact that our paradise was gone, my writing routine was wrecked and a new home would take months to find. I didn't even own my record any more – I'd given it away to Ian Brown.

I phoned the big house in Ashmore and asked if they'd let out the little one-bedroom cottage that stood in their grounds. It was a long shot but we liked each other and they despised my former landlord, which was a stroke of luck. They agreed and it was a fantastic place to live, with the best view in the whole village, overlooking the pond – and it was classy. Dee visited as I was considering it and she thought we could do better in another village. We viewed one place that would have worked but I was reluctant to leave Ashmore, loving it as I did, and we struggled with my decision. I felt my new material was born of the vibe in Ashmore and I couldn't bear the thought of leaving all the magic behind. She helped me move in and stayed a few nights until the subject of our future cropped up again.

Robbie and I appeared at The Barrelhouse Club for music promoter and blues guitarist Paul Hart in a neighbouring town and sold so many tickets they had to turn people away. It was 28 April 2001. We all had an inspiring night. Back at the cottage, Dee said, 'You're going to be successful and I'm going to be left looking at those ducks.' I argued that, if I was successful, we would come across a lot more opportunities for her and she might find a job in music that she enjoyed.

Coming so soon after *Look Out* had caused so much anger, she quite logically said, 'Why would I want to work in the music business? Look what it's done to you.'

I couldn't find any answers. We were both mentally and physically exhausted by our jobs, our housing problems, our money shortages and, most painful of all, our relationship.

'Can I stay one more night and I'll leave in the morning?' she asked, with tears running down her face. In the morning, I hoped we could forget all about it but she had noticed I'd separated her CDs into a pile. I don't know why I did that, I didn't want her to leave, but she read it her way and got into her car. As she said goodbye, I said, 'I can't do this.' I meant I couldn't let her go. She read it as 'I can't do this *relationship* any more' and drove off. I wouldn't see her again for two years.

The girl who had inspired me to write what would become a huge hit wasn't going to be there to enjoy it. The girl whose only crime was to want to do a job 'where I can make a difference' had no idea that thousands of people would write to me in six months' time saying *I* had made a difference to their lives. She should have had that praise, not me.

Robbie and I were getting noticed. Although my album was the victim of yet another distributor going bust, the little press I had got had been good and credible. Robbie's album was even better received and as a double act we were great value whichever way you looked at it. He was rated as the guitarists' guitarist and his material was good. Robbie has been fortunate to have been able to support his family all through his married life and lives for his wife and four children. Visiting their home in Weymouth was like visiting the Waltons. He loves his family, he loves all sport, particularly football, and he loves to play his guitar. He commands a top fee because he's the top session guitarist in the country and has been for years. As this book reaches publication, he joins one of the best acts in the world, Norah Jones.

He loved comedy and had the largest collection of shows on tape I've ever seen. We had to drive up to Ullapool in the west of Scotland for a guitar festival and laughed for the entire 650 miles going up. We did three days of gigs and, because he wanted to drive all the way back straight after the last gig for his son's birthday, we drove non-stop home to Shaftesbury in eleven hours, laughing all the way. Dr Robbie had prescribed comedy for my condition and I was soon on top form again. I think I fell asleep once but Robbie kept going.

As we approached Ashmore, I asked him to slow down. I wanted him to see the man who sat on a chair in the hedge all day. Because we'd been listening to comedy for so long, he didn't believe me, but he slowed down as asked. Monty was there. Monty presides over a field full of old fridges on the A30 just outside Shaftesbury, sitting on a large Gothic chair in the middle of the hedge by the roadside. With a long, ginger beard and large, staring eyes, he peers out at the passing traffic. If he sold the land he sits on, he'd probably be a millionaire but he likes it there in the hedge, watching this silly world go by. I wrote a song about him on the album *Look Out* called 'Self-Made Man'. It was a great ending for Robbie after driving all night and half the day. Robbie named him 'Hedgeman'.

Working with Robbie and Hamish was taking me away from most of the bars I'd been playing and I felt confident that my life and career were moving in the right direction. After Scotland, I landed the support gig to Eric Bibb, playing large theatres. It all seemed so easy after doing bars and, having only 35 minutes onstage, I could play the cream of my material. Dee was the subject of all the songs, so she was always with me whenever I sang. The audiences loved it and I loved the company of fellow pros like Eric; Dave Bronze, the bassist; and Janna Peterssen, the keyboard player. It was the high spot of the year for me and I was relieved to know that big theatres are easier than bars because, having done 20 years of bars, it would have been awful if I'd been nervous.

The first gig in Cambridge at the Corn Exchange should have been a disaster, as the PA had been stolen and the audience had to wait. I went on as calm as ever to an impatient crowd and said, 'It's all my fault.' That got a laugh. I did the first song while they were still soundchecking. The stage manager was so knocked out at the impromptu performance, he recommended me for the Cambridge Folk Festival.

As soon as I had finished the Bibb gig, I landed the support for the nationwide Errol Brown tour, which was even bigger.

One day, whilst travelling with Ian Brown in the car, we talked about our pasts. I started telling him about my Hollywood days with Susan George and he told me of his days as a pig farmer. When I said I felt I could produce a record for Susan, Ian's PR brain went into overdrive and I enjoyed listening to the endless insane stories he was creating with every mile we travelled. He had quite an imagination and a complete understanding of what the tabloid press meant by a story. Within ten minutes, he had the whole Susan George press campaign clearly laid out in his mind. His stories are always ridiculous, and I told him Susan would never allow it, but it was great entertainment and I enjoyed his company whenever we had to travel together. He could cure me of my negativity faster than any analyst and we had great creative sessions driving along the M3 at 5 a.m., preparing me to 'smile and be positive at all times!'

Being together so much with an ex-pig farmer brought back memories of Reggie Perrin when he'd quit Sunshine Desserts and worked at Pelham's Piggery. I began to think of that whole series and my pen pal for 20 years, David Nobbs. I just had to meet the man who continually popped into my mind and who seemed to be following me around. Reggie was at West Bay, as I was; he talked of Godalming all the time, where I'd lived with my wife; he mentions Mickey Fudge from Bournemouth, who sang on my records; he mentions Scandinavians on their way to Marks & Spencer. He was always getting bored with it all and now here I was working with Ian Brown, a pig farmer like Reggie.

We continued our Susan George conversation as the 6 a.m. traffic ground to a halt. 'Six lanes of stationary traffic and nowhere to pee.' Now there's a song title. No wonder men suffer with their prostate glands. We could save the National Health Service thousands if we weren't so bashful.

I had done TV with Susan George, we had jammed in LA together and we liked the same kind of artists. There was always a warm feeling between us, which had survived for 20 years, so I gave it some thought. It could be my way of thanking her for the good times in 1978 and fulfilling some of the dreams we'd had back then. After calling her, there were a couple of meetings and my friend Nigel Slater was keen to finance the production. I booked the Warehouse again at Oxford, along with all my favourite musicians, whom I'd been working with over the past four months. Sam was on drums, Dave Bronze, bass, Paul Yeung, saxophone, and Janna Peterssen on piano. Hamish played a nylon-strung Spanish guitar and arranged the backing vocals.

I spent three weeks routining with Susan, combing through 30 or 40 songs. I knew how I wanted to produce her, and she was very excited and thrilled with the musicians. The backing tracks were a joy to produce and, to this day, I maintain the quality of the feel, the playing and the brilliant sense of harmony that was brought together on those tracks by the crème de la crème of London beats anything I've heard in the genre of the Latin-flavoured music I've always loved. Sitting in the control room with Steve Watkins, the engineer, all day for a fortnight listening to my favourite players was the best therapy I could ever have had. Coming so soon after recording *Harry's Bar* there, I knew I would never need to record anywhere else. It was heaven. Susan and I were on cloud nine. Every musician was superb. I felt connected to a higher plane every time we listened to the playback. Hamish's backing vocals were a masterpiece, using jazz progressions in five-part harmony. I felt privileged to be the producer. With this team and Steve Watkins anything was possible and Nigel Slater began to get excited about his investment.

Stan Getz and Antonio Jobim chose Astrid Gilberto to sing their music. It was a perfect sound. They weren't looking for a Barbra Streisand; it wouldn't have been so delicate. The ego of the singer would get in the way. So it was my idea to treat Susan in a similar way. She was sexy – so bring it out. Don't let her be an aspiring singer, there are hundreds of those. Let's go for a sound that fits the spiritual elements of these tracks. That's how we had routined it and it was working. Marilyn Monroe pulled it off, so could Susan. We did all the vocals in a week and I was happy. I listened at home to the monitor mixes and told Nigel I was ready to complete the record. He called to say that Susan had played it to her friends and they'd all said they had heard her sing much better, so she wanted to do all the vocals again. I told him her friends were theatrical and would expect a theatrical performance from her, which wouldn't work. Elvis was sexy. Peggy Lee was sexy. They didn't show off. They understood seduction. Susan was a natural.

Norah Jones appeared a year later with exactly the same vibe that I was going for. It remains in limbo but I had enjoyed working as a producer for a second time. Working with such brilliant musicians, who were also becoming my friends, eased some of the emptiness I felt living without Dee in my life.

With a busy gig schedule of theatres and clubs, I was focused entirely on my performing career.

I'd heard there was a lady living in the village who worked in the advertising business and, as the record was technically in the hands of the receiver, I posted it through her letterbox at Stud Cottage with a note submitting the songs for her consideration in her capacity as advertising executive. I didn't hear back, but as I was walking round the pond one day, she stopped me on her horse and introduced herself as 'Tiggy, the lady in Stud Cottage'. She quickly explained that she was a producer and music wasn't her department, but why not come over to dinner?

She was the most positive and cheerful person I'd ever met and I felt happier each time I saw her. I wasn't likely to see Dee again because she felt she had tried her hardest with me and hadn't been able to make me happy. I had given up. Tiggy and I had a very pleasant neighbourly dinner and I told her I was appearing at the Larmer Tree Festival in a couple of days. She had a crowd of friends coming down from London at the weekend and the festival was only two miles up the road. I might see her there. I didn't give it a lot of thought. I was focused on my job and the last thing I wanted was a distraction.

I was booked with Robbie to support Van Morrison but Robbie's house was struck by lightning, caught fire and was gutted, so he couldn't make the gig. He would have gone to pieces if it had happened while he was playing with me and hadn't been there to get the kids to safety, so in a way the timing was fortunate. It happened at midnight and the family had been left homeless. As Robbie stood watching his life's work go up in smoke, he caught sight of a page from a book floating out of the roof. Thinking it might be a page from the Bible with a prophecy or an enlightened piece of wisdom, he ran over to where it landed and retrieved it, dabbing out the lighted edges. It was a page featuring Biffo the Bear. The whole family stood in their dressing gowns at the roadside, looking at the remains of their once-lovely home, smiling, shaking their heads and reading *The Beano*.

Hamish stepped in to do the gig with me and, afterwards, Tiggy invited us back to the cottage. The second day, I played solo. Tiggy and I left the festival just as Johnnie Walker arrived backstage. Johnnie asked the stage crew if he could put out a message over the PA for Gordon Haskell. We missed each other by minutes. At this point, Johnnie hadn't met Tiggy and I hadn't seen him since the '80s, but it was one of those spooky moments. It was July 2001. Two months later, he'd be playing my record.

Tiggy had an apartment in Marylebone, along with one of the loveliest cottages in the village, so she was clearly loaded. And she was single. She was 40 and had her own sad stories, menwise, having escaped an unhappy marriage in her 20s. She lived life to the full, knew all the shows opening in London and all the directors and was a combination of all the good things I had enjoyed with Sally without any of the bad. We enjoyed each other very much and laughed a lot, each trying to get over our last big romance.

She invited Hamish and his partner down for another weekend and we all had a great time together. By coincidence, they all belonged to The Union Club in Soho, so we arranged to meet them again the following week. I stayed up in London for a few days at Tiggy's flat and bumped into Ian Brown in a café in Marylebone High Street. We got into a heated conversation about the fact that I had made yet another album for the benefit of dodgy distributors to help them maintain their shiny motor cars. I'd had to pay off £7,000 on one credit card plus interest and a further £21,000 from other bankrupt firms that had taken, and still legally owned, my music. My question to him was, 'Why am I bothering and why shouldn't I be angry?'

His standard reply was, 'If you don't like the music business, fuck off.'

I found myself falling for his charm.

He gets to the point quicker than anyone I've ever met. We agreed that the roots thing had meant diddly-squat. I hadn't made the broadsheets or radio, or the mainstream music press. They only want to review the fashionable and they were unaware that I had played in every trendy club in London in the past three years and knocked out audiences. I was 55 and no one was going to touch me. I might as well have carried on selling direct at gigs; there was no hope of winning them over. No matter that The Borderline, a music club well known for picking up on talent, had just called me the best act they'd seen in years; no matter that I was working more than anyone in the neighbourhood; no matter, no matter. The doors of opportunity were closed to me.

'Let's go with "How Wonderful You Are",' I said. 'We'll get Michael Parkinson and Jazz FM. It suits my age and style and it sets me apart from all the competition.'

He agreed. 'It's so wrong . . . let's do it!'

'How's the Thea Gilmore record?'

'I'm going to see Johnnie Walker with it next week.'

I casually said, in all innocence, 'I've known Johnnie since 1966. We're old mates. He plugged Les Fleur de Lys and my song "Lazy Life" and he was at the Larmer Tree Festival looking for me the other day.'

Ian went nuts. 'All this time I've been fucking about, and now you tell me?'

I said I'd sent him stuff in the past and grown tired of hassling him and, anyway, if people don't get this record, they shouldn't be in the music business. I bet they'd soon get it if Tom Waits was singing it. Then what will they say? What a great song, who wrote that?

Over a few drinks, I told him about Tiggy. A week later after he had pressed up the single, I added the punchline, 'By the way, when you see Johnnie today, you may as well know we shared the same girlfriend in 1966. I'm not sure if he ever knew, so he might throw the record back at you.'

Ian sighed, and said, 'For Christ's sake, I've just spent £500 on pressings. Any other gems for me today before I get thrown out of the BBC?'

I got a message from Johnnie to call him on his private number, that he wanted to meet up. I suggested The Union and we met on 10 September. I was with Tiggy. Hamish was coming later and we were going to spend the following day writing at Tiggy's flat. I was telling her all about my history with Johnnie and the Stratford Place days with Janet and Judy when Johnnie walked in. Over dinner and a bottle of wine, we all got stuck into a deep conversation about our lives, with Johnnie telling me to read *Positive News* on the Internet, as I was whinging on about the music business. It was great to see him again and when Tiggy went to the ladies room, he leaned over and said, 'She's fantastic. Don't fuck it up.'

A few days later, Tiggy and I had our first fall-out when I caused a scene by spouting anti-Thatcher politics at a posh dinner party.

'This isn't going to work too well, is it, Tiggy?' I said.

'No, Gordy, it isn't.' And we hugged each other and started laughing. We weren't suited but it had been a lot of fun that summer. After she'd broken up with her ex and I had lost Dee, we were good for each other. We didn't hurt.

When Johnnie left The Union Club the night of our reunion, he called Tiggy and Tiggy called Johnnie. It was love at first sight, though they didn't quite know it then. The following day, I was in the middle of writing a song with Hamish at Tiggy's flat when we got a call to turn on the television. It was 11 September and we saw the second plane go into the Twin Towers. Hamish and I never did finish the song.

Johnnie had by now listened to the single that Ian had left with him the week before and decided to take a risk and play it. He was quoted as saying that after 9/11 people needed something comforting and real, and this record encapsulated that. Without 9/11, he might have missed the point.

CHAPTER 16

🐚 🐚 🐚

Pub Singer Signs for £2.8 Million

It had been an extraordinary year so far. Was this part of my extraordinary year too and if so what did it mean? Robbie Williams with his newly released 'Something Stupid' and the giant EMI were certainly the Goliath, and Ian managing a 55-year-old grandfather was undoubtedly the David. We were being dismissed at the very gates of freedom and refused entry into the world at large. It creates resentment and anger. Success in England means global acceptance. We were locked out, peering through the perimeter fence. It wasn't fair. Here comes that movie *Havana* again. Redford says, 'Nothing's fair – where the hell have you been?'

The record prompted an instant response from the public. They began sending in emails. Johnnie played it again and the switchboard was jammed. They had to hire another girl to handle the dozens of emails coming in. Johnnie called me to tell me to try to get it on the playlist. The man responsible for making that decision was Colin Martin. He'd heard it on Johnnie's show as he was driving home from the BBC, which was another twist in the story. He always commuted by train. It's a ten-minute car ride from the railway station to his home. In that ten minutes, he heard me on his car radio. He decided to put it on the playlist without any prompting from anyone. He loved the record. Johnnie said I might have a hit if it got onto the A-list, where records are played in heavy rotation, guaranteeing maximum exposure. He continued playing it and the public continued to respond. The following week, it was Colin's record of the week and automatically went onto the playlist. Now it was on every Radio 2 music programme. The record had sold itself just like all the '50s records had in the age before marketing men. My strategy of making a record the way they were made in 1957 had worked. Knowing Johnnie as I had for 30 years, I had even told Ian to package the disc in an old-style paper record bag. I hadn't really needed a manager so far. I'd had an amazing piece of luck.

The Errol Brown tour started and I went to do my first show at Reading. There was no billing, no money and I was supposed to feel privileged to be on the bill without paying the promoter thousands to go on it. There was a hostile sound crew talking about how great it was on the Hear'say tour that they'd just finished. I had to pay for food because they'd only catered for the main act. There were no drinks on offer. I sat in my dressing-room listening to Johnnie's show and hoping someone would hear my record and change their attitude, but when it came on they said nothing. I did six shows in fabulous theatres but it was costing me petrol money I couldn't afford and it was hours and hours of travelling without a hotel. I couldn't sell much merchandise as there wasn't anywhere I could do it and no one offered to do it for me, so I called Ian Brown to tell him I was going to quit unless they started paying me. I was earning £800 a week in the pubs and I didn't need this nonsense. Ian went very silent and then said, 'OK.'

'You'll never work again,' came the familiar line from Errol's manager and I started to laugh. *You'll never lay bricks in Bournemouth again.* Frankly, my dear, I don't give a rat's crap.

The sound crew was getting paid, the usherette was getting paid. It may have been thrilling once but it is simply the exploitation of a musician's weakness: the longing for a decent platform. The only thing I really enjoyed was the soundcheck on my last night. Checking the microphone, I said 'Kiss me.' I waited for the response and in my best Al Pacino voice quoted his famous line from *Dog Day Afternoon*: 'Kiss me . . . When I'm being fucked, I like to be kissed.'

The record was into its sixth week on the playlist and Colin Martin was asking Ian what was happening, as the release date kept moving. No one at retail wanted to stock it because there was 'no plot behind it'.

'What chance has a 55 year old got of selling more than 500 records?' they argued.

'It's on the A-list at Radio 2. It was their record of the week,' Ian had responded.

'So what? Everybody knows Radio 2 doesn't sell singles. Does he have TV? No. MTV? No. The commercial stations? No. *Top of the Pops*? No. Is the music press behind him? No.'

Today's retail trade doesn't have any experience of natural hit records. Each record they look at has to have a marketing budget of thousands of pounds behind it. Retailers never listen to the records. They haven't the time. Records in 1958 only had radio behind them. The public chose whether to buy what they heard or not. I was being heard and people wanted to buy, but nowadays that's irrelevant.

'We don't get it. We'll take 500,' came the reply from retail.

We had 230,000 people trying to buy a record that no shop would stock, in a marketplace where the industry cries, 'The single is dead!' The public was getting angry.

I decided to submit the songs to Warner Publishing for a laugh, knowing they wouldn't be listening to Radio 2 and that they'd be completely unaware of the action. Sure enough, it boomeranged with the usual rejection letter saying it wasn't commercial. I would have taken £20,000 for it then.

Ian hired a good team of pluggers for the regions. Neil Cossar and Liz Sanchez were doing fine with the BBC stations but the independents wouldn't touch it. The distributor was Vital, who are mavericks like Ian, and they loved anybody who tried to take on the majors. Alan McBlane, a BMG Records consultant, was Ian's undercover man, informing us of things we weren't privileged to know as outsiders. He knew retail personally and kept chiselling away at them. It would cost me £20,000 for his valiant work. He must love retail's attitude; they keep him employed.

Warner was trying to buy Thea Gilmore from Ian's label. She had sold 3,000 records. Ian took a call from Sarah Conacher in the Warner legal-affairs department. 'I'm too busy right now, Sarah,' he said. 'I'm considering whether to press 250,000 singles.'

Sarah's ears pricked up and Ian told her about the record. Her boss, Christian Tattersfield, called him and said, 'I think it's time you brought this little record into us, Ian.'

His lack of magnetism and charm was to be expected. It was in stark contrast to the warmth I was bringing him with 'How Wonderful You Are' and I felt the first blast of cold air coming across my bows as my ship entered the hostile waters of the music business. It's nothing personal, they say. It's all business. Music, unfortunately, for most executives in the industry, only represents money. They appear to be deprived of the pleasure it gives to the rest of us. For that reason alone, I pity them.

Christian neither liked nor disliked the record. It was irrelevant. He saw a profit. Artists live in a strange world. Surrounded by the coldness and ruthlessness of their record companies, they are expected to express their emotions to the world, maintain their integrity and reveal none of the truth to the media. *We're all in it for the money.* That attitude has created the public's mistrust not only in music, but throughout society. Accountants, marketing managers and PR people are the new red, white and blue. They make it almost impossible for anything genuine to penetrate the fortress they have built to maintain their own living. In politics, we now call it spin. Thirty years ago, we called it lies.

Warner Records made an offer that amounted to £2.8 million over five years. I met the Warner staff and felt there was no emotion or warmth in anybody's eyes. These people appeared to dislike their jobs; maybe they didn't like the idea of having to sign a grandfather. I was unimpressed. It felt no different to entering a morgue. The business was discussed while I was interviewed by a journalist in another room. My emotions weren't required, so I didn't show any.

I drove home to Dorset deep in thought. Before I went to bed, I looked out of my window at Ashmore and saw the ducks gliding across the pond in the moonlight and I felt very fortunate.

Johnnie Walker, meanwhile, was visiting Tiggy a lot and we were hanging out together more and more. He was a gentleman. They had fallen in love and he wanted to be sure I wasn't hurt. I told him the story and assured him I was very happy for them both. We spent many evenings together and in the mornings when Tiggy was out riding her horse, Johnnie and I would go up to the little airfield on top of the Downs a mile from Ashmore. The view was stunning on a sunny day. We'd have a full English breakfast and watch the aeroplanes landing and taking off, and talk about everything but the music business. I felt I'd found a soulmate. It was all very easygoing.

191

I enjoyed the fact I'd introduced him to the love of his life. They looked great together and that was good enough for me. Magic happens in Ashmore.

From his desk at the *Leicester Mercury*, one critic was saying the support at Radio 2 for Haskell was contrived and that I didn't deserve all the attention. Ashmore was amazing. The rest of the world continued pumping out their negativity at me; they all seemed so very bitter and twisted.

Ian asked Warner Records to fax through their £2.8 million offer on 3 December and a day after it arrived, they backed out; probably after talking to the retailers, who were still refusing to stock the disc. A classic song that people wanted to buy was set to fail. It was a real hit song and the public was passionate about it. My website was receiving 35,000 hits a week, up from its previous figure of 600. But no one could buy the record anywhere.

I was hearing from strangers via email who were saying how it expressed everything they were feeling and had felt for years. Cars were pulling onto the hard shoulder on motorways as soon as the record came on and texts were flying into the BBC to find out who it was. Greetings cards came to me with messages like 'the most beautiful record I've heard in years'. A British army major in the battlefields of Kosovo wrote and asked where he could buy the record as the men in the mess all drew comfort from it, that it was a morale booster. 'How Wonderful You Are' wasn't a bad thing to hear if you were likely to be shot at. Couples were falling in love to it and making it their song for future weddings. Leslie Grantham, 'Dirty Den', came up to me at Granada Television and said it was his favourite record. Of course, the industry has repeatedly argued with me over the years. They all use the same phrases: 'Yeah, but what does the public know?' and 'This would be a great business without the artists.'

Record executives have been having a private party for years. They take the credit when the public loves an act like The Beatles and blame the public when they lose millions of company money on their idea of the next big thing. 'The public are morons, so, with the aid of our marketing managers, they buy what we tell them to buy' is another one they're proud of.

'How Wonderful You Are' was saying the exact opposite. It's no wonder they tried to stop it. I had made them look in the mirror.

Colin Martin was making Radio 2 the most popular radio station in the country. Because he was a musician and had an ear for music, he knew 'How Wonderful You Are' was a classic song. The stations around the country that Neil Cossar took me to for interviews were mostly BBC-owned, so weren't under the pressure of ratings, and were a joy to work with. There are some outstanding exceptions in independent radio and I expect they will be the stations to survive. The rest will go the way of America, which has giant corporations controlling the airwaves; record sales continue to plummet as audiences register their boredom.

Christian Tattersfield at Warner reckoned it wasn't going to be a hit after all and had a change of heart about the deal. Radio 2 didn't count in the record industry at that time. My record, rapidly followed by Norah Jones, changed all that.

It was 7 December. Time was running out. Ian didn't give up.

He called the *Sunday Times* and told them of the £2.8 million offer and that I was a semi-retired pub singer living in Ashmore, doing a bit of part-time gardening to make ends meet. I had to go along with his degrading inventions to get attention. Despite being on the radio with a popular song, the record industry was intent on ignoring it. It was absurd but their absurdity was contagious. So I bought a gorilla suit.

Ian had sent me to a warehouse in Christchurch to pick up 100 CDs. There was a party shop next door. At the point of sale stood a gorilla suit of the highest quality. I'd never seen one before. In fact, the only memory I had of one was from the movie *A Suitable Case For Treatment* starring David Warner. It catches fire on his motorbike and is one of the funniest scenes of the movie. Buying it to wear to Warner would keep me warm. It was certainly no sillier than they were and the thought of it amused me. It was way too subtle for anyone to suss, even Ian. Jurgen had called all artists monkeys. Now I was going to be Ian's monkey. Making a beautiful record wasn't enough. Let them believe I was a benighted fool with a straw hat. Let them believe I was the fool on the hill. I could keep quiet while Ian did the job I'd paid him to do. *I've made a good record. Now you sell it. Show me you're worth the 50 per cent you're charging me.* Ian had a family to feed too and there were other considerations apart from my own. *Don't be selfish, don't be egotistic, don't be an artist, set an example and be a tame ape.*

This was the time to be Redford, the poker player in *Havana*, which I had seen 79 times by now. When Redford is asked what he is doing in Havana and he replies, 'Looking for the Big One like everybody,' I knew how he felt. When he says, 'I've played every moose hall and elk's club in America, Joe, and now I want a shot, one shot where the players don't even think about how much is at stake,' I knew how he felt.

I had been sincere when I wrote the song and sang it. Now it was war and it had nothing to do with music. I had to do something to relieve the boredom and when asked later on TV and radio what I had bought with all my new-found wealth, I always said a gorilla suit. Nobody asked me why.

'How Wonderful You Are' had officially become the most requested record ever on Radio 2, beating 'My Way' and 'Hey Jude'. The thousands of emails were real enough. It was bound to be a hit regardless of all the resistance from the industry.

The *Sunday Times* asked for some kind of written proof and Ian forwarded the fax from Warner detailing the deal. They wanted to send a photographer down to Ashmore and Ian called me and said, 'Put on your oldest clothes and a straw hat, if you've got one. You're retired, and act surprised and doddery, like you don't know what day it is. Look and act like a village idiot. Put on your old wellies. Don't let on to the reporter, whatever you do. The more gormless you are, the better they'll like it. None of them know your real history.'

I told my landlord that the press was coming and asked permission to be photographed in his garden with a spade. The landlord agreed and was highly amused at the deception. He was a retired major and had fought and won a few battles himself.

Ian was still having conversations with Sarah Conacher at Warner, who said on the Friday before the story was published that she still wanted the record and she'd talk to the MD over the weekend, but Ian played hardball and said we were considering going with BMG, who had offered £750,000 in our hand. The *Sunday Times* ran the story, 'Pub singer signs for £2.8 million', with me posing like a buffoon. Warner smelt the money and came back on board immediately, arranging a meeting for 5 p.m. on Monday, 10 December.

Colin Martin at Radio 2 had been a saint and stayed with the record, and it was still on the A-list, increasing its number of plays. The release date was set for 17 December. It had first been played on 26 September. At no time had it been intended as a Christmas record.

It's just a strong song with a large appeal. Robbie Williams was getting ten times the exposure with his record. We had no money for a video but Ian found a willing team to do one for £500. I arrived in an old coat full of holes. It was ridiculous and I played it like an old tramp in a bar leering at the young girls. *Top of the Pops 2* thought it was the worst video they'd ever seen, which was kind. Even kinder, because they liked the record they put it in the show. It was a fantastic result and a welcome relief to know someone, apart from those at Radio 2, had got it. Thank you, Mark Hagen of the BBC. You have taste. I can eat now.

A long-standing fan and friend of mine called Martin had a taxi in Southampton and did us a cheap deal driving us up to London at 5 a.m. on the Monday morning and staying with us all day. Ian explained it was a day when anything might happen. Ian called his father, who was an early riser, to go down to the paper shop and see if the dailies had picked up the *Sunday Times* story.

'It's in every single one, son,' said Farmer Brown senior, president of Pigs 'R' Us, incorporating Men in Sheds Limited.

I was on the way to Stiffs 'R' Us at Warner.

We got into Kensington at 7 a.m. and looked for a paper shop and a coffee bar. Ian eagerly bought all the newspapers and we were in every single one, including the *Racing Post*, which was running bets on my record being No. 1.

I couldn't bear to look. I saw the photograph and shook my head. I looked like an amateur with a silly grin. It only took one day to wipe out the 20 years of self-respect I had earned. That was the price I had to pay. I felt like a whore, but it was either that or lose the chance of a hit record. My past 20 years in hell being true to myself meant nothing to anyone.

Ian had found a mansion flat behind Harrods that a friend of his hadn't used since the '60s. There was still a box of matches there priced 1d. The place may have had four bedrooms and a lovely view of the trees in Lennox Gardens but it was freezing cold, damp and full of fleas. The gorilla suit was perfect and kept me warm. Ian and I woke up laughing every single day in that penultimate week. It may have been the first time in his life that a gorilla had brought him a cup of tea in the morning, but I can't be sure. As a farmer, he'd only ever worked with animals.

Paul Yeung, the wonderful saxophonist on the record, stayed one night, and Ian rang in and asked how everything was going. 'It's jumping,' Paul said. He'd been bitten all over, so he knew what he was talking about.

I rose early and went to the tobacconist's in the gorilla suit. Passers-by in the Brompton Road ignored my 'good mornings'.

I began doing interviews while Ian was running round town seeing other interested parties and booking appointments with all the major publishers who were calling him. He phoned on the mobile every now and then to check if I'd screwed it all up yet. The story that Ian had invented was that I wrote the song whilst shopping in Safeways with my mother. The television companies loved it and wanted to reconstruct the scene. This meant the humiliation of playing my guitar in the fruit and vegetable section and walking round with a basket pretending to make notes as I picked up the gherkins. Apart from that extreme piece of idiocy and utter fiction, it was great fun. I had never had to live a lie in 35 years of being a musician. If I wanted my record to be stocked in the shops, I had to do what Ian told me to do. I should have told him to go to hell but I quietly went along with it, degrading the song and myself as each hour went by.

The scene would come to life in my mother's supermarket in Verwood a few days later. Ironically, I no longer had time to do her shopping there on a Thursday and wished I could embarrass them for not offering to deliver to her free of charge in return for the nationwide publicity I was giving them. Ian stopped me just in time. He said 'NO!' in a voice that reminded me of someone training a dog to come to heel. I laughed at the sound of it for the same reason I had been amused when Jurgen had called me 'Youfuckingoldman'. These people hated honesty.

I was a very good little boy until the 85th interview, having thought there were only 84 in any single week. When the phone rang in my room at the hotel, I mistook the caller for an old friend of the same name. When asked about Warner, I was completely honest about my reservations, but the story never appeared anywhere.

I arrived with Ian and Martin, the driver, at the Warner office to see Sarah Conacher at 5 p.m. A man from the publicity department met us and on being introduced to Martin assumed he was part of the management team. While Ian and I went up to Sarah's office to discuss the deal, Martin was given a guided tour of the building, meeting every employee and all the individual heads of departments.

I signed where I was told to sign. I figured by paying £20,000 to Ian's lawyer and having a manager charging me 50 per cent, I was pretty well protected. We met Martin afterwards in a nearby pub in Kensington High Street. Ian gave me a cheque for £100,000 plus VAT. We had a drink and he said, 'Not a bad day's work for a Monday, Rodney.' We were all smiles; we were friends together, celebrating our success and it felt absolutely beautiful. Martin drove us home and I smiled all the way back to my starlit Ashmore, where it had all been created. I was out of debt at last.

Over the next seven days, we sold 280,000 singles. Retail had changed their tune to my tune. There were huge displays in every store across Britain. Warner certainly had the muscle and was already in profit. There's no money in singles apparently. It may have seemed to Ian not a bad day's work, but to me it represented 35 years of dedication. In my haste to get out of debt, I'd sold myself short, but I was grateful nonetheless – naturally.

In the following days, it all went nuts and we had to move into the flat properly to keep up with it all. Ian bought some fan heaters from Harrods to try to dry it out a bit but I still needed the gorilla suit to keep warm. Martin came too because I had to start going round the country to a few radio stations that were slowly coming on board.

My favourite moment was on the Friday night in the Finchley Road. The police stopped the car because they spotted Martin's taxi plate and were suspicious. Two officers asked Martin to get out of the car and began questioning him.

'What's that on the seat?' said the young rookie as the older one backed off.

'It's a gorilla suit. Do you want to try it on? It's great. Look.'

As I said this, I opened the car door and put the gorilla's head on. Martin started laughing. The novice policeman wasn't smiling.

Martin said more sombrely, 'He's going to be No. 2 in the charts. He's been doing a radio show in Newcastle.'

The older policeman said, 'Oh, I see. You're a musician.' That seemed to explain everything to him. He saw the humour but the younger one was still deadly serious. Martin and I were told we could go because passing motorists were slowing to look and the flow of traffic was coming to a standstill, curious to know why two policemen were questioning a gorilla at 9.30 p.m. in the Finchley Road.

I couldn't stop Martin laughing for hours after that. Forget the thrill of the No. 2 record. That young policeman's face without a glimmer of a smile on it as he stood talking to a man with the head of a gorilla in the crowded Finchley Road remains the defining moment of the whole campaign. Bliss.

CHAPTER 17

≋ ≋ ≋

The Single is Dead

Meanwhile, Ian had arranged for ten publishing companies to visit the flat to discuss selling the publishing rights. This didn't happen until the day of release.

There is a computerised sales system called CIN that you can subscribe to for £1,500 per year if you're a serious player in the record business. It will tell you every record that is selling and where it is selling and the position in the daily sales chart. What did they do before barcodes? They had to use their ears. Now, you don't need ears; you only need eyes, a computer, £1,500 and an accountant to calculate the odds.

On Monday, 17 December, the record went on sale and we went straight in at No. 3 on their secret computers. The other two records had that Sunday's sales to beat me. All anyone has to do in publishing is buy the act's publishing before the chart is released on the following Sunday. It's not rocket science and there's no risk at all, as it has already earned what their first offer will be. To the unsuspecting novice songwriter, £30,000 is a dream, £100,000 is a pools win and anything else is unheard of. I had told Ian that Warner had turned down my songs for publishing and I wouldn't sell for less than my friend Don Gallacher had procured for P.J. Harvey, which was £400,000.

Ian had arranged for the morning publishing appointments to start at 8.30 a.m. – unheard of in the music business, and three hours later than he usually started. Farmers work hard before going bankrupt. The first caller was the head of Sony Music. He hadn't heard the record (naturally – only the public listens to radio, executives are too busy). Ian put it on a portable ghetto-blaster and the Sony man asked what we wanted.

'I want a million,' said Ian.

'That's outrageous! I thought you were serious. Our company is interested in the development of an artist,' said Mr Sincere golf player.

'Development?' said Ian. 'He's 55, for Christ's sake!. He's developed already. He needs a pension, not development. Give us your fuckin' money.'

'You can't talk to me like that. I'm the head of Sony.'

Ian replied with style. 'So fuck off, then. I didn't ring you, you rang me. I didn't ask you here. You wanted to come.'

Our man from Sony stormed out, passing the man from Warner Music on the stairs, just to humiliate him further. He rang 30 minutes later with an offer of £750,000. Ian said it was so outrageous he couldn't possibly accept it. I wanted *developing*. I could hear Reggie Perrin saying it.

'Let's hear it, Ian,' said Richard Manners of Warner Music, obviously no fan of Radio 2 either. It had been on the playlist for three months. Ian repeated the exercise. It was only Monday and we had six days to make it No. 1.

'What are you looking for?' asked Richard.

'Sony just offered £750,000 but they want to pay half now and half in six months' time. Give me £500,000 now and it's yours,' said Ian, thinking of my figure of £400,000 that he had to beat.

'Let me think about it,' said Richard, then left, passing the EMI guy on the stairs, scratching his arms. Ian had forgotten to sort out the flea problem.

The guys from EMI went through the same routine and made an offer of £350,000. They knew it wouldn't make No. 1. Robbie Williams is on EMI. They had five days to stop it in its tracks and they knew they had the power to do it.

One by one, they all came and Ian was done by 5 p.m.

He'd turned down the Sony offer and Warner had backed out yet again. We had nothing for about an hour. The record was being tipped heavily now for No. 1, so Warner came back on board and we signed the deal for £500,000.

The press and TV spots were coming in all the time as it got bigger and bigger and closer to chart day. I loved being on the Michael

Parkinson show and hearing him say he would play the record again and again and again. I loved the repartee between Jonathan Ross and me, and the surprise I got by liking him immensely and recognising his talent. I had him down as a punk and I was wrong.

We got the big one, *Top of the Pops*, on the Wednesday. The show would reach four million people who probably don't listen to Radio 2. We only needed 5,000 more sales and we'd beat Robbie Williams. We went to Shepherd's Bush to do the show and hired tuxedos to create the same stylish image as the video I'd made on the Tuesday for Warner. It's still on Magic TV 50 times a week. The show went well and I came off the stand and felt a huge drama unfolding around Ian and the producer. I asked what was wrong, wasn't it any good?

'Its nothing,' he said. 'Everything's fine.'

But there was something. Sam Kelly had a word in my ear. 'My mate is the assistant producer. He was my bass player once. He says Robbie Williams *will* be No. 1. We're not going to be on the show tomorrow.'

I didn't believe him and asked Ian what was going on, but he still wouldn't tell me anything. He told me to never mind, so I left it alone.

The following day I rang my family and said I'd be on *Top of the Pops*. I told them that, in the midweek sales, I was No. 2 and just 5,000 records behind. With *Top of the Pops*, the manager at HMV reckoned I'd pull it off.

Friday came, with more TV in the morning and at lunchtime, and I enjoyed every second. Everybody at the television studios was beautiful to me – it felt as if I'd entered a world where people were warmer to one another. I could do it all with such ease and I was being admired for being so laid-back on TV. I had a chance to use some wit, which was wasted on the gormless music press. I didn't screw up once. The TV technicians enjoyed it as much as I did. It was a refreshing change for us all. After the unpleasantness of the record-business personnel, these people were a breath of fresh air. Much as I loved music, it had been so hard on me throughout my 35 years that the idea of becoming something else was very appealing. I was either ready to retire or ready for a complete change. If classy music was to be frowned on and regarded as wet, then I was no longer in the right job. My song suited me perfectly – it was jazzy, classy and, most of all, full of optimism. I'd lost interest as soon as the knives had started coming out at Warner. The head of promotion had said, 'I don't get it.' I didn't expect any spiritual awareness from them but I had hoped they could still hear a good song.

All the top musicians I associate with recognise the song's merits, as do the audiences to whom I play. Apparently certain executives or critics don't, but that was why I had removed them from my life. Hearing their voices again after so many years and reading their ugly remarks merely confirmed what I already knew. I had learned to live without their approval but they are, after all, the doormen to the privileged club they run. It is they who prevent so many from making a decent living. It's ironic that for 50 years artists have been robbed of their potential royalties by these people and now the record companies are having a taste of their own medicine as piracy escalates.

All I had to do at this stage on television was to talk and be natural, so it was an ideal way to demonstrate how contented I had become without fame or fortune. It was an extraordinary position to find myself in because, at the very moment I had broken through with my music, I knew I had grown out of my need for success. I didn't need the hostility that came with it. I don't love money that much. I was finally vindicated but I had so wanted to feel that I'd been reading the record business wrong for the past 25 years. Now that I knew I had always been right, I wanted to leave it all behind. I had climbed to such a height at Ashmore and now I felt the descent into rampant materialism; a world of back-stabbers with lousy taste in music and an unawareness that I found repellent.

The *Evening Standard* financial editor wanted me to advise his readers on what property I was buying and what investments I was making. I couldn't believe they weren't having a laugh. Every single person I spoke to believed the press story that we had picked up £2.8 million. The begging letters began. Ian said I'd be a millionaire within six months. I believed him and gave away over £80,000.

Very few media people talked about the song. They seemed more interested in the story. They would say 'such a simple song' while musicians were writing to me for the sheet music because they were having trouble working it out. It wasn't a simple song at all. It was the best-selling piece of sheet music for ten years, according to some people I spoke to in the business. They told me it had outsold 'My Way'.

On 19 December, the *Financial Times* called Ian for an interview. He claimed that they wanted to know how a man working from a garden shed in rural Dorset was causing fluctuations of the EMI share price. The shareholders were concerned that EMI was considering paying millions for the new Robbie Williams contract due for renewal. Somehow we were involved and seen as a possible humiliation to all concerned if we beat Robbie at this delicate time. An article spread over pages two and three didn't appear until 28 February 2002.

At 4.30 p.m., Paul Yeung and I had to prepare for a live radio broadcast at Virgin Radio. It had an audience of a million and, like *Top of the Pops*, they'd be new potential buyers for the record. We jumped into the car Warner had sent for us and, as we drove past Harrods, Ian called.

'It's cancelled, Gord,' he said. 'You can go home again.'

'Why?' I asked. He replied that Virgin had decided the record wasn't right for the programme.

'So, it was OK yesterday but not OK today?'

'Leave it,' said Ian.

'No, I bloody well won't,' I replied.

I told Paul Jackson, the programme controller, to grow up and was photographed outside the radio station in the street in my gorilla suit, putting two fingers up at them. Nobody published that picture. Two hours later, I learned that I wasn't going to be on *Top of the Pops* either. I had been cut from the show. My performance wasn't aired until February 2003, a total of 14 months too late. I was never shown on *Top of the Pops* throughout the success of either 'How Wonderful You Are' or *Harry's Bar*, which reached No. 2 in the album charts. I'd like to know why. The records I sold were due to exposure from Radio 2 and *Top of the Pops* 2 and a clutch of regional stations.

A hell of a lot of influential people seemed to want the record to fail and did everything in their power to stop it charting. On three separate occasions in three separate locations I heard of people complaining that the record was being kept under the counter in some stores and a 'sold out' sticker put in the chart rack.

Below is an extract from the industry magazine *Music Week* dated 22 December 2001 in its chart commentary. You can see that even the day before it was No. 2, the industry was longing for a flop.

> According to the tabloid press, Gordon Haskell's 'How Wonderful You Are' is expected to be there or thereabouts in the battle for the Christmas number one with its quoted odds tumbling by the day.
>
> This is despite the fact the record is still getting very little exposure.

When we first logged its progress here four weeks ago before the hype kicked in, we noted it was in the airplay charts thanks to Radio 2 with almost no support elsewhere. That remains the case. Its exposure from other stations increased by 90 per cent last week but only from a paltry 3 plays to a still pathetic 30. Radio 2 meanwhile has upped support from 16 plays to 23, a move which propels the record 5–1 on its most-played list and provides more than 98 per cent of the 25.8 million audience which sees it climb 38–33 on the overall airplay chart.

It is not unknown for the combination of major press support, Radio 2 patronage and shortening odds to result in massive flops at Christmas. Anthony Hopkins had the same pieces in place in 1986 and belly flopped to a number seventy-five sales chart peak.

Haskell, of course, has considerably more going for him and is unlikely to fail so badly . . . the press picture of him as an amateur pub singer is somewhat at odds with his distinguished past with King Crimson.

Ian had me busking in Oxford Street outside the HMV store for an even more degrading bit of press because he was trying to make up the losses caused by the sabotaged shows. Several tabloids together would amount to another five million potential buyers. The pictures were totally unrepresentative of me. I looked like a tramp with a demented expression and my heart sank because I knew everything was spinning out of control. People who bought my record bought it after they heard it and liked it . . . not because they saw a picture of a tramp in the *Daily Star*.

Radio 2 took out full-page advertisements with a picture of my single, the first single that the station had ever broken, proving it to be the most popular station in the country, a position it has maintained ever since. They had given me a hit and in return I had brought the station lots of publicity. Colin Martin put up the gold disc in his office and I was the golden boy whenever I walked into the building at Portland Place. Four months later, every major record company was trying to copy Ian Brown's methods. Covers abounded of old '50s standards. Ian was deemed the genius for making my song a hit, the only reason for my success, while I was deemed 'uncool' by the other stations. My 'old-style' song was only a year old. Robbie was singing Sinatra's 'Something Stupid' at the time and songs that were around 50 years old. The irony escaped everyone. Rod Stewart followed suit with *The Great American Songbook*. Eventually Norah Jones emerged and did better than any of us. She delivered in the same style as *Harry's Bar* and she didn't have to degrade herself to do it.

The weekend came. It was Christmas and we went home on the Sunday morning. I asked Ian when he'd know the chart position and he said he'd call me. The difference between a No. 1 and No. 2 record is worth at least £100,000 in kudos, compilation sales and airplay, so it would be an important call.

I heard the news alone at Ashmore. I had entered the chart at No. 2. I was grateful. I really wasn't disappointed. How could I be, after travelling to hell and back? It was a magnificent victory and it had inspired so many people in the country. I had told everyone of their own potential in the song and by doing so I had fulfilled my own.

The mail I was receiving showed me how distorted one's impression of the world can become if all you read, see and hear is the newspapers, television and radio. These good souls, who were communicating with me directly, wrote in the thousands and they all worshipped the same beauty and had the same aspirations as I did. They had never had anyone to fight their corner and there was so very little in the media that was representative of them any more. I had the confirmation I had been seeking for years that the world is still a beautiful place full of beautiful people. They were the antithesis of the tiny, blinkered, music-business world I was forced to inhabit to get my message through. Without Colin Martin at Radio 2, there would have been no exposure at all for Gordon Haskell or Norah Jones. Now the voices say, 'The single is dead.' If a record is exceptional, it can still sell over 250,000 copies, as mine did. I was very lucky to get my hit before all the doors close for good on music like mine. It will be equally hard to repeat my success, no matter how great a song I might write tomorrow. The hostility is overwhelming, but it's hard for everyone – even for the executives watching their own backs.

I felt like a warrior returning home from a battle. To be No. 2 at my age was a miracle. I had got through a hole in the fence; I felt like the prisoner escaping in *The Shawshank Redemption*. Nobody had thought it was possible, least of all the music business. Muff Winwood at Sony had said for five years, 'I love your stuff, Gordon.

I listen to it in my car but I can't sign you because I don't know how to reach your audience. You'll always work, though.' Rob Dickins, the former Warner chairman, had said, 'You're sounding great, Gordon, but it's not quite right for our label.' And so on and on and on you go as the years go by and your whole life ticks away until the day comes when you'll be told, 'It's good but you're too old.'

But I had done it. And, to be fair, some of them were pleased for me. Rob Dickins sent congratulations. His saying 'you have turned the record business upside down' was now proving to be true, with record companies all having major successes with similar music.

There were so many phone calls to my house when the chart show on the radio finished that the answer machine gave up time and time again. My daughter pointed out to me that it was 23 December, exactly 12 months to the day since she walked into The Old Mill for our reunion. Yet another strange coincidence to add to all the others that had occurred in the most extraordinary year of my life and the most dramatic year in the history of the world. It was a year for surprises. Everyone was still reeling from 9/11.

It was eerie in Ashmore when I returned to my own place on my own, knowing my face was all over the papers and TV. I was interviewed out. If I visited my mother, she'd interview me. And the same would happen with everyone else. I felt very tired. But the relief of being out of debt . . . oh, what heaven that was and how grateful I was to Johnnie Walker, Colin Martin and Ian and the team for making it happen.

I took the book of sheet music that Warner had published featuring all the songs and wrote a dedication in it for Dee. 'You always said you wanted to make a difference in the world. 250,000 people are saying you did. Thank you for saving my life.'

On Christmas Day, I had breakfast alone at The Royal Chase Hotel in Shaftesbury. I was waiting to see my son – I'd got up too early and his household wasn't awake. I felt ridiculous eating solo in such a public place when I was at No. 2 in the charts but my whole life had been ridiculous. I went back to school in my mind, to the fives championship against Robert Fripp, and it suddenly dawned on me who managed Robbie Williams – David Enthoven, Robbie's manager, had managed Robert in King Crimson. I shook my head in amazement at how Robert and I were still playing that game 40 years on. What had I said? 'I loved the game too much to care about winning,' and here I was again coming second to his ghost. This time, though, I *had* fought to win. The game was rotten and I was rich, and Ian and I had, in the words of Rob Dickins, 'turned the music business on its head'. There was some satisfaction in that. Robert Fripp didn't communicate at this time, which was very honest of him. But he probably noticed his old manager was at No. 1 and his old sparring partner was at No. 2. At least now the first question I would be asked wasn't going to be, 'Didn't you used to be with King Crimson?'

I thought of all the people I knew who loved me – and vice versa – and realised I was choosing solitude as a holy man might, to contemplate and listen to the silence I so needed. Soon I would be with my son and later I'd visit my mother and sister. On Boxing Day, I would join my daughter, her husband and my two grandchildren. I was shared out over the next few days and I'd almost certainly fall asleep in somebody's chair and tell myself it had all been worthwhile. After seeing everyone, they'd wake me and I would return to my solitude at Ashmore.

CHAPTER 18

⪼ ⪼ ⪼

. . . And this Little Piggy Went to Market

Four weeks later, in January 2002, *Harry's Bar* went into the album chart at No. 2, beaten by The Stereophonics. Richard Branson's label V2 had reduced the band's album to £6.99 to hold on to the coveted No. 1 spot.

It was still a brilliant result to have a No. 2 single followed by a No. 2 album. I received a gold record for the album and a silver one for the single. Sales were terrific and Europe was sitting up and taking notice. Warner in Europe had suffered a bad year financially and saw *Harry's Bar* as a possible salvation. The emails continued in their hundreds, encouraging me and convincing me that I had found my place in the scheme of things. I had no way of replying personally because I was so rushed off my feet. Occasionally, they'd enclose a phone number and I'd surprise them by calling to thank them personally. I wished that every single fan had received a reply. I was so grateful.

The critics had been divided 50–50. The good ones called the record 'timeless', including David Sinclair, the music critic at *The Times*; the bad ones called it 'fabricated world-weariness'.

My job for Warner was now an international one and I was sent to Europe almost every week to promote in every country. I cancelled the last three pub jobs in Ringwood and Southampton and I was sorry to let them down. A tour of England with my buddies, Hamish Stuart and Robbie McIntosh, had been booked months before the record came out so the promoters rubbed their hands with glee as we worked to packed houses for just £100 each.

At every venue, they'd changed the billing to headline Gordon Haskell instead of Hamish Stuart, Robbie McIntosh . . . and Gordon Haskell. In some places, they moved the show to a larger venue to take more money. It was human nature.

Ian didn't seem to care and stayed away from the gigs. He loved doing the big deals. He always used the phrase, 'It's better than shovelling pig shit.'

I began to say, 'And this little piggy went to market.'

We'd had so much fun breaking the record and I was very laid-back about the whole success. Alan McBlane, head of the team behind the single, said it was the best fun he'd had for 20 years. We had all laughed non-stop for three weeks but I was on my own now. Ian and Alan were close and I barely saw them. Had I managed my own affairs, I would have booked 200 art centres and small theatres and earned myself a cool £200,000. Ian had other ideas.

Ian was doing a deal for a nationwide tour with the giant promoters Clear Channel. I felt that it was too ambitious and told Paul Fenn, the agent at Asgard whom Ian had appointed. He replied, 'You've sold more records than James Taylor this year. We think you'll do OK.' I shrugged my shoulders and made the mistake of not arguing. I had handed over control of my life to Ian and decided to be a good boy and remain silent. I was still very grateful to him. Who wouldn't be? I really was content and trusting. When Ian made a mistake, I ignored it. He never attended gigs and I was still humping gear about, just as I had always done.

I went to Europe, where the press greeted me with open arms, proclaiming *Harry's Bar* a classic, full of class, style, intelligence, spirituality and that rare quality, longevity. Every country seemed to have a Harry's Bar. In Munich, Paul Yeung and I walked into a pub called Pusser's and started talking with the barman. He began to tell us his life story. He was from Philadelphia. His father was in partnership with a guy called Harry MacElhone, a Scotsman who established a bar in Paris in 1911 and another in Venice in 1931. They called them Harry's Bar. My record wasn't out yet in Germany. I was anonymous and our meeting was a pure coincidence. I listened with fascination. The Harry's Bar name became synonymous with Ernest Hemingway, who spent a lot of time in them and helped to make them famous. He loved their Martinis. Pretty soon, they opened another in New York and then wanted to start another in Berlin, but they fell out. This guy tried to open one there in Munich but was forced to use another name, hence Pusser's bar, the place we had walked into by chance. Paul smiled and said to the barman, 'Have you heard of a record called *Harry's Bar*?' and the barman shook his head.

When I wrote the words for *Harry's Bar*, I was writing about my own life. I hadn't been thinking of the famous chain of Harry's Bars across the world. I wasn't familiar with its celebrated history but it certainly conjures up the same pictures. It was an incredible accident to learn of its history directly from a member of the Harry's Bar family.

According to the official story, the Venice bar is credited with being started by Giuseppe Cipri in 1931, but the Paris bar was indeed started by Harry MacElhone in 1911 and was the birthplace of the Bloody Mary in 1921 and the Sidecar in 1931. Hemingway not only drank in both of them but lived in Havana, the name of the film I had seen 79 times. Weird.

On my arrival back in London, I read in the newspapers that I had only sold 39 tickets for the Hammersmith gig. I called Ian, who said they had only advertised it once and tickets had just been on sale for a fortnight when he decided to cut a deal and pull me out. 'You and the musicians will all get £5,000,' he reassured me. 'It's the easiest £5,000 you've ever earned.'

'I've got two questions for you, Ian,' I replied. 'Why am I getting the blame for your incompetence and who tipped off the press?'

'Don't know,' he said.

'So, let me get this straight. I go to Europe, where the quality press is raving about the record, I'm in the charts in every country and Warner in Europe have said I am the easiest artist they've ever worked with, yet I come back here to a complete shambles. Is that about right?'

'Fuck off! Loads of acts have their tours cancelled. It's normal. They just thought you'd fill the big theatres and wanted to have a punt at it.'

I suddenly hated his couldn't-care-less attitude. It was exasperating and I was beginning to smell a rat. 'What's next?' I asked him, too tired to dwell on the bad side of things.

'Warner has added strings to "There Goes My Heart Again" and edited it and is releasing it as the follow-up single. Jon Sweet has produced it and you have to approve it. I'll pick you up at 6 a.m.

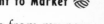

from Ashmore.' Here comes the second major mistake from my new employer . . . and a £10,000 studio bill for me.

From that moment on, I knew I had lost control. Ian was big news in the industry now and every door to every major record company was open for him. Other acts were queuing up to sign to him. He had taken his eye off the ball.

I told him that 'Freeway To Her Dreams' was the obvious follow-up. It had already been well received at radio. I had never played 'There Goes My Heart Again' in public. It was too slow for my set and I knew it would be too slow for radio. I had road-tested all my songs, and I knew better than anyone which were potential hits, but nobody wanted my opinion.

Ian took no notice and started flattering me to soften me up by saying, 'It's a classic song. A guy called me up and said he'd just heard it on the album and it was his favourite song. It's brilliant. Willie Nelson could have written it.' I saw that I was losing the Ian Brown I had loved. He was on a roll, hobnobbing with the industry while I went to work.

I'd brought Warner a hit single that I'd written, financed, produced and sung. The audience had made it a hit. Ian had enabled it brilliantly but they were only in it for the market share, according to Ian. My debts were paid. I had to be grateful.

When my birthday came on 27 April, Ian hired a stretch limo to take me to the pub. It wasn't my style but again I had to be grateful for the thought. Misrepresentation was by now the norm. Nobody really knew me. They were playing rock-star games and had assumed I wanted to join their club. The beauty I had found in Ashmore had lowered my guard. Now I had to put my armour back on. How utterly boring.

Europe was looking healthier so I had very little to complain about and absolutely no time to waste on negative thinking. I had the respect of its people and they had a deeper understanding of my material.

In England, I was a 'brand', as they say in corporate language. I didn't feel like an artist any more, but in Europe everything was as it should be. London was just so unmusical; they had missed the spiritual message.

I was well on the way to having a worldwide hit and eagerly awaited the release of *Harry's Bar* in America. It could go to No. 1 there. The American public has always recognised quality songs like 'How Wonderful You Are'. As it was proving itself all over the world and being added to dozens of compilations, I couldn't believe it when I heard Warner was refusing to release it in the States.

Ian put it with a small label in Nashville and it managed to climb to 44 on the Triple-A stations with a tiny promotional budget. With Warner's muscle, it might have reached the top 10.

Financially, I was secure. The old feelings of gratitude came back and I did have rather a lot of money. I'd settled £28,000 of credit-card debt, the £65,000 mortgage on the house my mother lived in and I was still happy to rent at Ashmore for £100 a week. I never wanted to leave. I didn't need a grand house. I deposited £350,000 in the bank. Its attitude change was amusing – they'd known me as a pauper for 30 years.

Then the local press started having a go. It couldn't reach me when I was away in Europe, so someone wrote a snide piece in the *Bournemouth Echo*. The reporter invented a quote saying that I wouldn't set foot in certain pubs any more and that the locals in Ashmore were snobs and driving me mad. He said I'd bought a Rolls-Royce. When I returned to my beloved Ashmore, the whole village had turned against me. I called up the paper to talk about it. The reporter said, 'A friend of yours told us.' I was calm but curious. I had delivered a message of goodwill and in return they spat in my face. Why? I had to be strong enough to turn the other cheek.

Gratitude begins to grate after a while. You begin to feel you're somebody's whore and you're grateful to your pimp for getting you tricks. Something in me wanted to scream at the sheer banality of it all. I longed for some honesty and a little decency. It was all so undignified. I had exchanged the prison of poverty for the prison of celebrity and riches, and I spent my time alone meditating on it.

I got on best with the drivers. We talked continually and they told me how I was the only artist who'd ever bothered to speak to them. I learned about their families, their love lives and problems, their struggles and bankruptcies and how they'd ended up chauffeuring spoilt brats around all day. I became close with my regular driver, Lawrence, and he'd pour his heart out over the hours we spent on the road together. He was built like the Incredible Hulk. I told him about having to make up the boss's fire and the sawdust story. We were kindred spirits.

I benefited from my close friendship with Lawrence one day in Warsaw when he saved me from being murdered. He was hired by Ian as a driver, security man and stand-in manager. People had derided the need for any muscle around me and would say,

'Frightened of the 75-year-old fans are we, Gordon?' The truth was that Ian was scared of flying. These extra costs for a chaperon were borne by me.

I had to use a different saxophonist in Europe when Paul Yeung had a death in his family. His stand-in became very agitated in Italy and, at one radio station, he suddenly threw his saxophone across the studio in a rage. I stayed calm and he muttered something to himself in Spanish. After the session we went to eat. Aurelio, the Warner representative, chose a beautiful Italian restaurant and El Saxo muttered to me, saying he wanted a McDonald's, adding, 'You can take the boy out of the estate but you can't take the estate out of the boy.' I loved his playing and I was prepared to put up with his lousy manners, so I stayed quiet. Things stayed calm for the meal and we left and flew to Warsaw. After checking into the hotel we all had a drink. We were on our third when El Saxo started freaking out again. It started with him saying £150 a day wasn't enough, that Warner was paying him and they should pay him more. I said if he wasn't happy, I'd make up the difference myself. He was getting over £1,000 a week to play one song a day, with all expenses paid.

'I don't want your money!' he screamed. 'They should pay.' His eyes were those of a madman. I said I was going to bed and left for my room.

Lawrence and El Saxo followed me up five minutes later and I asked him if he was all right. He hugged me, apologised and then he flipped again. He threw his cases down and the saxophone case burst open. He picked up his sax and lifted it above his head in a violent rage. He was over six feet tall and had already told me he'd served time for grievous bodily harm, so I had no doubt he was serious and more than capable. He slammed the saxophone down towards my head with all his strength, screaming, 'I'm going to kill you!'

As the instrument neared my skull, Lawrence threw himself between us, diverting the blow, and the saxophone hit the coffee table and bent in half. It was solid brass. My brains would have been mashed potatoes. 'Calm down, man,' Lawrence called out. 'Everything's OK.' He held him in an iron grip and ushered him to his room next door. Lawrence watched El Saxo as he sat on a chair twisting and turning, his body in agony as he ached for the medication he longed for. His eyes remained possessed by a demon. He texted me all night, threatening to kill me and destroy my career in any way he could. He was sent home. The pain I was feeling was one of sadness for a giant talent suffering torment.

Lawrence had saved him from a life sentence for murder. He had saved two people's lives in one single night. Bands would benefit greatly from talking to such a man. He's not just any old driver.

The love that had created 'How Wonderful You Are' had turned into a never-ending nightmare of hatred. Comments were appearing on websites from strangers saying if they saw me in the street they'd kill me.

I had difficulty understanding how such a song could attract such ugliness. It was being trashed and despoiled, and it saddened me. There was obviously a long way to go before I could put my feet up and say, 'The rest will be easy.'

I decided to leave behind the cottage and the three years of bliss I'd known in Ashmore. The locals believed the press story and had shunned me; outsiders wanted to kill me. As soon as I found a house to buy Ian organised for me to stand outside it to be photographed with my gold records . . . I looked like an arrogant prick. The picture went into the newspapers. Ian said we needed retail to stock the new record and 'We need to show them you are news.' I found another place and hid from the world. Ian told the press I had bought a castle in Scotland. I was forever having to explain to my friends and try and straighten out the stories, but I had the awful feeling that they all believed I had changed. I hadn't and now I felt very isolated.

The beautiful thatched cottage I had bought was near Fordingbridge in Hampshire. It had a stream running through the most exquisite garden I had ever seen. It was how I imagined the Garden of Eden to be. It had taken the previous owner 18 years to create and was filled with wonderful shrubs and trees, and every kind of flower imaginable. There was a separate vegetable garden with fruit trees. I went back to the world of nature that I loved and understood. There were locks on the garden doors and high hedges ensuring privacy, and a security system. Living behind locked doors just wasn't me and I became restless. There was also a dead rat in the loft that stank the whole house out.

It could never be like Ashmore, with its openness. I missed the local people. I missed Ashmore's pure air and that glorious sky filled with stars at night. The new air I was breathing had a stench that turned my stomach and I was down in that long cul-de-sac heading nowhere, being misrepresented by everybody. All I wanted was my old life back now that I was out of debt. I put the place back on the market. And I sold it to Ian.

I moved to Shaftesbury, on top of the hill. It's a terraced cottage in the middle of the town. I see people every day. It's a lot better and, although I can no longer live in Ashmore, I can see it from my garden.

By August 2002, I was back on Ian's label. I was not privy to the conversations between Ian and Warner. He claims I was sacked because I called the MD an android in a magazine. I doubt if that would have bothered the man who had just made £2 million out of me for his bosses. I had to put up with a lot worse in the press.

Ian wanted me to record another album straight away and dump *Harry's Bar* after only four months of promotion. I did as I was told out of gratitude and it was enjoyable being back at Oxford for the couple of weeks' studio time he gave me. Other acts plug their albums for two years in every corner of the world and spend months in the studio preparing their follow-ups. We had barely started with *Harry's Bar*. It was a massive wasted opportunity and stripped me of any desire to follow it up but I did a good job considering the circumstances.

Recording *Shadows on the Wall* so soon was incredibly stupid but it's a strong album nevertheless. It isn't the jazz road that I had started to go down so easily on *Harry's Bar*, the natural direction to follow considering its popularity. Ian was determined to build his record company up and sell it for millions to a major. He wanted product quickly. Half of the material was drawn from my past and it feels like a back-catalogue album to me.

Everything about the early days of *Harry's Bar* had been honest and sincere, which is what the public recognised more than anything. I turned down offers of £75,000 from other interested labels out of loyalty to Ian. He released *Shadows on the Wall* and it charted at 44 but to maintain the promotion would have cost him too much. He had failed as an independent with the single and now he was struggling against the giant record companies again. It was a fair result in a falling market. Bigger names than Haskell sold less that month. Mine were being pirated now along with all the others. It has sold over 45,000, yet I have earned nothing from it. He could have played safe by managing me and placing me with another label, but I wasn't going to bring him down by leaving him. I still had a degree of faith in him.

According to Ian's calculations, I have to sell 100,000 albums before I can start earning again. It means everybody on the production line, all the way to retail, earns a living except the creator of the work, something I've seen become a general practice with the majority of record companies. I know of a recent case where the artist sold two million albums, but his earnings were nil. It is a convenient way to get artists to work for nothing. When the royalty statements for *Harry's Bar* went to Ian and not me, I discovered I had personally never been signed to Warner. My contract had been with Ian and it was he who was signed to Warner; he'd cut me out of the deal. This explained why I'd never had any contact with the label or the publisher and many of my suggestions had been met with a stony silence. Ian was building up his own record company, not my career. He had taken *Harry's Bar* from me and sold it as if he had created it. He hadn't; I had. It had never occurred to me. We had been friends and laughed together every day for months. I liked him. In the end, it was nothing personal, it was just business. After 40 years of struggle, it should have been a beautiful thing, but it was spoiled. In four little words: he stole my joy.

The last gig I did for Ian and Paul Fenn before I finally decided to change my representation was the most cruel joke of all. Again, it was my fault because I agreed to it and I'd fallen into the appalling habit of doing as I was told. I'd slipped back ten years to being dominated just because I wanted a reputation of being 'easy to work with'.

The worst job I had ever done in my whole career as a struggling troubadour had been the booze cruise out of Helsinki. In May 2003, having put all the bad old days behind me, I was booked to play there again for two nights. It was the opposite of what I had worked so hard to achieve and I was finally forced to do something about it.

The good times Ian and I shared began when my old friend Johnnie Walker started playing the record. After that, getting the track into the charts against impossible odds was the best fun we could possibly have had. I'd loved the music business in 1966 and, with Johnnie on board again, we had brought back the spirit of the '60s in a big way. I had felt right at home with a record that was tailor-made for me and my beliefs, but the laughter had stopped as every song I had ever recorded was sold off. There were four albums on the market, all at the same time, and a wealth of potential hits were buried in poor productions.

I'm listening again to my inner voice and it tells me I'm right to lie low and wait. I will write again. I will record again. But it will be from a cloudless sky.

It all reminds me of a Greek fable of the time Alexander the Great visited a poor philosopher he admired called Diogenes, who lived inside a Greek urn. Alexander told him if there was anything he could do for him, he would do it. Diogenes, looking up at the big powerful man, then at the sky, replied, in a nutshell, 'Yes, there is something you can do for me. Move over. You're blocking the sun.'

At the end of the day, all I can rely on are my instincts.

Time and time again they have proved reliable and enabled me to survive. A lot of my opinions over the years have been based on misinformation, rendering them worthless; nevertheless, my instincts always managed to protect me and lead me on to my goals, teaching me valuable lessons as I grew up. I could hear alarm bells ringing.

My recording contract had promised me statements every three months. For almost two years, I had not received any. It looked suspicious. My childhood dream of being a detective was about to be fulfilled after all.

I met with a lawyer, who read my contracts, then looked up and confirmed my suspicions. 'You've been had,' he said. After going into complicated details, he asked me how I felt about it all.

'It's simply a case of whether I feel the bottle is half full or half empty,' I said. 'In my case, I feel it's half full.'

I can see I have lost a fortune and most of my former reputation. But no one owns me any more. The crime committed was perhaps mine for trusting too easily and not caring enough about the small print. I would have taken any offer to get out of the debt that had nearly driven me crazy for 20 years and I didn't look for potholes.

Before my success, I had been my own man. I had discovered a wonderful life at Ashmore, full of truth and beauty, and out of that purity had come *Harry's Bar*, bringing my salvation along with it. What was to follow was rumour, speculation and manipulation, and a lot of money flying around, fuelling greed, deceit and betrayal.

Oh, and fame. I'd almost forgotten fame.

All I had to do was go back to the Ashmore state of mind, regain my equilibrium and start writing and recording again. I had always been successful by being true to myself. Anything less than that felt like failure, regardless of the money I could make by being dishonest.

It was extraordinary to me that such beautiful songs, written from the very depth of my soul, had brought with them an attempted murder, a robbery and so much venom from total strangers. It made me look even more closely at myself to see if there was some justification for it. Getting over the experience was my next task and I thought it would be the most challenging of my entire life. I found it quite easy. It is just another part of my journey towards wholeness and I welcomed the change in my circumstances.

Harry's Bar made thousands of people happy. And making people happy is a good way to live life. I felt I had been robbed along the way but it doesn't matter; I didn't rob anybody. That's what counts. The wisest course is to move on and leave the past behind. I'll put all the trash into the incinerator with the rest of the garden refuse and watch it burn. I'll rake out the ashes and use them for next year's compost. As my song predicted, 'It was all in the scheme of things.'

My experience proved to be a magnificent lesson for me, filled with irony. I may have believed in the message for the world encapsulated in 'How Wonderful You Are' but I hadn't quite believed it of myself.

I sold 280,000 copies of 'How Wonderful You Are' and about 300,000 of *Harry's Bar*. They are still selling well all around the world. The 50–50 deal with Ian meant that we would share £5.50 per sale when Ian was to release the record on his own Flying Sparks label. When Warner came aboard, with its much greater sales potential, that came down to £1.80 . . . 90p a record for me. So far so good, because even at that modest 90p, initial sales alone would have netted me half a million pounds in royalties – and they were paying up front. Ongoing sales would have been my pension. In a nutshell, it leaves me in the odd situation where my success has left me not a penny richer.

As a young lad working with Reg and Uby, I saw the template for happiness. I was just the delivery boy but my days were filled with humour and I was surrounded by good-natured people full of the subtleties of life. The milk of human kindness I'd witnessed then was a constant reminder of how it is possible to get through life without turning sour. I believe I am succeeding in doing that, step by step; it takes so long because I believe it is meant to. For what is a lifetime but a journey in which to learn to love, understand and forgive our fellow man in all his complexities, and in the process learn to love and value and forgive ourselves? I never played the star. I was always the observer, aware of each and every one of us stumbling around in the dark playing blindman's-bluff.

I pick myself up a lot quicker these days and know I have no one else to blame but myself for my cock-ups. But I am still so fascinated by life and what strange creatures we all are. There is this knowing inside that assures me we are all connected to one another in some other dimension. Real art inspires us and gives us all hope. The art of music remains as beautiful as we wish to make it, as spiritual as we wish it to be, a reflection and expression of our hopes and dreams. Or it can become a distortion of our neuroses that relates to another's distortion of the truth. It finds success in all its various forms. Success has taken me a lifetime. But at long last I am a free man, as I knew in my heart I would be.

It's gratifying to know that the good are all still out there quietly going about their daily lives. They may never believe they are powerful but ultimately they are the *most* powerful, as history has shown and will continue to show as another tyrant bites the dust. I hear their voices loud and clear above the continuous din and clatter and stupidity of modern life – and it is they who keep my faith intact. I hope they'll remember just how wonderful *they* are.

As I was putting the finishing touches to this book, an army officer was convicted for running a brothel two doors down from me. This morning I passed the woman I'd deduced was the prostitute involved. I felt sorry for her because her picture was all over the newspapers and I offered my home to her as a refuge from the reporters, remembering how uncomfortable it had been for me.

It was the wrong woman.

I'm still going to get things wrong. But I think I'll always see the funny side when I do. Before I sat down to write the story of my life I had never quite realised just how wonderful it is. Harry's Bar will always be a good place to go to whenever I need to pause and think about a few things.